ALLEN CARR'S EASY WAY TO CONTROL ALCOHOL

ARCTURUS

ALLEN CARR

In 1983, after countless failed attempts to cure his own addiction to nicotine, Allen Carr discovered what the world had been waiting for – the Easy Way to Stop Smoking. Since giving up a successful career as an accountant to help cure the world's smokers, he has built a global reputation as a result of his phenomenal method and a network of clinics spanning the world. *Allen Carr's Easy Way to Stop Smoking* became an international bestseller and has been published in over twenty different languages. This has been followed by *The Only Way to Stop Smoking Permanently*, *How to Stop Your Child Smoking*, and video, audio and CD-Rom versions of the Easyway method.

In 1998 Allen Carr was invited to speak at the 10th World Conference on Tobacco & Health, held in Beijing, an honour that the most eminent physician would be proud of. His method and reputation could receive no higher commendation. He is now widely accepted as the world's leading expert on how to help smokers quit.

The success of Easyway encouraged people with other problems to approach Allen for help. This has resulted in the publication of *Allen Carr's Easyweigh to Lose Weight* and *The Easy Way to Enjoy Flying*. After tests with some of his patients it was discovered that the simple logic of Easyway also worked well for people with a drink problem.

A full list of Allen Carr clinics appears at the back of this book. Should you require any assistance, do not hesitate to contact your nearest therapist. All correspondence and enquiries about Allen Carr's books, videos, audio tapes and CD-Roms should be addressed to the nearest clinic.

**DEDICATED TO
THE FELLOWSHIP**

AND

**My special thanks to Crispin Hay,
whose expertise and assistance
have been invaluable.**

ARCTURUS

Published by Arcturus Canada
A division of Arcturus Publishing Limited
26/27 Bickels Yard
151-153 Bermondsey Street
London SE1 3HA

ISBN-13: 978-1-905555-06-2
ISBN-10: 1-905555-06-7

British Library Cataloguing-in-Publication Data:
a catalogue record for this book is available
from the British Library

This edition printed in 2006

Printed in England

CONTENTS

CONTENTS

INTRODUCTION

On 15 July 1983 Allen Carr, a confirmed chain-smoker for a third of a century, extinguished his final cigarette and announced that he had discovered a method of stopping which would enable any smoker to find it easy to quit: immediately and permanently, without using willpower, gimmicks or substitutes; without suffering withdrawal pains or gaining weight; and, most important of all, without spending the rest of their lives resisting the craving, believing that social occasions will never be quite so pleasant and that stress will not be so easy to handle without a cigarette.

At the time few could believe that such a seemingly magical cure was possible. After all, it was common knowledge that quitting smoking required the use of immense willpower, was usually accompanied by weight gain and horrendous withdrawal symptoms, and was about as easy as climbing Everest. Sadly, millions of smokers still suffer from this illusion.

Considering the thousands of hours and the millions of pounds the medical profession had spent on searching for an effective method to quit smoking, it is understandable that no one could believe that a lone ex-smoker, with no medical training whatsoever, had succeeded where they had failed. Members of Alcoholics Anonymous will find this concept easier to accept. As a former member of AA, I can confirm that literally millions of alcoholics would testify that they owe their very lives not to medical experts, but to fellow alcoholics.

Allen Carr is now widely accepted as the world's leading expert on helping smokers to quit. His first book, *The Easy Way to Stop Smoking*, has been a best seller every year since it was first published by Penguin in 1985. It is now translated into over 20 languages and has been the No. 1 best-seller in Germany, Austria and Switzerland. There is also a world-wide network of clinics based on Allen Carr's method.

I originally heard about Allen Carr from friends who had attended his clinic and were overjoyed by the result. I was completely sceptical, after all some had only quit for a few days. I assumed that they had spent a fortune on the latest 'miracle' cure and were trying to make me fall for the same gimmick, but I knew that time would tell. It seems hardly credible now, but I actually wanted them to fail. It annoyed me that it didn't seem to bother them if I smoked in their presence, and as time went by I began to realize that they were genuinely free and clearly enjoying the fact. Instead of pitying them because they could no longer smoke, I began to envy them. For years I'd felt like a social pariah because I still smoked. As a regularly faltering member of 'The Fellowship', I was fully aware that alcohol was ruining my life. But my justification was that it was an essential social prop. Now I began to feel a social pariah because I was drinking. So I attended an Allen Carr clinic. Still convinced that it wouldn't work for me, I didn't even tell my wife let alone my friends. When I left the clinic four hours later, I couldn't wait to tell the world.

Allen claims that his method is equally effective for all drug addiction and chemical abuse. I am indeed delighted of the opportunity to testify that he not only enabled me to quit smoking but helped to release me from a nightmare that was controlling and ruining my life: alcoholism. I once believed that there was no cure to alcoholism. Allen proved me wrong. My only regret today is that I didn't learn about Allen Carr earlier. Don't worry if you are also sceptical. Allen will expect you to be. I won't try to tell you how or why his method is so effective. All I will say is that by the time you have finished reading the book, the great mystery in your life will be why you couldn't see it so clearly before. Enjoy the book.

Emanuel Johnson

1 *The Easy Way to Control Alcohol*

It has been more then twenty years since I proved that any smoker can find it easy to quit. When I discovered my method, I fully expected that smoking would be a thing of the past in a few short years. Indeed since then, at a conservative estimate, over five million smokers have been cured by my method. The vast majority of them found it easy and enjoyable to quit. Nonetheless, there are millions of smokers worldwide who have never even heard of Allen Carr or his method. I can only put it down to the fact that it takes time to turn generally accepted dogma on its head. After all, everyone knows that it is very difficult to stop smoking.

For the majority of human history we all knew that the world was flat and lay at the centre of the universe. Likewise it is common knowledge that for anyone with a drink problem to put it behind them requires a phenomenal effort of will, usually involving several abortive attempts. There is a general belief in society that the only people who really need to control their drinking also happen to be the very ones who find it hardest to do so. If I found it difficult to convince people that there is an easy and enjoyable way to stop smoking, how much harder a task will I have to convince you that anyone can control their drink problem easily, immediately and permanently? Whether your fear is that you are in danger of becoming an alcoholic, or you suspect that you are already one, my task is not helped when Alcoholics Anonymous (AA), the organization widely accepted as the leading authority on the subject, categorically states:

'Alcoholism is a fatal illness for which there is no known medical cure.'

Unfortunately, this opinion is widely supported by many eminent members of the medical profession, and by the media and society generally. So ingrained is this belief that there is no cure for alcoholism, that you might be excused for despatching this book to the rubbish bin without even reading it. I beg you not to do that. There are many doctors who do not support AA's view, but they seem reluctant to admit to their doubts on national television.

If you happen to be a member of AA or a similar organization, and in your 20th year of 'recovery', you might be wondering how I can commence this work by contradicting the very cornerstone of AA philosophy, while at the same time dedicating it to 'The Fellowship'. It is because I have the deepest regard for an organization that has saved the sanity and the very lives of literally millions of alcoholics: people who were in the depths of despair, having lost their job, friends, home and family, without any semblance of hope or self-respect. AA welcomes and whole-heartedly supports such people, regardless of race, class, colour, religion or creed. What is more, it does so without judging or incriminating them. Many members attend meetings after a particularly bad day. The atmosphere before the meeting starts would make a dentist's waiting room appear like a party. As each member unloads their tale of woe, so the mood changes: laughter becomes more and more frequent and it actually feels like a party, even without alcohol!

I'm not a Roman Catholic and am aware that many regard the confessional as blatant hypocrisy. Like all such issues, I'm sure there are two sides to the story, and I have no intention of discussing it further, except to say that it must be very comforting to be able to unload your conscience. If a problem shared is a problem halved, how much more of a relief to be able to share your problems with a roomful of people, all of whom can empathize with you and who will not judge you or ask you to do penance.

Although alcoholism is the common enemy that has united all these people, the matters addressed often bear no relation to alcohol and involve the everyday stresses and indignities we all buckle under from time to time, whether we have a drink problem or not. In fact, so impressed am I with the support and genuine benefit that AA gives to alcoholics, that I believe that it is time that someone set up APA – Any Problems Anonymous, run on similar lines to AA. In fact I'm convinced that if such an organization existed, many victims might not have fallen into the alcohol trap in the first place.

One of the sad effects of alcoholism is that it generally leaves its victims penniless. It's fine for rich people who have a drink problem and can escape to a health farm when they can no longer cope with the situation, but for the vast majority of alcoholics, AA is the only effective help available. So why do I contradict the cornerstone of AA philosophy: the idea that alcoholism is a disease for which there is no known cure?

BECAUSE IT IS BASED ON A FALLACY!

The aspect I most admire about AA meetings is that each speaker is given the floor, can make outrageous statements, get as angry or as tearful as they like, use language that would make a drill-sergeant blush, and all without the slightest interruption or remonstration. Politicians should be made to attend AA meetings to learn how debates should be conducted.

I'm aware that some of the assertions I make might cause you feelings ranging from relief to anger, fear and disbelief. But whether you regard yourself as someone with a slight drinking problem or as a full-blown alcoholic, recovering or otherwise, I have nothing but good news for you. All I ask is that you allow me the same courtesy as you would extend to any other speaker at an AA meeting.

Let me make it quite clear that, no matter what I might say about AA, in no way am I opposed to it on principle or even in competition with it. To most alcoholics AA is the only source of help available. But according to its own doctrine there is no cure for alcoholism and the road to recovery can be a long and painful one. Imagine if there was a complete, easy and inexpensive cure that would work for anyone with a drink problem, a cure that was:

- IMMEDIATE!

- PERMANENT!

- DIDN'T REQUIRE WILLPOWER!

- INVOLVED NO SUFFERING OF WITHDRAWAL
  SYMPTOMS!

- ENABLED YOU TO ENJOY SOCIAL OCCASIONS MORE!

- LEFT YOU BETTER EQUIPPED TO HANDLE STRESS!

- INVOLVED NO FEELING OF SACRIFICE OR
  DEPRIVATION OR NEED TO RESIST TEMPTATION!

Perhaps you'd find it easier to believe in fairies. But just assume for a moment that such a cure did exist. Imagine AA were to use it. How long do you think alcoholism would remain a plague on this planet? What rational person would not use it?

Well, the cure does exist. It is in your hands. The fact that you have read thus far indicates that you believe you have a drink problem to some degree. Wouldn't it be rather foolish not to finish the book? Surely it's worth investigating a cure for that problem, particularly when that cure claims to be instant, easy, enjoyable and permanent!

Why should you trust me? I don't even ask you to. On the contrary, I not only expect you to be sceptical, but an essential requirement of my method is that you question not only every statement that I make, but every belief about alcohol and alcoholism that you have hitherto accepted as fact.

When I first claimed my method would enable any smoker to find it easy to quit, I was treated as a joke by my closest family and friends. They were kind enough not to laugh in my face, but it was blatantly obvious that they regarded me as a candidate for the funny farm. Perhaps this was not surprising when you consider that I'd failed to quit on umpteen previous attempts, and that I made the claim immediately after I extinguished my final cigarette. Today I have people stop me in the street and thank me for saving their life, or that of a friend or close relation. Daily I receive letters telling me what a genius I am, that I should be knighted or made a saint. It has even been suggested that I should be allowed into the royal enclosure at Ascot: personally I believe that would be carrying things too far. The accolades are far greater than I deserve. Like all great discoveries, Easyway was more the result of luck than any genius on my part. In truth the awe and respect in which I am held today is sometimes an embarrassment. Even so, I wouldn't be human if I didn't relish those accolades. In fact, I thrive on them and no way would I risk my reputation by making statements that I couldn't back up.

If you are discerning, you will already have asked yourself:

"If Allen Carr's method is the magic that he claims it is, why isn't it used by AA, ASH, QUIT, the established medical profession etc.? Surely with modern communication techniques, such a cure would spread through the world like wildfire?"

That situation has both frustrated and puzzled me for years. It is because those organizations are large and powerful. They not only regard themselves as the experts, but are accepted as such by the government, the media and society generally. They also have access to vast public and/or charitable funds. Why should anyone listen to the voice of a lone individual who contradicts practically everything these respected experts say? When the subject of alcoholism comes up in the media, have you once heard the views of Allen Carr? More often you hear the views of some doctor or psychologist, often a heavy drinker themselves, or the latest star who has just been released from the 'health farm', spouting cheap Californian psychobabble, and perpetuating the same fallacies that we have been hearing for years.

In the late 1990s the British government appointed a drug 'Czar.' Who did they appoint? A policeman. Did prohibition cure the alcohol problem in the USA? On the contrary, it merely created another problem – organized crime! Did policemen solve either problem? The Czar's name was Hellawell; it might just as well have been Canute.

The question you should be asking is why people fly from all over the world to consult this rather insignificant, lone individual, an individual with no medical training, who doesn't even advertise his method; and why is he widely regarded as the world's leading expert on the subject? There is just one simple answer to that question:

,EASYWAY WORKS!

You might have formed the impression that the established medical profession is opposed to my method *per se*. It is true that initially I was regarded as a 'quack' or a charlatan. But today more members of the medical profession than any other seek help from our clinics, and most of our recommendations come from doctors and nurses. The medical profession is an intensely responsible and stressful vocation. As such, its members are more vulnerable to the drugs trap than the average person, particularly as they tend to have ready access to them.

Even if the average general practitioner wanted to use my method on his patients, it wouldn't be practical. It takes a minimum of four hours' therapy to complete the cure, and it takes a year to train as a therapist. Organizations like DRINKLINE, ASH and QUIT are charitable institutions run by well-meaning amateurs, many of whom have never experienced the problems themselves. Their advice tends to consist of the hackneyed platitudes that guaranteed your failure in the past.

However, I do believe that members of AA, all of whom have been into the pit themselves, would have the necessary experience, knowledge, motivation and dedication required. Add the correct information to that recipe and perhaps alcoholism could be on the schools history curriculum in a few years' time.

Does this mean that Easyway will not work unless backed by an organization such as AA? No it doesn't. Clients arrive at our clinics in various degrees of despair, convinced that if they do succeed in breaking free it will only be after weeks, months or even years of torture. Most believe that even if they do succeed, social occasions will never be quite as enjoyable, that they won't be able to handle stress and that they will have to spend the rest of their lives resisting temptation. They leave four hours later. Over 90 percent of them are exhilarated, completely cured of their problem, knowing that right from day one they will enjoy social occasions more and be better equipped to handle stress.

"Hey! Hold it right there a moment. I've been abusing my body with alcohol for over 30 years. Please don't insult my intelligence. No way could I recover in four hours."

I didn't say you would recover in four hours. I said your problem would be cured in four hours. Have you noticed that if you've suffered toothache for weeks, the moment you pluck up enough courage to visit the dentist, it miraculously disappears? It's 'Sod's law'. Have you also noticed the miserable expressions on people's faces when they enter the dentist, and how difficult they find it to keep the smile off their faces when they leave? Toothache itself can be cured immediately by filling or extracting the tooth. Recovery from toothache can take longer. Your gums might remain sore for several days. But no matter how sore your gums are, when you walk out of the dentist you feel great, particularly if it is the final visit.

This is true of any problem whether it be physical or mental: once you know you have the solution to the problem, you feel great. The greater the problem, the longer you have suffered it and the more convinced you are that there is no solution, the more exhilarated you will feel when you find that solution.

"But surely there cannot be quick and easy solutions to long term and highly complex problems like alcoholism?"

Imagine you were imprisoned in a cell with a combination lock. You could spend years trying to discover the combination and never succeed. But if I gave you the combination, you would be freed easily, instantly and permanently.

"But surely alcoholism isn't like that?"

Alcoholism is exactly like that and Easyway is the key to that prison.

Is this book merely an advert for Allen Carr's clinics? No. It offers exactly the same cure and is complete in itself. The clinics and the book are separate methods of communicating the same cure. The clinic has the advantage in that you can ask questions and dispute points with a trained therapist. You cannot do that with a book and some people find this frustrating. The therapist is also trained to detect if you have missed an important point. Clearly a book cannot do this. I have stated that the cure is immediate. Obviously it is only instantaneous from completion of the cure. The therapy at the clinic usually consists of just a single session lasting about four hours. The cure with the book will take as long as it takes you to finish reading it. The book has the advantage in that you can read it at your leisure. But this can in reality be a disadvantage. I frequently receive letters saying something like:

"My daughter bought your book for me three years ago. I finished it ten days ago. How right you were. It's so wonderful to be free. Why did I waste those three years?"

Why indeed? There can be many reasons why someone doesn't start or finish a book. In a session a person is more likely to stay the course. I've personally given therapy to over 25,000 people who have sought my assistance. Only one walked out of the session, and that was only because the lady's husband had tricked her into attending it. Like most people, I loathe instruction books, most of which are about as exciting as watching paint dry. So I have made every effort to make the content of this book interesting. I hope I have been successful enough for you to finish it, because this book is in fact a guaranteed self-help cure to your drink problem. In fact, your problem is over once you understand the information contained herein. To do that you need to be fresh and sober, so you can concentrate. Some people read the book at a single sitting, however that is not something that I would recommend.

I have stated that the cure is guaranteed. At the clinics we give you your money back if we fail to cure you (you will find information about this at the end of the book). I regret that it is not practical to give a money-back guarantee with this book. You are no doubt wondering why some people fail and whether you are likely to be one of the unlucky ones. Luck doesn't come into it. The cure is guaranteed in that it will work for anyone provided they follow all the instructions. If they do follow all the instructions, they will find it incredibly easy to solve their drinking problem with Easyway. Most people actually find it enjoyable. You might be thinking:

"I'm beginning to smell a rat. The instructions will be something like: make a solemn vow that you will never drink alcohol again, stick to it, and if ever you are tempted just say to yourself – 'Isn't it great, I'm free!'"

In fact, if you did follow that simple instruction it would certainly solve your drinking problem. But I doubt that you would be very happy and no way would we receive recommendations, or achieve a success rate in excess of 90 percent, if the method went no further than that. Perhaps you are now thinking:

"I see the snag. The instructions are so complicated that it will take an Einstein to follow them, and Allen Carr will blame me for not being intelligent enough to understand his method and succeed."

No, I won't. If you have the intelligence to read this book, you have the intelligence to succeed. All you need to do is to follow the instructions. Picture each instruction as one of the numbers of that combination lock. Miss one, or take one out of sequence, and the lock won't open. Your first instruction is to:

FOLLOW ALL THE INSTRUCTIONS

Remember, over 90 percent of clients who attend our clinics succeed. They do so because they follow all the instructions, which are for use during the session. Likewise, the instructions are for use as you read the book. As I said, I loathe instruction manuals and, if you feel the same, I'm pleased to inform you that there are only seven of these instructions, and all will be dealt with during the next two pages. Your second instruction is:

DON'T JUMP THE GUN

By saying "Don't jump the gun" I mean don't refer to them, or to any subsequent part of the book before you get there. Read the book as you would a detective story. That is in fact what it is. The drugs trap is just about the biggest confidence trick in the history of mankind. Abraham Lincoln said:

"You can fool all the people some of the time and some of the people all of the time, but you can't fool all of the people all of the time!"

I believe drug addiction did just that, until I discovered Easyway. I don't mean that everyone became hooked, but that all the people were fooled by the illusion all of the time. Like all confidence tricks, drug addiction can fool intelligent people. But once he has seen through a confidence trick, even a simpleton won't be fooled.

This book differs from most mysteries in that it has alternative endings. For some it's a sad ending, tragic even. For many it is the happiest moment of their lives. The beauty is that the ending is yours to choose. To choose the happy ending, all you have to do is to follow the instructions. Your third instruction is to:

START OFF IN A HAPPY FRAME OF MIND

How can I expect you to do that if you are one of those people who believes that there is no cure for alcoholism, let alone an easy one? I have to admit that we have a chicken and egg situation here. If you could travel forward in time, just for a few moments, and experience a fraction of the elation you will feel when you have completed the book, then you couldn't help but start off in a happy frame of mind. It's a little bit like learning to dive. The water in the pool is eight feet deep but looks about two feet. The board you stand on is only two feet high but appears to be eight feet. You are convinced that you will smash your skull and, no matter how hard your instructor tries to assure you that you won't come to harm, it takes a great deal of courage to launch yourself.

The thought of attempting to control their drinking can be equally frightening to someone who has already made several abortive attempts. You might feel as though you're in a similar position to the diver. But you're not. In fact, you are in the enviable position of having so much to gain with absolutely nothing to lose. The worst thing that can happen to you is that you don't succeed. If that happens, you are no worse off than when you started. But follow the instructions and you will succeed.

Some people believe that Easyway is really an exercise in positive thinking. You know the sort of thing: if you believe you can achieve something, then you can. That is not necessarily true. I've always been a positive thinker, but that didn't enable me to escape from the drugs trap any more than it would have helped me to escape from a prison cell. However, you are far more likely to succeed if you do think positively and are almost certain to fail if you don't. So your fourth instruction is to:

THINK POSITIVELY

Let's cast aside all feelings of doom and gloom. There is no need to be miserable. You are about to achieve something marvellous, something that most people believe is impossible – a permanent cure to your drink problem. See your journey through this book as it really is – an exciting challenge. Just think how proud of you your family and friends will be. Most important of all, just think how proud you will be. One of the beauties of Easyway is that you can actually continue to drink while completing the course. This might sound incredible, but I promise you that all will be made clear. In fact, your fifth instruction is:

DO NOT QUIT OR CUT DOWN UNTIL YOU HAVE FINISHED THE BOOK

There is one notable exception to this rule. If you are in recovery or have abstained for longer than a whole day, remain abstinent if possible. Your sixth instruction is:

ONLY READ THE BOOK WHEN YOU ARE SOBER

The seventh instruction is the last and the most difficult to follow. The seventh instruction is:

KEEP AN OPEN MIND

2 Keep An Open Mind

I have said this is the most difficult instruction of all. Perhaps, like me, you are very lucky in this respect. Isn't it amazing how you and I are scrupulously fair, will always judge matters on their merits, never jump to conclusions, and wouldn't dream of passing judgement until we have heard both sides of the argument? Yet the rest of the world seems to be bigoted, prejudiced, incapable of seeing that they are wrong, in spite of the fact that you have explained the matter so clearly that it would be blatantly obvious to a two-year-old that you are right.

I cannot over-emphasize the importance of keeping an open mind. Some people believe my method is a form of brainwashing. Nothing could be further from the truth. But it does include counter-brainwashing and it is not an easy matter to reverse views that from birth you have regarded as fact. At one time everybody believed the world was flat. Now we all know it to be round. Do you think I could persuade you that we are wrong and that it is in fact flat? Of course not. But when you are in England, do you actually picture Australians standing upside down? Galileo was imprisoned for having the impertinence to suggest that the earth moved round the sun rather than vice versa. Nowadays we know he was right. But when you watch a beautiful sunset, do you visualize the earth rotating until you can no longer see the sun, or do you watch the sun sinking in the west?

Do you see how easy it can be to know a fact yet still have a distorted view? Perhaps I've oversold my case and convinced you that you won't be able to change your views about drinking. Don't worry; the reason we choose not to perceive Australians hanging upside down in relation to ourselves, or the earth revolving round the sun, is that we would get no benefit from seeing the situation as it really is: in our day-to-day lives the distortion doesn't affect us. But whether you are a confirmed alcoholic or just have a slight drinking problem, you have nothing to lose and so much to gain from seeing the alcohol situation as it really is.

I've asked you to be sceptical. How will you know I'm not brainwashing you? Don't worry, provided you keep an open mind, you will know. Successful clients will often say to me:

"I can't understand it. I already knew 99 percent of the things you've said to me, so why do I see things so differently now?"

It is because alcoholism is actually a very simple subject once you understand it completely. But because the people whom we regard as expert on the subject *don't* understand it, they make all sorts of false assumptions. This simple subject is therefore made to appear incredibly complex. One of the first things we are going to do is to unravel all the fallacies and illusions. I won't be trying to blind you with science, all you have to do is open your mind and use your common sense. You will be the judge.

An optimist sees the bottle half-full. The pessimist sees it half-empty. Either way there is exactly the same amount of liquid in the bottle; neither view is distorted. Optimists tend to be happy people and pessimists tend to be miserable. Since in this case you have a choice, you might just as well regard the bottle as half-full – that's positive thinking. Distortion is when you see a bottle as full when it is in fact empty, or vice versa. We are going to be dealing in fact. I recently met a recovering alcoholic who had been dry for over 20 years. During a relatively brief conversation he said at least three times: "I'm just one drink away from being a drunk!" He clearly still felt vulnerable, even after 20 years' abstinence. You won't have that feeling of vulnerability. Once you see the truth, no one will be able to brainwash you again about the facts of alcoholism; you will be in complete control, and you won't have to wait 20 years. By the time you have finished the book, you will feel completely secure.

The bottle half-full or half-empty was perhaps an unfortunate example. You no doubt assumed it contained your favourite tipple. In fact, this particular bottle contained a powerful poison. Incidentally, whenever I refer to a drink, drinking or a drinker, I'm referring to alcohol unless the context is obviously otherwise.

If you live in a democracy you tend to respect the opinion of the majority. But have you ever heard the statement:

'THE MAJORITY IS ALWAYS WRONG'?

The only time I ever heard it was during a discussion at the nineteenth hole, after several rounds of drinks had already been consumed. The statement appeared to be completely illogical to me. The fact that it had been made by a man we'll call Bloggs made the hairs on the back of my neck prickle. Bloggs was a particularly single-minded and bombastic person. I'd had several previous heated discussions with him, but even though I knew I had been right in each case, I somehow never seemed to win the argument. However, this time he had gone over the top and I positively relished the prospect of shooting him down in flames. Needless to say, in spite of the fact that I was supported by every other person involved in the discussion, which occupied the entire evening, I not only failed, but had to eventually concede that he was right.

I'm not saying there are no exceptions to that rule, but I have yet to find one. The rule is based on the following criterion. If nine people all agree, that is strong evidence that they are right. Therefore the tenth person will not disagree with them unless he is absolutely sure that he is right. Supposing the nine are all intelligent and expert on the subject? This is even more reason for the tenth person to be absolutely sure of himself if he is going to disagree. Supposing 999 people all agree? The more people that are unanimous and the more expert they are, the less likely you'll find someone to contradict them. If you do, that person is either a fool or is absolutely certain of his facts. I hope I've already proved that I'm not a fool.

If you are wondering what this has to do with controlling your drinking, the point is that it can be exceedingly difficult to accept that the vast majority of established experts could conceivably be wrong, especially when you have accepted a particular view as an established fact throughout your life. Let me make it clear, I am not stating that 'the majority is always wrong' in the expectation that you will automatically accept my view whenever I disagree with the majority. On the contrary, just as Bloggs could only convince me by the use of sound logic, so I will use similar logic to convince you. However, I will not be able to do that unless you can accept the possibility that the established experts might be wrong. Your acceptance of this is an essential part of the mind-opening process.

You might wish to discuss with other people some of the statements that I make. This can be of great help. But it can also be a hindrance, unless you are conscious of just how ignorant the bulk of the population is of the true facts about alcohol. For example, I will prove to your satisfaction that no one actually drinks a glass of wine purely because they enjoy the taste. But if you tried to convince a thousand wine enthusiasts of that fact, I very much doubt if even one would agree with you. Even after you have completed the book and are certain that what I say is correct, you will still find it difficult to convince such people. One of the ingenuities of the alcohol trap is to exaggerate the so-called benefits and to underplay the downside. No matter how intelligent, logical or open-minded drinkers might be on other subjects, on the subject of alcohol their minds are closed. To attempt to discuss the matter with such people would be completely unconstructive and might even be destructive. Unless, of course, they have reached the stage that you have and accepted that they have a problem. If you need to discuss points with other people, do so with somebody who is at least prepared to listen to the points you make.

You will find no one more willing to help you to solve a drinking problem than AA members in recovery. The trouble is that the very cornerstone of AA philosophy is a fallacy. AA was created on the premise that there is no cure for alcoholism, let alone an immediate and simple one. I'm not saying that you should not listen to their advice, but if it contradicts my instructions, don't follow it. I won't ask you to do – or not do – things just because I say so. I will explain the reason for all my instructions so that you won't have to follow them blindly. You will be the judge.

Another part of the mind-opening process is to try to separate the message from the messenger. You'll probably find me as single-minded and arrogant as I found Bloggs. I will say this for Bloggs, however: he helped to open my eyes and I can do the same for you. If you don't appreciate my style or sense of humour, let that not distract you from the important messages that I'm trying to convey. Remember everything that I write has the sole object of helping you to solve your drinking problem. I'd like to apologize in advance for statements like "As an alcoholic, he . . ." , when it should strictly be: 'he or she'. I'm fully aware that drink problems are not restricted to the male gender. I'm also aware that chauvinism is another evil that I could help to eradicate by altering my style. However, if I attempt to solve two problems at the same time, I run the risk of solving neither. So please excuse me if I concentrate on the alcohol problem. If you find that I tend to repeat certain points or over-elaborate, remember there are two basic constituents to a drink problem. One is alcohol, which is constant and never changes. The other is the drinker. Every human being is unique and my job is to help everyone who has a drink problem. So please bear with me, your patience will reap ample rewards. Now let's start to unravel some of the illusions and mysteries. How do you see yourself? As a social drinker with a problem or

ARE YOU AN ALCOHOLIC?

3 Are You An Alcoholic?

Obviously there's a great deal of difference between a normal drinker with a slight problem, and a chronic alcoholic. OK, heavy drinkers drink more than they should and perhaps they do become boisterous at times, and maybe even argumentative or aggressive. But what drinker doesn't? After all, 90 percent of adults drink, and why not? They are mainly hail-fellow-well-met types. It's a sociable pastime which helps us to relax and is one of the few genuine pleasures that helps us to cope with the stresses of modern life. But an alcoholic? That's something quite different. That's a very serious disease similar to being a heroin addict, but with no hope of a cure. Alcoholics have a real problem and tend to be a menace to society.

Now that's quite a marked difference. Normal drinking appears to be a very pleasant pastime, whereas alcoholism seems to be the exact opposite. AA states that:

'The unhappiest person in the world is the chronic alcoholic who has an insistent yearning to enjoy life as he once knew it, but cannot picture life without alcohol. He has a heart-breaking obsession that by some miracle of control he will be able to do so.'

It is obviously important to you to know whether you are just a drinker enjoying the pleasures of alcohol or 'the unhappiest person in the world'. With such a marked difference, it should therefore be a relatively simple matter to establish. Let's find out what the experts say. There can be few more eminent physicians than the pioneer of heart transplant surgery, Dr. Christiaan Barnard. Let's examine his views:

'*The process of becoming an alcoholic can take anything from 2 to 60 years, although 10 to 15 years is the average. You may think you are immune, but do not be complacent.*'

Now, 2 to 60 years is a pretty wide span. I wouldn't have thought many alcoholics started heavy drinking before their teens or that many lived to reach 70. So, according to Dr. Barnard, you could become one at almost any time in your life.

Dr. Barnard invites the reader to give honest answers to a series of questions. The answers are what I believe I would have replied during the period when I wasn't sure whether I was an alcoholic or just a normal drinker. Some would have described me as a rather heavy normal drinker.

Q: 'Do you take a drink before facing up to a problem?'
A: Usually no, but I'm sure there are times when I have.

Q: 'Do you drink for the taste or for the effect?'
A: Sometimes for the taste, sometimes for the effect, sometimes for both and sometimes for neither reason.

Q: 'Do you sneak away from work for a "quickie" before lunch?'
A: I have drunk before breakfast, let alone lunch, but sneak away? Never. If I had to sneak away for a drink, I wouldn't need to answer any other questions, I would know that I had a serious drinking problem. On reflection, I might have got into the habit of a sandwich with a pint rather than eat at a café. And lunch might have started earlier and ended later as the years progressed, but there was nothing sneaky about it.

Q: 'Do you drink by yourself?'
A: Yes, whenever I feel like it.

Q: 'Do you have memory lapses after drinking?'
A: Frankly I don't remember, but I'm told I do!

Q: 'Do you find other people slow to finish their drinks?'
A: Sometimes, particularly when I've bought the first round and the other person sits there all evening sipping that one drink. That's almost as annoying as the person who buys the first pint, gulps it down in one go, then expects me to get up and buy another before I've had the chance to take the head off mine.

The questionnaire concludes:

'Exercise extreme caution if you have answered "yes" to one or more of these questions – it could mean that you are drinking too much. Seek medical advice. You may not necessarily have to stop drinking, but you would be well advised to control your drinking.'

For the first time the subject of 'controlling your drinking' has reared its ugly head. We will address this matter later. The above are extracts from *The Body Machine*. The cover gives no author. The only name mentioned thereon is Dr Christiaan Barnard: Consultant Editor. I find it sad that such an eminent 'path-finder' should have endorsed such drivel. The approach would be more suited to a subject like: Does the opposite sex find you attractive?

I have genuinely attempted to answer the questions honestly and in the way I would have at the stage of my drinking career I described earlier. At that stage none of my acquaintances would have hinted that I had a drinking problem, let alone that I might have been an alcoholic. Yet I answered 'yes' to five out of the six questions. I would suggest that if they were being completely honest, any normal drinker couldn't possibly come up with fewer than three affirmatives. The logical conclusion would be that nearly every drinker in the world should seek the advice of their doctor including, of course, the vast majority of doctors. Supposing we did seek medical advice, I wonder what help or advice we would actually receive? I strongly suspect it would be identical to the advice that the book gives if you answer 'yes' to just one question:

CONTROL YOUR DRINKING

Dr Barnard doesn't seem to be of much assistance in helping you decide whether or not you are an alcoholic. Let's examine some extracts from AA literature. How do Alcoholics Anonymous describe themselves?

'We are a fellowship of *men and women who have lost the ability to control our drinking* and have found ourselves in various sorts of trouble as a result of drink. We attempt, most of us successfully, to create a satisfactory way of life without alcohol. For this we need the help and support of other alcoholics in AA.'

The italicized words appear to me to be quite a sensible definition of an alcoholic. At a recent birthday celebration, I posed the question: What is an alcoholic? I deliberately did so at the beginning of the dinner before too much alcohol had been consumed. Of the six people present, two were casual drinkers – the type that you sense do not really enjoy drinking but do so because they feel they are not quite normal if they don't – one person was what society generally would describe as a normal drinker, and three were alcoholics. I should emphasize that none of the three even hinted that they regarded themselves as being alcoholics, but it was obvious to an outsider that each of them had long ago lost control of their intake. Isn't it amazing how easy it is to see that one of our friends is an alcoholic, yet we ourselves won't accept that we even have a drink problem, let alone that we might be an alcoholic?

The conversation became a little heated and somewhat incoherent. If you are ever at a dinner party and the conversation starts to lag, I recommend that you pose the same question, but don't blame me for the consequences! Not one of those six people defined an alcoholic as someone who has lost control. One of the alcoholics did admit that he drank, not out of enjoyment, but because he needed it as a social prop. Another of the alcoholics avoided the question and spent the rest of the evening explaining how he could control his drinking. The third alcoholic, although still physically present, was already in a world of her own. Five of the six were adamant that they drank purely because they enjoyed a drink. The alcoholic who admitted that he needed a drink said:

"There's grandma who'll have a glass of ginger wine at Christmas at one end of the scale; and at the other end there's Uncle Ted who has a 'hair of the dog' the moment he gets out of bed, and continues to drink until he is paralytic. Somewhere in between lie the billions of other drinkers in the world."

I don't think anyone could query that statement. The AA booklet refers to normal drinkers who can control their intake; unlike alcoholics, who have a physical and mental illness which dictates that, should they allow just one drop of alcohol to pass their lips, they are compelled to have another, then another *ad infinitum*. The booklet even refers to it as:

'Similar to the manifestation of an allergy. It is compounded by an overwhelming craving for the very thing that can only worsen the effects of physical suffering, irrational behaviour and increasing isolation.'

I find that a strange comparison. People with allergies usually have an overwhelming desire not to get within a mile of the cause of the allergy. They certainly have no desire to actually take it non-stop. Alcoholism seems to be much more comparable to nicotine or heroin addiction. However, I suppose the comparison with allergies does help to give some credence to the AA belief that the true alcoholic has a congenital physical defect. The booklet also states:

'Alcoholism is a progressive illness often of gradual onset.'

'Alcoholism is a fatal illness for which there is no known medical cure, and many of its victims are forced to wage a losing battle.'

'If we take any alcohol whatsoever into our systems, something happens both physically and mentally . . .'

The AA booklet actually groups alcoholism with heart disease and lung cancer! On the one hand, AA are saying that the actual physical make up of an alcoholic is different from that of normal drinkers. On the other hand, it is widely accepted that with heart disease and lung cancer someone might well develop either of these diseases purely as a result of their lifestyle, and not because of any innate physical difference in their make-up. Strange, therefore, with a disease like alcoholism, which appears to consist purely of a lifestyle of drinking too much alcohol, that AA should attribute it to a congenital physical defect.

I've several times heard the rumour that it is possible to establish whether a two-year-old is an alcoholic! How do I know it's just a rumour? Because if it were possible, it would be standard practice to have our children tested on their second birthday.

The implication that alcoholics are genetically different to normal drinkers is quite astounding when you consider it. It means that the actual alcohol is really just a side issue. You can be an alcoholic without ever having drunk alcohol!

'We in the Fellowship of AA believe there is no such thing as a cure for alcoholism. We can never return to normal drinking ...'

'If you repeatedly drink more than you intend or want to, or if you get into trouble when you drink, you may be an alcoholic. Only you can decide. No one in AA will tell you whether you are or not.'

I find this just as vague and frustrating as Dr Barnard's comments. If I repeatedly drink more than I intend to or if I get into trouble when I drink, I MAY be an alcoholic. No one will tell me. I've got to decide for myself!

I don't think that anyone in their right mind could dispute that alcoholism is a serious disease, least of all alcoholics themselves.

Imagine taking Dr Barnard's advice and seeking your doctor's help. He tells you that you might be an alcoholic and that if you are one you are incurable. Naturally you would then expect him to establish whether you had the disease. To which he responds:

ONLY YOU CAN DECIDE!

You might be wondering why you paid all those National Insurance contributions. If you haven't got the disease, you don't need his help and if you have got it, it's incurable, so he *can't* help you. On second thoughts, it's not such a bad deal. What a pity all diseases aren't like that. Since, according to AA, a chronic alcoholic is 'the unhappiest person in the world', and since there is no cure for the condition, it follows that I'm doomed to remain the unhappiest person in the world for the rest of my life. I think I'll decide that I'm not an alcoholic but just an accident-prone normal drinker. I apologize, I'm just being facetious. But this does help to explain why drinkers who clearly do have a problem are so reluctant to accept the fact. Isn't the doctor's response really a cop out? You seek the help of your doctor or AA because deep down you know you've got a drink problem. What you really want is a solution to your problem. Far from solving your problem, they merely confuse the issue by giving a name to the problem and then passing the buck back to you.

Of course it doesn't help one iota to condemn someone who has a drink problem with the stigma of being an alcoholic, and the doubt of whether you are one or not merely exacerbates the problem. Imagine having your annual medical check up and your doctor informs you that you are suffering from advanced seborrhoea. Can you feel the blood draining from your face? All he needed to say was, "By the way, I'd like to recommend something to treat your dandruff."

Alcoholism is an extremely simple subject that has been complicated by the perpetuation of clichés, fallacies, illusions and misconceptions. You might have come to the conclusion that, far from clarifying the situation, I have actually made it more confusing. Please be patient, it is all part of the counter-brainwashing. Columbus could not have convinced the world that the earth was round without proving that it couldn't be flat. In order to accept the truth about alcoholism, we must first dispel the misconceptions that you've been brainwashed with since birth.

For the moment, let's just play along with the idea that alcoholics are physically different from normal drinkers, and that if they allow one drop of alcohol to pass their lips, they are compelled to have another, and then another, *ad infinitum*. If that were the case then how could it be a progressive illness often of gradual onset? How could it take from 2 to 60 years to become an alcoholic? Surely, the very first time an alcoholic drank alcohol they would have to go on drinking until they passed out. AA states that it is a fellowship of men and women who have lost the ability to control their drinking. This implies that they were once in control, which means it cannot therefore be a genetic disorder.

AA clearly contradicts itself. On what scientific grounds can they say with such authority that there is no cure for a disease when they are so vague about the disease itself and cannot tell you whether you are suffering from it? There's no cure, but there is recovery. What is the difference between cure and recovery? Why does a man who hasn't allowed a drop of alcohol to touch his lips for over 20 years, and who intends never to drink again, commence his monologue: "I am an alcoholic"? Yet a man who gets paralytic after drinking ten pints is not regarded as an alcoholic, but is merely spending a relaxing weekend. On the other hand, a clerk known to take occasional sips from his flask during office hours is automatically branded an alcoholic.

The whole subject does seem to be very confusing and contradictory. However, no one could accuse grandma of being an alcoholic because of her annual glass of ginger wine, and I think most of us would agree that Uncle Ted clearly is an alcoholic. But what about the rest of us? Somewhere we have to draw the line. I believe Dr Barnard and AA did make a positive contribution. Isn't the important question not so much the volume, type of drink or occasions that I drink, but:

HAVE I LOST CONTROL OF MY DRINKING?

So let us for the moment accept the definition of an alcoholic as: someone who has lost control over their intake. Neither the medical profession nor AA would argue with that definition. But are we any nearer to establishing whether you are, in fact, an alcoholic? In fact we are. At least we now have a specific yardstick rather than a series of confusing questions. At first sight it might appear that AA and I are at complete loggerheads. In reality our philosophies have much in common. But if alcoholism was a physical disease then a doctor could diagnose it. If an alcoholic is someone who has lost control over their drinking, then surely the person best equipped to make that diagnosis is the alcoholic themselves. So when a drinker has lost control, why is that blatantly obvious to his friends and relatives, but the one person who cannot see it is the drinker himself?

This is common to all drug addiction, whether the drug is heroin, nicotine or alcohol. Perhaps it isn't so much that we cannot see it, but more that we cannot face up to it. That isn't so surprising. No one likes to admit that they have lost control, particularly if it automatically brands you with the stigma of being an alcoholic, and with the unenviable prospect of being 'the unhappiest person in the world'. In fact the question of whether you are an alcoholic is a complete red herring, and merely adds to the confusion. Isn't the answer blatantly obvious? Why would anyone seek the help of AA, or Allen Carr for that matter, unless they had already admitted to themselves that they had in fact lost control? If they were in control, they wouldn't have a drink problem. People don't generally seek solutions to problems they haven't got. The three alcoholics at the dinner party were all reasonably intelligent, educated and strong-willed people who couldn't accept that from now on life can only be satisfactory, and that they can never return to normal drinking. I don't blame them; after all that is a rather dismal prospect.

THANK GOODNESS IT ISN'T TRUE!

Although I detest the word 'alcoholic' and the stigma that attaches to it, for convenience I'll continue to use it to identify a drinker that has lost control. Perhaps you feel that equal stigma attaches to the phrase 'a drinker who has lost control'. Before you castigate yourself, pause for a moment and try to decide the exact moment that you lost control. Don't confuse it with the moment when you realized that you had a problem, like the time you smashed up your car or lost your job, or when your partner finally gave up on you. Such moments are not only easily identifiable but difficult to forget. But there is a great difference between losing control and acceptance of the fact, and the two are usually separated by many years and many unpleasant incidents caused by heavy drinking.

Nor should you confuse the moment you lost control with a period when you greatly increased your intake to help you over a tragedy, like a broken marriage or whatever. You were actually in control at such times. You deliberately chose to drown your sorrows. In fact, aren't we always in control? After all, normal drinkers only drink when they choose to, nobody forces them to drink. Alcoholics are in exactly the same position.

"But alcoholics drink more than they want to."

Are you telling me that normal drinkers never drink more than they want to?

"Of course they do, but not as often."

And are you telling me that alcoholics don't have periods when they abstain?

"True. But again, not as often as a normal drinker."

Doesn't this suggest that the difference between an alcoholic and a normal drinker is merely one of degree? After all, both AA and Dr Barnard agree that it is a gradual process – just like growing old. We actually start to grow old the moment we are born but we don't feel old for many years. Have you considered the possibility that the reason we can't work out the exactly when we lost control is because we were never in control in the first place? Perhaps all the billions of drinkers in the world that lie between grandma and Uncle Ted are on the same downwards slide. Hard to believe? Before you dismiss the suggestion, let's examine another of nature's ingenious traps:

THE PITCHER PLANT

4 *The Pitcher Plant*

Perhaps you are not as fascinated as I am by nature programmes, and have never heard of a pitcher plant. What is so unusual about a pitcher plant? Like the Venus Fly Trap it reverses the usual process of nature, by which animals eat plants, and supplements its diet by trapping and consuming insects. But whereas the Venus Fly Trap works on the same principle as a bear-trap, a pitcher plant is far more subtle and akin to drug addiction.

As its name implies it is shaped like a pitcher. The inside of the plant is coated with a sticky nectar. The odour permeates the surrounding atmosphere and flies are drawn to it like bees to honey. The nectar tastes as good as it smells and the flies cannot resist tucking into this delicious free meal. Unfortunately the meal isn't free. On the contrary, the wretched fly will pay with its life. Rather like the unsuspecting missionary, who was invited to the feast as special guest of the chef, but ends up as the chef's special, so the hapless fly is not the guest, but the meal itself!

It is not just coincidence that the slope at the top of the plant is almost imperceptible, nor that the inside of the plant is coated with minute hairs which grow in one direction only: downwards.

Gravity, the supply of uneaten nectar and the direction of the hairs all conspire to ensure that the unsuspecting insects will travel further and further into the trap. Are you beginning to smell a rat? Are alarm bells ringing? Can you sense the similarity to drug addiction? The poor fly is so intent on enjoying the banquet that it is completely oblivious to the fact that the slope of the plant is becoming ever steeper, and that it is gradually being lured into the depths of the pit.

But why should the fly worry? He has wings. Even if he can now see the partly digested remains of dozens of other flies floating in the juices at the base of the pitcher, he knows that won't happen to him. Why look a gift-horse in the mouth? He's in control and can fly to safety whenever he wants to. Or he thinks he can, that is until he tries to take off. Unfortunately, he has gorged himself so much that he is twice his normal weight. His wings and legs are coated with the sticky nectar and the more he struggles the worse it gets. The sides of the plant are now hairless, slippery and practically vertical. Nothing can prevent that fly from joining his luckless companions.

Perhaps you find the comparison with alcoholism somewhat far-fetched. But just consider it for a moment and I think you'll agree that certain aspects are remarkably similar. Bear in mind that the life-span of insects tends to be measured in days and weeks rather than years.

Can you picture the fly alighting on the plant as the teenager sampling their first shandy? Can you visualize the lager lout just about to throw up as the bloated fly before it tries to take off? And when the alcoholic can no longer close his eyes to the fact that his life is being dominated and ruined by drink, doesn't he try to cut down and control his intake, rather like someone who is grossly overweight attempts to cut down on food. But does dieting make food appear less precious? Quite the contrary. The more you cut down, the more hungry you get, the hungrier you get the more deprived you feel, the more deprived you feel the more precious each morsel becomes. Exactly the same happens when you try to cut down on your drinking. At the times when you won't allow yourself to drink, you feel miserable because you can't drink, and when you do allow yourself to drink, you still feel miserable because you can't drink enough. Aren't the struggles of the fly similar to the abortive struggles of the alcoholic who is trying to control his intake? Drinking hasn't become less precious to him. On the contrary, it now dominates his whole life.

The more both the fly and the alcoholic struggle to escape, the more imprisoned they become.

Are the semi-digested insects not comparable to the down-and-out meths drinkers of skid row, whose entire existence is now confined to begging or stealing the next fix, and trying to find somewhere warm to sleep off the effects? Does the fact that the fly can see the partially digested bodies prevent it from joining them? Who knows? Perhaps some of them smell danger and just fly away. When we were innocent, healthy children, fully capable of enjoying birthday parties and handling stress without the assistance of alcohol, nicotine or any other drug, did the Uncle Teds of this world prevent us from joining the 90 percent drinking majority? Who knows? Perhaps his continual pawing and obscene breath did prevent some of us from falling into the trap. After all 10 percent don't fall into the alcohol trap; but once you fully understand just how ingenious that trap really is, you will wonder how anyone manages to avoid it.

Even if you find my comparison of the pitcher plant with the alcohol trap difficult to accept, the main object of the analogy is to consider the possibility that we were never, ever in control; or to put it another way: there is no innate difference between normal drinkers and alcoholics. Aren't all drinkers just flies at different stages of the slide down the pitcher plant?

"But if drinking alcohol is an inevitable gradual decline to disaster, how come most drinkers never reach the alcoholic stage, and how do you explain grandma, who is 70, drinks one glass of ginger wine at Christmas and doesn't touch another drop for the rest of the year?"

I'm pleased you asked me that question. If I sound like a politician, I promise not to evade the answer. My wife Joyce tells me that on TV and radio interviews I often don't answer the question that is put to me. It is a deliberate ploy that I have copied from politicians, and a very useful one. Of course their motive is to evade the question, whereas mine is altruistic. It is to avoid wasting valuable air-time by answering stupid questions that only make the audience switch programmes, such as 'Does smoking harm your health?'

Fortunately, I have no need to resort to such tactics in this book because I'm in the enviable position of both asking and answering the questions. You might suspect that I'll avoid the questions that

I can't answer. I promise I won't do that, for the simple reason that it won't help either of us. How could I enable you to understand the alcohol trap completely if I didn't answer all the important questions, or explain points that to you just don't add up? The questions that I put are the ones that I anticipate you might be asking at the time. No doubt you have many others. If they are relevant, they will be answered in due course. This is another advantage of the clinic: burning questions can be answered immediately. With the book you have to be patient.

Neither Dr Barnard nor AA explain why it can take from 2 to 60 years to become an alcoholic. If there were a pitcher plant for human beings, we would all slide down it at much the same rate. But the alcohol trap, though based on similar principles, is far more complex, chiefly because every victim that falls into the trap is unique. The rate at which you descend will depend on a myriad of circumstances. The more obvious ones are your upbringing; whether your parents drank and encouraged you to drink; your friends and colleagues; your hobbies and pastimes; your physical resistance to poisons and your finances. Even your religion can have a profound bearing: alcoholic Muslims are few and far between for obvious reasons.

How has grandma managed to sip the nectar without sliding down a single inch? Well, fortunately many of us can remember that our first alcoholic drink didn't taste like nectar at all; far from it, it tasted foul. It doesn't take much observation to notice that grandma isn't sipping that drink because she's enjoying it or it tastes marvellous. She might be doing it because she feels she is missing out. More likely she does it to make the rest of the family feel comfortable. You must have observed how uncomfortable smokers and drinkers feel when there's a non-smoker or non-drinker in their company. It's rather like the strained atmosphere at a wedding breakfast while the vicar remains present. Once he has left we can all let our hair down and act normally. You might also have noticed that grandma doesn't even finish that drink. She might also have a token cigarette for exactly the same reasons. If she does, observe the length of the ash.

Now forget about alcohol for a moment and concentrate on the fly and the pitcher plant. Ponder this question: at what stage did the fly lose control? Was it when it slid into the digestive juices? No, it was obviously before that. Was it when it tried to fly away and discovered it couldn't? No, that was when it realized it was out of control.

THE FLY WAS NEVER IN CONTROL!

The moment it got the waft of the nectar, it was being controlled by the plant. That is the nature of the beast and it had no choice but to follow its natural instincts. As for the pitcher plant, it is so ingenious it doesn't even lose the bait.

"But we are intelligent human beings and we have free choice. We could cheat the plant. We could eat the nectar and fly away before it was too late."

I'm afraid you are overlooking some very important differences between alcoholism and the pitcher plant. With the alcohol trap, there is no nectar. Alcohol is a powerful poison. You are not cheating the alcohol. On the contrary:

ALCOHOL IS CHEATING YOU!

"But surely there can't be any doubt that drinking alcohol in moderation has many advantages."

I'm afraid there are considerable doubts. But let's not confuse issues by addressing matters out of sequence. We are comparing a human being who drinks alcohol to a fly in a pitcher plant. The alcohol trap is designed to trap human beings and 90 percent of adults drink alcohol. That is a fact, so let's not waste time by questioning it. The trap is designed to imprison them for life, by making them believe that they drink because they choose to and that they are in full control. After all, why should any drinker want to quit if they enjoy drinking and it doesn't cause them any problems? But when they reach the stage where they have lost car, job, family and home – when it is blatantly obvious that alcohol is ruining their life – why at such a time, when they should most want to cut down or quit, do they not exercise their free will and do so?

"Because they left it too late?"

No, they didn't. This apparent loss of control didn't happen overnight. It has been blatantly obvious that they've been fighting a losing battle for years: obvious to everyone but the drinker themselves. Isn't it the same with all drug addiction, whether it be nicotine, heroin or anything else? That's the nature of all such drugs: the more they drag you down, the greater the apparent need for them. The greater this need seems the more you have to try and justify it by pretending – to yourself and to everyone else – that you are in control. But why would you need to do that if you really did feel in control? You didn't lose control:

YOU WERE NEVER IN CONTROL!

We have defined an alcoholic as a drinker who has lost control. Let's now adjust that definition to:

A DRINKER WHO REALIZES THAT HE IS NOT IN CONTROL

Perhaps you are still not convinced that you were never in control. If so, don't worry, we will address this in a later chapter. But is the concept so difficult to accept? After all, it's not a million years ago that adult men who didn't drink and smoke were widely regarded as being somewhat weird and unsociable. Perhaps we weren't unkind enough to actually accuse them of being sissies and weaklings, but that's how they were generally regarded. But in the last few decades the general attitude to smoking has changed completely. The vast majority of smokers themselves regard it as an anti-social pastime, and you won't find a parent on the planet who doesn't hate the thought of their children or grand-children getting hooked. Even smokers openly discourage their children from smoking. Doesn't that mean that every one of those smoking parents wishes they hadn't started smoking themselves? Doesn't it follow that they are not smoking because they choose to, but because they're trapped.

Before smoking became generally anti-social, a friend of mine was advised by his doctor that if he didn't quit he would soon be dead. He openly admitted that he envied us smokers, and we secretly pitied him. Today the position has completely reversed. Nobody envies a smoker, and although many smokers won't admit it, we all know the only reason that adults continue to smoke is either that they've failed to quit, or that they believe they couldn't enjoy life or cope with stress without smoking. When you see a youngster experimenting with his first cigarettes is your reaction: keep working at it son, it'll provide you with years of pleasure; or is it: you poor sap, if only you could see what you are letting yourself in for? Don't we see that youngster as we would a fly alighting on a pitcher plant?

What would you say was the more realistic perception of smoking: the Hollywood concept of a few years ago, or the filthy, disgusting and unhealthy pastime of today? Is it too much to ask you to believe that youngsters experimenting with their first alcoholic drinks are no more in control than a fly alighting on a pitcher plant? For the moment, just accept that this is the true position. If so, our definition of an alcoholic as 'a drinker who realizes that he is not in control' enables us to see the alcoholic in a completely different light!

To begin with, it means that you are already way ahead of all these normal drinkers that alcoholics envy so much. After all, most of these normal drinkers don't even realize that they have a problem. So their chances of solving it are nil – people don't set about solving problems that they don't realize they have. If they do suspect that they might have a problem, they will lose even the illusion of enjoyment.

They will spend many years regarding themselves, and being

regarded by others, as normal drinkers. It's not only AA or your doctor who can't tell you whether you are an alcoholic or not. Part of the ingenuity of any addictive drug is to fool you into believing that life without it won't be as enjoyable, and/or that you'll be less able to cope with stress. This is why, even when we suspect that we might have a problem, all of our ingenuity is focussed on searching for excuses to convince ourselves that we are indeed in control. The next stage is to realize that you do indeed have a problem but that it is not yet serious enough to address. The following stage is to realize that it is now serious enough for you to address, but that now isn't the right time.

Of course, I'm merely telling you what you already know. All drinkers go through these stages of suspecting then realizing they have a problem and pretending to themselves they haven't got it: AA call it 'denial'. It's all a nonsense really – how can you pretend you haven't got a problem unless, at some level, you realize you have? The point is it can take years for you to decide whether you are indeed an alcoholic. What I want you to realize is that already you have made tremendous progress. Not only are you ahead of the normal drinkers in realizing that you have a problem, you have also made the very important step of accepting the fact and deciding to do something about it. The fact that you are reading this book is proof of that.

"Every day is the first day of the rest of my life." It's a hackneyed phrase but it happens to be true. I want you to put aside any self-recrimination for anything alcohol has caused you to do in the past. You haven't been abusing alcohol; on the contrary, it's been abusing you. At this stage no one can expect you to do more than you are attempting to do now, including yourself, so let's concentrate on success.

I have already stated that I detest the word 'alcoholic' and the stigma that attaches to it. Although I will continue to use it, I do so purely to assist accurate communication. Let me emphasize that it is the word itself that I hate and not the individual so branded. To me, no stigma whatsoever attaches to any person described as an alcoholic. This might not be so in the eyes of other people, but to hell with them! All that concerns me at this stage is that you remove the stigma in your own eyes. I have no doubt that, like me, your drinking has caused you to do many things of which you are ashamed. You may feel even more ashamed of the things you have left undone, including perhaps your inability to solve the problem by yourself. It might be difficult for you to accept at this stage, but you have no more cause to feel guilt than the fly enticed by the nectar. I remind you that your third instruction was to start off in a happy frame of mind. It is an essential part of the cure and you won't stay in a happy frame of mind if you are despising yourself. Perhaps you suspect I'm asking you to absolve yourself of your sins just to increase my success rate. If I thought that would help you, I would do so. Fortunately, I have no need to do so. By the time you have completed the book, you will realize that the true perpetrator of those sins was not you but alcohol, and that you were the victim not the villain. One of the real joys of using Easyway is that you not only solve your drink problem but lose the feeling of guilt and reclaim your self-respect. When you've done that the respect of others will follow.

I would like to define two other terms that I will be using, not because I have no dictionary but because of society's general ignorance about alcoholism and addiction. Different dictionaries give varying and often misleading definitions. I give these definitions purely for the purposes of accurate communication, so that you at least understand what I mean by them:

RECOVERING ALCOHOLIC: A person who intends never to take alcohol again.

EX-ALCOHOLIC: A person who suffered from alcoholism and is completely cured.

The fact that I have defined an ex-alcoholic does not mean that I expect you to accept at this point that there is a simple and easy way to become one. I probably still have much to do in order to convince you.

The real purpose of the pitcher plant analogy is simply to

demonstrate how a fly is fooled into believing that it is in complete control when the exact reverse is the reality, and to show that drugs have the same effect. The fly's problem is physical and there is no escape. The effects of drinking alcohol are also physical, but fortunately for you the solution to the problem is purely mental, and it is never too late to escape from the alcohol trap. It is also very easy once you know how! Also please bear in mind that:

IT IS NEVER TOO SOON EITHER!

This is an opportune time to consider the advice offered by the other experts, the medical profession, and to take a closer look at:

THE PRISON

5 *The Prison*

Imagine that you are the Count of Monte Cristo, that you've been locked up for 25 years in a damp dungeon, that the Countess is worried about your health and she has persuaded your GP to pay you a visit. Supposing he said to you:

"Look it's terribly damp in here, there's a distinct possibility that you'll catch pneumonia, and you are clearly under-nourished. You are being extremely inconsiderate. Have you the slightest idea of the consternation you are causing your family? Now why don't you be a sensible chap and leave this place permanently. Or if you don't want to leave permanently, at least try to cut down on the time you spend here."

You would not only regard that advice as incredibly patronizing, but you would regard that doctor as a complete moron and I've no doubt that you would tell him so.

A doctor is being just as patronizing, and equally stupid, when he tells a heavy drinker that he won't live to be fifty unless he abstains, or cuts down on his intake. Perhaps you would argue that such advice is neither patronizing nor stupid; on the contrary, it appears to be excellent advice. It is patronizing because the doctor knows that his patient is already fully aware, both of the effect that his drinking has on his health, and of the solution to the problem. The doctor also knows from bitter experience that the advice, sound as it might be, will probably go unheeded. From his point of view, it is the patient who is being incredibly stupid.

In reality neither doctor nor patient is being stupid. In truth there is only one real culprit. No it's not alcohol, but the ignorance that surrounds it. It is this misconception that we drink because we choose to. If drinkers, smokers and other drug addicts take their respective drugs because they choose to, why do they find it so difficult to abstain or cut down? If you are choosing to do something, you must, by definition, be able to choose not to do it, or to do it less often.

If an alcoholic has tried to abstain or cut down but can't do so, then surely he is as trapped as the Count of Monte Cristo in his dungeon? The reason we can't see it so clearly is that in addition to this fallacy that people drink because they choose to, the alcoholic appears to be both prisoner and gaoler. It isn't true! He is an unfortunate victim of the most ingenious trap that man and nature have combined to lay: THE DRUGS TRAP, and he is as effectively imprisoned as if he were locked behind steel bars.

Perhaps you feel my argument is a cop out. After all, millions of people have managed to quit drinking and/or smoking, and I cannot refute that obvious fact. These people will be only too pleased to tell you that it might not be easy, but that by using a bit of willpower and discipline, you too could succeed. And your relatives, your friends and your doctor will all say the same thing.

This is another generally accepted fallacy: that it takes willpower to control your intake or abstain. So ingrained is this belief, that you will probably find it very difficult to believe that willpower has absolutely nothing to do with it. This is something that puzzled me greatly. Many of my friends and colleagues, who I regarded as rather weak-willed, were able to control their drinking or quit altogether. Why couldn't I? I knew that I was a very strong-willed person from other aspects of my life. But I was in good company in that respect. Go to any AA meeting and you will quickly realize that the majority of members are dominant and successful people, or were before the drink took control. This is perhaps one of the reasons why AA believe that alcoholics are innately flawed, physically and mentally.

I will explain later why willpower will no more help you than it would help the fly to escape from the pitcher plant. But knowledge of the trap would have enabled the fly to escape before it was too late. And even if willpower did help, does that really change anything? Suppose our failure to control our drinking *is* due to our lack of willpower. What possible help is it to be told that all we need to use is something that we don't possess? Though intended to give us hope, such advice is worse than useless. So why don't we castigate the 'experts' that offer such advice? Because we too believe that willpower is the solution. Our self-respect is already somewhat deficient, and it doesn't help to be regarded by others, or indeed by ourselves, as a weak-willed jelly-fish.

Have you ever tried to quit by listing all the disadvantages of drinking? It seems to be a logical approach, and is often recommended, but as you will soon discover, the advice that society generally gives you to help solve your drinking problem, including that of the so-called experts, actually makes it harder. The list consists of such things as:

1. The average life-span of a heavy drinker is twenty years less than that of a non-drinker.

2. The average drinker spends £100,000/$142,000 in their life on alcohol.

3. Alcohol destroys the brain cells.

4. Alcohol is a major cause of impotence.

I won't go on, because you might suspect that I'm using scare tactics. Nothing could be further from the truth. The very point I am trying to make is that the list actually makes it harder. It might help you to resist temptation for a few days, and I don't deny that some 'recovering alcoholics' manage to remain dry using such techniques. But they do so in spite of them and not because of them.

The reasoning behind making the list is that whenever you are tempted, you take it out, read it and think: "Don't be stupid!" This helps to remove the temptation. But only temporarily. You are relying on willpower and eventually a day will come when your resistance is exhausted. You are tempted and you think: "To hell with the list – I NEED A DRINK!" You take out the list, not to read it, but to tear it up.

Why doesn't it work? For exactly the same reason that the doctor's advice is worse than useless: because we don't drink for the reasons that we shouldn't! Such advice might well make us *want* to solve our problem, but it doesn't help us to do so. The only real answer is to remove the reasons that cause us to drink, or to drink too much. In fact, all reasons for quitting actually make it harder to do so. Some people find it very difficult to grasp this point. But do the facts about the dangers of obesity remove the temptation to eat? Of course not! It's the forbidden fruit syndrome: they just make food seem ten times more precious than it was before. The more you concentrate on the terrible disadvantages of drinking alcohol, the more another part of your brain will say:

"So alcohol must provide enormous pleasures or benefits, otherwise I wouldn't drink it, nor would the rest of the 90 percent."

Or if you've reached the stage where you can no longer kid yourself that it gives you any pleasure or crutch whatsoever:

"This evil must hold tremendous power over me, otherwise I could quit and so could all the other chronic alcoholics."

The more you concentrate on the reasons you shouldn't drink, the more deprived and miserable you will feel during the periods when you aren't drinking: the forbidden fruit effect, and the more stupid you will feel when you do drink: the guilt effect.

But the main reason that concentrating on the evils of drinking makes it harder to control your intake, is that you concentrate all your efforts on to the problem, as if that in itself will provide a solution. You might find this point difficult to accept, but it is very important that you understand it from the outset. Let's return to the Count. Suppose he heeded his GP's advice and spent the rest of his waking life concentrating on just how miserable prison life was. Would that help him to escape? Of course not! It might increase his desire to escape, but he already has that. What he needs to concentrate on is *how* he is going to escape – and every moment he wastes concentrating on *why*, prevents him from doing that, and thus actually makes it harder for him to achieve his goal.

In the case of the Count, the situation is quite obvious. Why is it more difficult to see with a drink problem? Because of this illusion of appearing to be both prisoner and gaoler. The prisoner is the part of our brain that wants to solve the problem. The gaoler is the part of our brain that prevents us from doing so. Because they are both part of one and the same brain, we believe that by concentrating our efforts on the miseries of the prisoner, the gaoler will have the good sense to set him free.

If you find this point somewhat obscure don't worry. If you already had the solution to your drinking problem, you wouldn't be reading this book. We both know that there are millions of other people on the planet who have the same problem. People who desperately want to control their drinking but find they are unable to do so. So let us accept the unquestionable fact that until you find a solution, you are just as effectively imprisoned as the Count of Monte Cristo. Does the Count need someone to tell him how miserable prison life is? Does a man who has lost his job, home and family really need to write a list? He has already lost all semblance of self-respect and the last thing he needs is to tell himself how stupid or weak-willed he is being. The situation is not helped one bit when a doctor rubs salt into the wound by telling him what he already knows.

There are three important points to this chapter which I will summarize:

1. The only solution is to remove the factors which prevent us from controlling our intake. What are they? Basically that we find alcohol an essential to enjoy social occasions and/or to cope with the stresses and strains of life. Perhaps you believe that those

factors also happen to be facts, and as such, cannot *be* removed. That remains to be seen. Remember it is essential to keep an open mind. But if you do believe they can't be removed, it is easy to understand why people find it so difficult to quit or to control their intake.

2. Accept the simple and unquestionable fact that if you have tried to abstain or to cut down but have failed to succeed, you are as effectively imprisoned as if you were incarcerated in Fort Knox.

3. The very last thing a man who has reached rock-bottom needs is to be reminded how stupid and weak-willed he is, either by other people or by himself. It only makes the problem worse.

So let's cast all negative thoughts aside! If you feel stupid and weak and lack self-respect, stop criticizing yourself right now. You are not the guilty party. You are no more to blame than the other 90 percent in the same prison, or the fly that follows its natural instincts. And remember that if you are at rock-bottom, there is only one way you can now go. All the Count needed to solve his problem, instantly and permanently, was the key to his prison. You already hold the key to your prison. Follow the instructions and finish the book and you too will obtain immediate and permanent release. Although alcohol is a chemical and creates physical effects, the solution to the problem is entirely mental:

EASYWAY IS THAT KEY!

By the way, have you heard about the latest drug? It's called:

EXHILARATION

6 *Exhilaration*

Don't be fooled by the name. It's a powerful poison and will shorten your life considerably. It is also highly addictive, will debilitate your immune system and impede your concentration. It will systematically destroy your nervous system, your confidence, your courage and your ability to relax. By the way, it tastes awful and will cost you about £100,000/$142,000 in your lifetime. What does it do for you? ABSOLUTELY NOTHING!

Hasn't got much going for it has it? Isn't the name somewhat misleading? No more than the name 'ecstasy'. But the manufacturers would find it much harder to sell 'exhilaration' if they named it 'misery'. Do you think I could persuade you to try 'exhilaration'? If you did try it, do you think you would become hooked on it? If you are in doubt, read the description again. Imagine you were hooked and that all you had to do in order to escape was to stop taking it, and that there would be no terrible withdrawal symptoms. Do you think you would quit? Do you think 'exhilaration' will catch on?

It already has. In fact 90 percent of intelligent, civilized Western society is already hooked on it. As you will no doubt have deduced, the drug I am referring to is our old friend alcohol.

Perhaps you think my description of alcohol is somewhat less than accurate. Let's go through it point by point. When you ask someone "What's your poison?" it's not merely a colloquialism. Alcohol is a very powerful poison. If you drank a relatively small quantity of neat alcohol, you would kill yourself. In fact, you are already doing that: slowly but surely.

Will it debilitate your immune system, impede your concentration and systematically destroy your nervous system? If you have doubts about this, don't take my word for it, consult your doctor.

He may not be much help in enabling you to solve your problem, but he is far more expert than me on explaining how alcohol destroys you physically.

Does it taste awful? Try just a teeny-weeny drop of pure alcohol. Why do you think we never drink it neat?

Will it really cost you £100,000/$142,000? I don't know. That's an estimated average. You can do your own estimate if you think it will help.

Is it really highly addictive? Is heroin highly addictive? How many people do you know that are addicted to heroin? Nine out of ten of the people that you know, including you, are dependent upon alcohol.

"But surely the vast majority of them are merely using it because they enjoy drinking."

Are they? Or are they just flies in the pitcher plant?

"But taking alcohol provides no advantages whatsoever?"

Let me make this quite clear. I don't mean that the disadvantages outweigh the advantages. I mean that there are no advantages whatsoever to taking alcohol. At this point I need to issue a warning. Part of the counter-brainwashing is to prove to you that this statement is true. This is in fact very good news, but you might not see it that way at this moment.

Allow me to elaborate. It's hard enough being an alcoholic, but at least you thought you were getting some compensatory benefits. Now I'm about to remove the illusion that there are benefits to taking alcohol, without having removed you from the prison. Those illusory benefits must seem pretty valuable; after all, they are your excuses to justify your need to drink. You might feel that I'm pushing you off the diving board before I've even taught you to swim.

This is the stage when panic can set in, when some people stop reading the book, out of fear. Have you noticed that before alcohol destroys people (physically, mentally and financially) they have no desire to cut down, let alone quit? So they don't. It's only when they are at rock-bottom, when they have lost the support of family and friends, that they wish they could control their intake. But that also happens to be the time when they feel least able to do so, when they feel that they most need what they now regard as the only friend or crutch they have left.

This is one of the clever subtleties of the alcohol trap. It is designed to imprison you until it's killed you. Please don't fall for that trick. Remember you have absolutely nothing to lose and so much to gain. There is no need to be miserable or depressed. In fact, I'm taking nothing away from you. Alcohol never did give you courage or confidence; you only thought it did. In reality, it has been imperceptibly and systematically destroying your courage and confidence for years.

This is another of the ingenious subtleties of the alcohol trap. The slide to rock-bottom is so gradual that we aren't even aware of it. It's rather like growing old. As we shave or apply our make-up each morning, we are looking at the same face as the previous day. It's only when we see a photograph taken ten years earlier that the ageing process becomes apparent. Even then we try to disguise it. What we are thinking is "Crikey! I'm getting old." But what we say to ourselves is "Gosh! Didn't I look young?"

It is exactly the same with obesity. Imagine going to bed with the figure of a gymnast and waking up with that of a Buddha. You would rush (or rather waddle) to your doctor in absolute panic, wondering what terrible disease had afflicted you. Imagine if he said, "Yes, this is a very serious disease and can be fatal, but fortunately I think we've caught it in time and all you need do is change your eating habits slightly". You would be so relieved that you would be delighted to follow his recommendations. Bear in mind that not only would the change in shape be a tremendous shock in itself, but you would have gone to bed feeling as fit as a fiddle and woken up feeling tired, lethargic and out of breath. But because the onset is gradual and each day we look and feel exactly as we did the day before, we accept our debilitated state as normal. We don't even regard it as a disease, let alone a serious one:

"Perhaps I have put on a few pounds, but I'm bound to at my age. A diet and some exercise will soon put me to rights, but I'll wait until after the holiday. Yes, I know I said that last year and the year before, but this time I really mean it."

It's exactly the same with alcohol. If I could transport you back to the time before you fell into the trap, better still if I could transport you just three weeks into the future to show you how great you will feel if you follow my suggestions, that is all I would need to do. And I don't just mean how good you will feel physically, I mean how much stronger and more confident you will feel mentally. Unfortunately, I can't do that. But you can! You've got an imagination:

USE IT!

It's not so difficult. After all it's easy to see it clearly with other drug addicts. Picture an addict who can't get heroin. Imagine the panic, and the resulting shivers and shakes and sweats. Imagine the utter relief when they force a hypodermic syringe into their vein and those symptoms disappear. Would you look at that person and think, "Injecting heroin looks like loads of fun, I must try that at the first opportunity!"? Would you think, "Heroin is obviously really good for the sweats!"? Would you go up to a sweaty bloke and say, "What you need mate is some heroin!"? Or would you know damn well that heroin causes the sweats and the shakes? Non-heroin addicts don't suffer those symptoms. To an outsider it is so obvious, but heroin addicts believe they are getting a genuine high. Do you think that addicts actually enjoy injecting themselves?

Non-drinkers find it difficult to believe that anyone could deliberately force pint after pint of poison down their throats, then throw up and render themselves legless. Then the victim says, "Why do I drink? Because I enjoy it, it relaxes me, it's sociable."

Do you think non-drinkers believe him? Who do you think has the true perception? The non-drinker or the alcoholic? Open your mind. Use your imagination. Once you can see yourself in the pit, it's easier to imagine just how great life will be when you have escaped from it.

In any case, I'm not trying to push you off the diving board before you are ready. Remember I instructed you not to attempt to cut down or quit until you had finished the book. I won't even try to push you when you have completed it. It will be your free choice, and by that time you'll be like a dog straining at the leash to exercise it. I mean, exercise the choice not the dog.

"But surely ignorance is bliss? Given that I'm in the trap, aren't I better off believing that alcohol relaxes me and gives me courage and confidence?"

If someone commences a sentence with "I'm not being disrespectful but ...", you can be certain that the one thing they will be is disrespectful. Likewise 'ignorance is bliss' is a cliché that we only use when it doesn't apply. If you have a serious problem and there is absolutely nothing that can be done about it, then obviously you are better off if you don't know about it. But if an employee was systematically stealing from you, wouldn't you rather know about it? Alcohol has been systematically stealing your money, your health, your courage and your confidence ever since you fell into the trap. If there were nothing you could do about it, of course you would be better off in ignorance. But the beautiful truth is, you not only can do something about it, you are going to do something about it!

You also need to be aware that I haven't actually taken anything away. Alcohol never gave you any advantages, you only believed that it did. Even that isn't completely true. Perhaps you noticed that I didn't say, "I'm about to remove your reasons for drinking." I said, "I'm about to remove the excuses you have been using to justify your drinking." All drug addicts make these excuses. They feel miserable without the drug, but don't understand why, so they invent excuses to explain their behaviour; that way they don't look quite so stupid to other people or to themselves.

In fact you don't even have to invent the excuses, you merely repeat the platitudes that you have been brainwashed with from birth. A classic example that is easy to explode is a smoker saying: "I smoke because I enjoy the taste."

Do smokers actually eat cigarettes? Where does taste come into it? Obviously it doesn't, but we hear it so many times that both smokers and non-smokers actually believe it. Or do they? When a smoker is nearing the bottom of the pit, he will admit that his reasons for smoking were in fact just excuses. When he fails to cut down or quit, the excuses miraculously turn into reasons again. This is another important aspect about drug addiction that you need to be aware of: all drug 'users' tend to sweeten the pill by seeing their 'habit' through rose-coloured spectacles. Let's not mince words:

ALL DRUG ADDICTS TELL LIES!

Not just to other people, but to themselves. It is not that they are basically dishonest people. It is self-protection: part of 'the ignorance is bliss' syndrome. In the early stages, when they have no desire to control their drinking, they sweeten the pill. Why do they need to do that if they have no desire to control their drinking? Because all drug addicts instinctively sense that they are being stupid, but as I will explain in due course, one of the ingenuities of the alcohol trap is to make you use all your ingenuity to put off the day when you will address the problem. At the chronic stage they believe they cannot solve the problem, so they have no choice but to sweeten the pill.

Fortunately, you can and will control your drinking, but you need to stop lying to yourself. This is part of the mind-opening process and one of the reasons why it can be difficult to open it. We have to lie to ourselves to defend our drinking. By all means continue to lie to other people about your drinking, if you wish to. Soon you will have no need to do that either. On the contrary, you'll find it difficult to resist enlightening other drinkers. But it will help if you start observing them more closely and recognizing when they are sweetening the pill. Nothing will help you to control your drinking more than observing and understanding other drinkers.

Supposing you did list all the disadvantages of being a drinker on one side of a sheet of paper and all the advantages on the other. If I could systematically prove to you that every one of those advantages did the exact opposite to what you thought, would you want to quit, or just cut down? If you are in any doubt about your answer, read the description at the beginning of this chapter again. If they could see it for what it was, the biggest idiot in the world wouldn't take that drug.

But am I seriously suggesting that alcohol doesn't help you to relax, that it doesn't give you courage and confidence, that it doesn't help relieve you of boredom and stress? Am I really suggesting that it doesn't quench your thirst and that it isn't an essential ingredient to any successful social function?

That is exactly what I am suggesting. Alcohol has several unpleasant and undesirable effects. Two of them create the illusion that it provides certain benefits while the reverse is in fact the case. The first effect is that alcohol, far from quenching your thirst, does the exact opposite:

ALCOHOL DEHYDRATES YOU!

Again you can check with your doctor if you want to. But you really don't need to. In all probability you have already heard that statement many times before. Even if you haven't, like every other illusion that I will help you to remove, it is a simple matter to prove it to yourself. Even on the hottest day after vigorous exercise, you will rarely need more than one pint of water to quench your thirst. So why, after drinking pint after pint of beer, do you still have a thirst? Bear in mind that when you drink beer or wine, over 80 percent of it consists of water. If you find such a drink thirst-quenching in the short run, it is because of the water content. The alcohol content, far from quenching your thirst, just exacerbates it. Why else would you wake up in the middle of the night, after a heavy drinking session, with a throat as parched as a dry river-bed? If drinking alcohol truly quenched your thirst, the last thing you should be after all that liquid is thirsty. And what do you drink when you wake up thirsty? Water usually. It is true that after a football match or a game of squash, a pint of beer will temporarily ease your thirst, but it's the water that does it and not the alcohol.

The other undesirable effect of drinking alcohol, an effect that creates the illusion of providing benefits, is that:

ALCOHOL INEBRIATES YOU!

It is this effect which hooks the drinker. Inebriation is a process of gradually deadening your senses until you are rendered insensible or, to use the vernacular, until you are blotto. True relaxation is having no worries, cares, tensions, stress or pain. It is impossible to feel truly relaxed, or anything else for that matter, if you have been rendered senseless. If you think being inebriated is relaxing, then you must think being knocked out is relaxing. It achieves exactly the same effect much quicker and with far less aggravation.

"But don't relaxants like Valium work in exactly the same way?"

Yes they do. And this is why many doctors are loath to prescribe them nowadays. I will explain this matter further in due course. I will also explain why drinking is a major cause of the ruination of social functions, and is about as unsociable a pastime as it is possible to imagine. And I will explain how it actually causes boredom and stress, and why its tendency to remove inhibitions is one of its major disadvantages.

If the description of alcohol that I gave at the beginning of this chapter is accurate, it is difficult to believe in this enlightened age that 90 percent of the population could fall into the trap in the first place, let alone remain in it. That is just the point. We are not enlightened and the object of this book is to do just that – enlighten you.

We have reached one of the key points to solving the problem. We also need to pause for a moment and allow it to sink in. It will help if you can reflect on one of those occasions in the early days of your drinking, when you had too much and became drunk and ill. We assume that the reason we drank so much was because we enjoyed the taste, or the effect, or a combination of both. Why else would we have drunk so much? But if we look back on the actual facts, we didn't enjoy the taste. And when we were young and carefree, we didn't need the effect. We made ourselves ill because the combined effect of alcohol was to cause us to be thirsty and deaden our senses.

Just consider what an ingenious and lethal concoction this is! We dance, which makes us thirsty, so we have a drink. The immediate effect of that drink is to quench our thirst. So our brains are fooled into believing that even a drink containing alcohol does actually quench your thirst. But once the alcohol takes effect, it actually makes you thirsty, so you want another drink. At the same time another part of your brain is saying, "Hold on a minute, if you drink too much alcohol you'll make yourself ill." The problem is that that first drink not only made you more thirsty but it began to remove your inhibitions, including the inhibition about drinking too much. Each subsequent drink just exacerbates the situation. You get progressively thirstier and your fear of drinking too much progressively dissipates.

This is the tug-of-war, or what I refer to as the schizophrenia, that every drinker suffers throughout their drinking lives. Part of you is saying "I need a drink" and another part is saying "But you musn't have too much!" The problem is, you don't satisfy your thirst by having a drink. On the contrary, you create a little monster inside your body that has an insatiable thirst, and the more alcohol you give him the thirstier he gets! It is not the flawed genes of alcoholics that, if they take just one sip, makes them want another and another, *ad infinitum*; that is the effect alcohol has on every living creature, including you!

Why do I refer to it as the little monster when it is the cause of so much misery in the world? Because the little monster isn't a problem, it is merely thirst, and can be satisfied by a glass of water or any other liquid that genuinely relieves thirst. It is not even the alcohol itself that is the root of the problem. The real evil is the Big

Monster: the belief that we obtain some genuine benefit from drinking alcohol, the belief that we cannot enjoy social occasions or cope with stress without it, and the belief that it is impossible for some people to control it. The real evil is the monster that creates these illusions:

THE BRAINWASHING

7 *The Brainwashing*

From the moment we are born, our young brains are bombarded daily with information telling us that alcohol quenches our thirst; tastes good; makes us happy; steadies our nerves; gives us confidence and courage; removes our inhibitions; relieves boredom and stress; eases pain; helps us to relax and releases the imagination. At the same time it is an absolute essential for successful social interaction. Whoever heard of a party without alcoholic drinks? It's almost a contradiction in terms. And then there's the most effective brainwashing of all: children drink lemonade, grown-ups drink beer, whisky and wine. With so much going for it, it doesn't really take a Sherlock Holmes to work out how so many of us fall into the pit.

My Collins dictionary-thesaurus defines 'intoxicate' as follows:

'1. make drunk 2. excite to excess.'

The two definitions would appear to contradict each other. It is blatantly obvious that 'intoxicate' is a derivative of 'toxic', which means poisonous. 'Exhilaration' is included as one of the alternatives to 'intoxication' in the thesaurus section. In fact, if alcohol really did do all the things claimed for it at the start of this chapter, then 'exhilaration' would be an accurate and rather apt name for it. Yet it is the same drug that I described at the beginning of the last chapter. An apt name for that drug would be

DEVASTATION

Which is the true description? It is not a question of: is the bottle half-full or half-empty? The bottle is full. The question is: is it full of exhilaration or devastation? From birth we are brainwashed to believe it contains exhilaration. When I was a youth, liquor advertising and Hollywood were the major causes of the brainwashing. Nowadays we don't even have to go to the cinema to be brainwashed. Today we can sit in our own living rooms and watch the box. Every time you watch a film in which the husband is waiting outside the maternity ward, someone will offer him a brandy to steady his nerves. When the baby is born, he'll crack open a bottle of champagne to celebrate.

In practically every Western film you've ever watched, half the action takes place in the saloon. Those tough pioneers who tamed the West seemed to spend all their lives drinking red-eye and playing poker. Their idea of a good night out was to be rendered unconscious in a drunken brawl or to get killed in a gun-fight.

At the other end of the scale, in *Dallas*-style dramas, what does the handsome tycoon do the moment he arrives home from a hard day in the rat race? He'll go straight to the bar, clink two lumps of ice into an expensive cut-glass tumbler and pour a generous measure of scotch.

Of course we were also being bombarded from birth with the seedy side of drinking. Well not exactly bombarded, but the evidence was there. You've probably watched those TV adverts enticing you to join the territorials. A handsome, golden-tanned young man is depicted surfing in tropical waters. Perhaps a more realistic picture would be to show him being shot in the eye, but we'd hardly expect that. It would be equally unfair of us to expect the liquor industry to spend their millions on depicting the occupants of Skid Row. We'd much rather see a successful executive or glamorous model enjoying a drink. Our own government seems oblivious to the seedy side. Not surprising really when you consider that the Treasury enjoys the major share of the profits.

Hollywood has been unscrupulously fair. Of the thousands of films I have watched, I can remember at least two that depicted the dark side of drinking alcohol. One was quite recent: *Days Of Wine*

And Roses. In case you are in doubt, I ought to point out that at my age, quite recent is anything made in the last forty years. The other film I remember vividly. I watched it when I was about ten years old. It was called *The Geek*. It starred the latest Hollywood heart-throb, Tyrone Power, and was about circus life. When he joined the circus as a boy, the manager showed him the various animals. One dimly-lit cage was not much larger than its occupant. As they approached, the snarling creature hurled itself at the bars and tried to grab the boy. It was the geek: half-man, half-beast. It was, in fact, a chronic alcoholic, unshaven and unkempt, who had once been a top international circus act. He had fallen for the demon drink and was prepared to suffer the indignities of playing the geek in return for his daily bottle of liquor. Both the circus boy and I were horrified. How could any human being be reduced to such a level? At the time I thought it was a classic case of Hollywood exaggeration.

Anyone who has been unfortunate enough to suffer from chronic alcoholism will know that it is not possible to exaggerate the depths to which you can sink. It was a most depressing film and had a profound effect on me. Unfortunately, it didn't prevent me from falling into the trap. Right from the beginning you could tell how the film would end. Needless to say, the boy also eventually became a top international act, also fell for the alcohol trap, and ended up actually begging the manager to give him the geek's job. He was lucky. The present incumbent had sunk so low that although he still looked the part, he was so spaced out that he could no longer act it. Such are the joys of drinking alcohol.

Even the films about prohibition give the exact reverse of the true picture. Does a single one even attempt to explain why prohibition was introduced in the first place? Isn't it obvious that society had recognized the misery caused by alcohol? But the authorities are depicted as killjoys. So precious is the poison, and so anxious are the jet-set to obtain it, that they are prepared to pay over the odds, to support mobsters who are ready to kill in order to provide the illegal liquor. Actors like Humphrey Bogart became heroes by playing such parts.

Do we idolize heroin pushers? Of course not, heroin is a real evil, we give long sentences to heroin pushers, and rightly so. Yet in the UK, for example, heroin kills less than 300 people annually, whereas alcohol decimates the population. Currently, in the UK alone, in excess of 40,000 deaths per year are due to alcohol, and the figures continue to rise. Actually, decimate is a very appropriate word for alcohol abuse. It comes from the Roman military practice of killing one in every ten soldiers in the event of any trouble in the ranks. One in ten of the drinking population also happens to be the official figure for alcoholism. I understand the practice was very effective as a means of disciplining those soldiers, but it appears to have no effect at all on drinkers.

How come the huge conglomerates that push alcohol are not only legal, but highly respected institutions? Why do we allow them to spend millions on advertising to push their poisons? Could it be because our governments take the lion's share of the profits?

"Surely alcohol isn't like heroin. Heroin pushers are evil men who hook their victims. Whereas the liquor trade is merely satisfying the legitimate demands of their clients."

Not true! Heroin addicts get hooked by copying their friends in exactly the same way that smokers and drinkers do. Their suppliers tend to be those same friends who are merely meeting their clients' needs, and are in turn supplied by the drug barons who, just like the liquor conglomerates, are merely responding to the demands of their clients.

You might find it difficult to accept this concept, but I did ask you to open your mind. It is really just common sense. Heroin pushers aren't even allowed to advertise. The only difference between the alcohol trade and the heroin trade is that one is legal and the other isn't. The reason we find it so difficult to see them in the same light is that we label heroin addiction as the evil it is and alcohol addiction as 'exhilaration'. We are looking at heroin from the outside, as non-addicts, so we can see it as it really is. But heroin users see heroin in exactly the same way as normal drinkers see alcohol. They believe that they take it because they choose to and that they are in control. They campaign for it and other drugs to be made legal. They have even persuaded many influential people that such a policy would be advisable. Just like the alcoholic, it's not until the heroin addict realizes the drug is ruining his life and that he is powerless to control it, that he sees it for the evil it truly is.

As I have said, the only real difference between heroin and alcohol is that alcohol is legal. It is only legal because 90 percent of us drink. The reason we fall into the trap is because from birth we have been conditioned to believe that drinking alcohol is normal, sociable, enjoyable and beneficial; and that we choose to drink and are in control. Advertising, Hollywood and television aren't the culprits. They merely depict western civilization as it is. It is true that they might exaggerate or distort the truth. But the truth as we see it is grossly distorted anyway. We see alcohol as 'exhilaration' when it is in fact 'devastation'.

We glamorize and emphasize the illusory benefits. One of the unfortunate features of icebergs is that 90 percent of them is hidden beneath the surface. With alcoholism, 99.99 percent of the problem is hidden. There is a stigma attached to being a pathetic alcoholic instead of a 'happy' drinker in complete control, so we are all forced to lie about our problem. We find it difficult to accept it ourselves, let alone admit it to other people. Even our closest family and friends join in the conspiracy. They become enablers. They too finally accept that they can't help us to solve our drink problem, so they start making excuses for us: "I know Ted is drinking a lot lately, but he has so much on his plate. I like him to let his hair down now and again."

Our society can't even see an alcoholic who has reached rock-bottom as someone suffering from a terrible disease. We like to depict a drunk as some sort of clown whose sole purpose in life is to entertain the rest of us. The comedian W. C. Fields made a career out of it.

Every family has its Uncle Ted. Ours was the life and soul of our Christmas parties. He would sit swaying in the middle of the floor because he could no longer stand. He had a huge red nose. Is that why clowns wear red noses and are always falling over? He would keep us children in fits of merriment doing funny things like slurring his voice and removing his false teeth. I find it difficult to believe that as a child I found that funny. For some reason his own children didn't seem to think he was so funny. Perhaps the swigs I'd been sneaking from the port bottle had something to do with it.

Uncle Ted's comedy routine was actually a double act. His wife, Auntie Mabel, was a natural straight man. All night, she would sit feeding him lines so that he could make his hilarious remarks: "I came in from the pub. She said, 'Your dinner's in the oven dried up and burnt.' I said, 'It must be me birthday.' "

It got such a laugh he repeated it five times. I've never met a couple that were so unsuited. The most miserable woman you can imagine. I can't ever remember her smiling, let alone laughing; yet married to the happiest, funniest man you could wish to meet. You've probably heard the expression: "I knew him for years and didn't even realize he drank until the day I saw him sober."

That was Uncle Ted. I had to stay with him for a week while my mother was in hospital. I was really looking forward to it. Talk about Jekyll and Hyde. It was the most miserable week of my life. It turned out that there were two Uncle Teds. They were both heavy drinkers. There was the life and soul of the party; and this miserable tyrant, who came home every evening reeking of stale beer, and spent the rest of the evening shouting at his wife, his children and me. There was only one Auntie Mabel, and it didn't take me long to work out why she was the most miserable person in the world.

That little episode also had a profound effect on me. But like the geek, it didn't prevent me from falling into the trap. Such is the power of the brainwashing to which we are subjected. However, I did find that the Uncle Teds served a useful purpose once I had fallen into it. It was during the early days. It troubled me greatly that my friends would boast about drinking eight pints while I struggled to hold down three. The pints would be arriving quicker than I could drink them. Obviously I didn't want to look silly, so I would craftily place a full pint on a table occupied by an Uncle

Ted. Lo and behold, my pint would disappear, as if by magic. It was a sort of symbiosis. The Uncle Ted could be a complete stranger yet knew his role without so much as a nod or a wink. I didn't give it much thought at the time. It seemed that I never had to. Miraculously, an Uncle Ted would always be conveniently nearby. It never occurred to me that the crafty so-and-so was aware of my predicament and had sought me out. It's rather like the phrase: a man chases a women until she catches him. Aeons later, when I had sunk to the depths of the pit, other people might have mistaken me for an Uncle Ted. How could they get me so wrong? I wouldn't dream of drinking from a complete stranger's glass. You never know what sort of disease you could catch. But anyone can make a mistake in a crowded bar.

Forgive me if I appear to be boasting, but I was a schoolboy boxing champion, and captain of the school rugby and cricket teams. I regard myself as reasonably intelligent and know that I am by nature very strong-willed. How could society have brainwashed me into believing that I was weak and deficient because I couldn't drink more than three pints of beer without being sick? Some morons actually boast that they can drink 16 pints. Is that really something to brag about? Just imagine a bucketful of beer swilling around inside your body. Could anything be more gross? I was grateful to be able to give pints of beer away, at a time when I couldn't afford to buy them. No doubt the Uncle Teds were grateful to receive my unsolicited charity at a time they couldn't afford to drink them. I wonder which of us was the bigger idiot. What difference did it make? We were both being conditioned by society.

Who was the most popular crooner of my generation? Who else but old 'Blue Eyes' himself, hard drinker and close friend of the Mafia. I was lucky enough to get a ticket to one of his concerts. During a pause he took a swig from a glass of some colourless liquid and immediately spat it out: "Ugh! It's water!" What a wonderful role model! His fellow rat-pack member, Dean Martin, perfected a singing style that sounded as if he was permanently sloshed. Little wonder we worked so hard to get hooked.

We didn't choose to drink any more than we chose to speak our native tongue. It was part of our heritage, our culture, our upbringing. Sooner or later we were bound to try our first experimental drink; we had been conditioned to do so. The difference between choosing and conditioning is a subtle one. But let us assume for a moment that you did choose to drink and for many years were genuinely in control and exercising your free will. You were still being conned. What you paid for was a pleasure and/or crutch called 'exhilaration'. What you actually received was a deadly poison called 'devastation'. We would all have an excellent case under the Trade Descriptions Act, but unfortunately we can't sue the liquor conglomerates. Or can we? The tobacco giants once thought they were immune.

The point is that if you bought a bottle of champagne and discovered that it was water, you probably wouldn't drink it. If you discovered that the water was poisoned, no way would you drink it. Yet we'll pay £50/£70 for a bottle that we know contains poison, and drink it; and describe ourselves as intelligent, civilized people. Powerful stuff this brainwashing. Actually, being both a sham and a pain, champagne is very aptly named.

Obviously there is no point in crying over spilt milk. The past is the past and there is nothing we can do about it. At the end of the day it doesn't matter whether we were conditioned or made a free choice. But we can analyse the past and learn from it. What is important is that you will soon be making a clear decision as to whether you are going to do something about your drinking problem in the future. But this time you will be in control and your decision will be based on solid facts. To do that we still have to establish to your satisfaction whether alcohol is 'exhilaration' or 'devastation'.

We have already started to examine one of the constituents of alcoholism: alcohol. Let's now take a closer look at the other: the alcoholic. Let's consider:

THE INCREDIBLE MACHINE

8 *The Incredible Machine*

Can you remember when you last woke completely rested after six hours' sleep, bursting with energy, feeling that you haven't got a care in the world, looking forward to another exciting day on this planet? Can you remember when it happened on a Monday morning?

I am now in my seventies. Can you believe that's how I wake up most mornings, including Mondays? I doubt it. In fact you are probably thinking: "How can Allen Carr ask us to open our minds and separate fact from fiction when he goes completely over the top by coming out with this evangelistic drivel? There's probably not a single person on the planet who doesn't have a care in the world!"

I agree with the last sentence. And we all have problems throughout our lives, but that doesn't mean we have to spend our whole lives dwelling on them, and it doesn't prevent us from waking up *feeling* that we haven't got a care in the world. Please bear in mind that I will never knowingly tell you something that isn't true. 'Be sure your sins will find you out.' I believe in that statement. If I was caught out in a single lie, Easyway would collapse like a house of cards. Sometimes I exaggerate deliberately. I do it not to mislead but because it is my style. How will you know when I'm exaggerating? Because when I do, I exaggerate so grossly that it will be blatantly obvious to you. No doubt you have concluded that the opening paragraph of this chapter is one of those exaggerations. It isn't. In fact, I originally typed 'every day'. But if I have a bad night because of toothache, I will wake up feeling sorry for myself, hoping the toothache will soon go. So I amended it to 'most days'. An example of a gross exaggeration would be: "I had a bump on my head the size of a football."

But let's get back to the opening paragraph of this chapter. Would you find it easier to believe that as far back as I can remember, before I escaped from the drugs trap, I would wake up feeling tired and miserable every morning, even after ten hours' sleep, and lie there as long as I could before I managed to drag myself out of bed to face the rigours of another day?

What a terrible state to get into! Is that what life is all about? The high point of my week was not the debauchery on Saturday night, but the lay-in on Sunday morning. Even though my throat felt like it was lined with sand-paper and a wheel-tapper seemed to be testing the inside of my skull for cracks. And what would I be lying there thinking about? "Oh God, tomorrow's Monday. How can I face another week?"

You might have difficulty in seeing 'exhilaration' in its true light. Even when we do see alcohol the way it really is, we try and block it from our minds as long as we 'choose' to remain in the pit. But most people admit that society tends to exaggerate the so-called benefits of alcohol, and underplay the bad side. However, most of us are completely oblivious to the more subtle and more damaging brainwashing we have been subjected to from birth. I'm referring to misconceptions about the other ingredient of alcoholism: the drinker. From birth we are brainwashed to believe that we are somehow defective: that we are feeble and fragile, and that it is natural for an adult of the species to feel permanently tired and ill.

The lay-in is a classic example. Surely bed is for sleep? Yes, I know there are other pleasant things you can do in bed, but just lying there isn't one of them. Hospital patients have to lie in bed, and they do it for exactly the same reason that I did, because they are ill and feel lethargic. Isn't it strange how we perceive two identical situations in such a different light? When we are ill, we don't pray to win the lottery; our only ambition in life is to feel well again, to get out of that hospital and to get on with enjoying our lives. So how could I see the identical Sunday morning lay-in as the high point of my week?

When I finally escaped from the misery of drug addiction, I fully expected a great improvement in physical health and in my finances. I'd always believed that these benefits would be tarnished to some extent in that social occasions wouldn't be nearly so pleasant without alcohol or nicotine. But my greatest fear was that I wouldn't have the courage or confidence to handle the stresses and strains of life. I knew that the booze and the fags were killing me, but whenever I tried to cut down or quit using the willpower method, I felt miserable. There seemed to be a permanent void in my life that I was convinced would be with me to the grave. So I took the attitude that I would rather have the shorter, sweeter and more exciting life of the drinker and smoker, than the longer more mundane life of the abstainer. I must emphasize that if that were the real choice, I would still be smoking and drinking heavily. Correction, I wouldn't be here. Incidentally, I define 'the willpower method' as any method other than Easyway.

Fortunately, that is not the real choice. In fact, to my amazement, the biggest gains were in courage, confidence, self-respect and energy. And the biggest of all was just feeling great to be alive! You've doubtless heard the hackneyed phrase: 'School days are the best days of your life.' It's only adults that seem to think so. I can remember thinking: "I can't wait to grow up and not have to go to school each day and be bored with subjects that seem to bear no relation to real life. It must be lovely to have your own home and money and to be able to do exactly what you want."

For some reason it didn't seem to work out that way. If anything life seemed to get more and more stressful. Mother Nature never intended it to become more stressful. For all creatures on this planet, including human beings, birth is the most stressful period of our lives, followed by babyhood, childhood and adolescence, because the chief causes of stress are doubt and not feeling in control, rather than physical pain. Test it out for yourself. Pinch your arm gently and gradually increase the pressure. You'll find that you can endure quite a high level of pain without suffering any accompanying stress whatsoever. That is because you know the cause of the pain and are in control. If a stranger were applying that pressure, you'd know the cause but be suffering stress long before the pain reached the level you applied to yourself, because you'd no longer be in control. And if a relatively slight pain suddenly occurred, without any apparent reason, the stress level would be intense; because in such a situation, you are neither in control nor do you know the cause or likely duration of the pain.

Have you ever watched children play and thought: "If only I could harness all that energy. I'd have free lighting and heating all year round."? I can remember bursting with energy as a teenager, rushing around for the sheer hell of it. I find it difficult to believe now, but I can also remember actually enjoying the regular medical. My attitude was: "There's no way you'll find anything wrong with my body." It all changed so quickly. Old age started in my early twenties. It was an effort to struggle out of bed each morning, and no matter how much sleep I had, I felt permanently tired. Apart from a smoker's cough and the occasional hangover, I didn't feel ill. In fact, I regarded myself as a healthy specimen. It was just that I seemed to have no energy. Each evening I would fall asleep watching television.

To what did my doctor attribute my permanent lethargy? I've no idea because I didn't consult him. That was something else that seemed to change overnight. I hated the thought of being examined by a doctor. It was typical Sod's Law. When I had no need of a doctor, I was regularly examined, and when I needed one, I'd avoid them like the plague. Adulthood wasn't the paradise I had anticipated. I hadn't realized that old age set in so quickly. Then there was the stress of setting up home and bringing up children: mortgages, bills and all kinds of hassle, plus the additional stress of holding down a responsible job. As I would often say to my children: "Schooldays are the best days of your life."

We have been brainwashed to believe that the human race is an incredibly fragile species. Pregnancy, giving birth and the rearing and training of a family are completely natural functions to wild animals, and they perform them without the aid of doctors or drugs. For human beings, childbirth tends to be regarded as though it's a disease requiring hospitalization. Both mother and baby need numerous pre-natal and post-natal medical examinations, and intensive care before, during and after the birth.

Please don't misunderstand me. I'm not saying this is wrong but merely pointing out the effect it has on how we perceive ourselves. The baby is regarded as incredibly fragile. The way father holds it you would think it was made of tissue paper. Yet a baby is often the only survivor in serious road accidents. The regular school medicals also help to form this overall impression of frailty. We have to boil baby's bottle, disinfect our toilets and food preparation surfaces, use soap and toothpaste. We have to be immunized and vaccinated. We even take medicines before we are ill. When I was at school, the daily spoonful of cod-liver oil and the weekly ritual of the opening medicine were compulsory. We regard doctors, pills and medicines as part of our everyday lives and believe we cannot survive without them.

How do wild animals survive without the benefit of doctors, pills or medicines? You might argue that most of them don't: that is why so many species are becoming extinct. But wild animals do not die from disease but from starvation or being attacked by other species. The main reasons for their death and extinction nowadays are the destruction of their natural habitat and the general pollution of the planet by homo sapiens. And how did the human species survive and prosper for millions of years without the benefits of modern medicine? How did we colonize and conquer the entire planet?

My object is not to knock doctors or their methods, but to emphasize how incredibly strong we are. I'm in absolutely no doubt as to which has been the happiest period of my life. It is the last twenty years or so. It is no coincidence that it was some twenty years ago that I discovered Easyway. What accounts for the great difference? Some suggest that it is because my discovery has provided me with wealth and respect. As a chartered accountant and a director of Triang Toys, I was already reasonably wealthy and respected. I have the same friends and material lifestyle as I had before I escaped.

We tend to believe that it is old age and the stresses of modern civilization that drag us down. Physically and mentally strong executives arrive at our clinics and say something like:

"I have a very responsible job and am under a great deal of stress. How can I answer the phone without a cigarette? And if I didn't have those couple of whiskies to help me relax in the evenings, I don't think I could handle the responsibility."

This is all part of the brainwashing that we just take for granted. In western civilization we've removed most of the real stress from life. The vast majority of us don't have to worry about where our next meal will come from or whether we'll have a roof over our heads tonight. Why do you think we take up hobbies like skiing and bungee jumping? Isn't it because we seldom experience real danger these days and we miss the excitement? We don't walk around in fear of being attacked by wild animals. Compare this to the life of a wild animal. A rabbit isn't safe even in its burrow. Its entire existence is a battle for survival. But it has adrenalin and other drugs. It can cope.

So can we!

Where's the great stress in answering the phone? It won't bite you or blow up. Why do we confuse responsibility with stress? We take on responsibility because we thrive on it and would find a more mundane job boring and therefore stressful. Why did I regard the mortgage and bills as such a hassle? I had a good job and could afford to pay them. I had a lovely wife, four healthy children, a nice car and a comfortable home. In fact I was a very lucky man and had a lot going for me. So why did I find life such a bind?

Because when you feel physically and mentally low, molehills become mountains, slight set-backs seem like disasters, and the smallest problem tends to be the final straw to break the camel's back.

The most important thing in your life is your health. Another cliché, but how true it is. When we are ill and in pain we are obsessed with just one thought: to get well again, and how quickly we take it for granted once we are. But I had never appreciated the tremendous difference between not feeling ill, and feeling positively great. During my years of heavy drinking and smoking, I didn't feel ill most of the time, but I'd forgotten what it was like to be bursting with energy: just to feel great to be alive! I thought that feeling ended with adolescence.

This is another illusion that society brainwashes us with from birth. Animals don't have the problem of counting how old they are each birthday, or being branded as old age pensioners. If you feel physically and mentally strong and healthy, you can truly enjoy the highs to the full. You'll still have tragedies in your life, and they won't be pleasant, but you'll be equipped to handle them. The minor set-backs that we all suffer won't even appear to be problems but merely part of the exciting challenge of life. There is no such thing as old age. If you are lucky enough to have good health and feel great to be alive, it matters not a jot whether you are 2 or 92. The important thing is how old you feel, not how many days you have lived. I felt like an old man when I was 46 and I feel like a young boy now I'm in my seventies. What's more, I look forward, without trepidation, to many more happy and exciting years. The only material change between then and now is that I ceased to poison my body on a daily basis. It was like escaping from a drugged, nightmare, black and white world of fear and depression into a world of sunshine, colour, confidence, health and freedom.

I regard this as the most important chapter in the book. The main reason that I would like you to cut down or quit is not because it is killing you, ruining your life and costing you a fortune. The reason that I would like you to do so is for the purely selfish reason that:

YOU WILL ENJOY LIFE SO MUCH MORE

The obstacle that prevents us solving a drinking problem is the belief that even if we succeed, the quality of our lives must inevitably deteriorate. Ironically, the greatest gain when you do succeed will be the complete opposite!

In my late 40s I felt physically and mentally weak. My friends and colleagues thought I was the Rock of Gibraltar. And I did feel confident and courageous, providing I had my flask and my fags.

Without them I was like Samson after he'd been shorn. In fact, I was convinced they were my courage and confidence, and I was prepared to die rather than be without them. But I also knew that with them I would shortly be dead. Even that thought didn't enable me to escape. No way could I kid myself that I was physically strong. When I consider that I spent a third of a century systematically and progressively poisoning my body, I find it a miracle that I actually survived the self-inflicted punishment for so long. The fact that I did set me thinking about what an incredibly powerful and sophisticated machine the human body is.

Do you think of a tiger or an elephant as a weak animal? Of course not. Yet both species are in danger of extinction. The human body is made of the same stuff and is equipped with a much larger brain. If I asked you to hold up your left hand, you might pause for a second before deciding which hand was your left, but you would not find the actual feat particularly complicated. In fact, you could train most dogs to do it. But imagine your task was to get every one of the millions of people that inhabit the earth to hold up their left hands simultaneously. Even with modern communications your chances of success would be zero. Yet that is virtually what is happening every time you perform the simplest of tasks, like scratching your nose.

Your body is composed of trillions of cells, each cell a separate entity, yet working in complete cohesion with all the others. Do you think you could peel apples, read your newspaper, play cards or answer the telephone? Of course you could: none of those tasks is particularly complicated. But would you complete even one of those tasks efficiently if you attempted to do them all at the same time? Those trillions of cells that make up our bodies undertake dozens of incredibly complicated tasks, and at one and the same time throughout our lives.

Whether you are awake or asleep, your lungs continue to breathe in oxygen, and your heart continues to pump that oxygen and other chemicals through the circulatory system to the parts of the body that require them. Your internal thermostat continues to keep your body temperature at the required level. Your body continues to digest food, absorb the necessary fuel and nutrients, and process the waste. Your immune system fights a constant battle to overcome injury and infection.

Because these functions are automatic and require no conscious effort on our part, we take them for granted. Although it is not necessary for you to understand the technical details, it is important that you are consciously aware of the incredible sophistication of the human body. In fact the human body is the most efficient survival machine on the planet: the pinnacle of creation. It is millions of times more sophisticated than the latest computer or spacecraft.

Perhaps you believe that we are the coincidental result of the 'Big Bang', followed by three billion years of natural selection and evolution. Perhaps you believe we were created by an intelligence millions of times greater than our own. Perhaps you believe that evolution is the process by which that intelligence developed the miracles of Mother Nature over three billion years, rather like mankind developed the modern Rolls Royce from the wheel.

It doesn't really matter what you believe. You don't have to have faith. Just open your mind ... and your eyes! Mankind is a fact. We didn't create ourselves, but are the product of three billion years of trial and error. We are the product of Mother Nature. Every natural instinctive function we possess is designed to ensure that we survive, whether we like it or not. Anyone who is stupid enough to contradict three billion years of proven intelligence has no right to describe themselves as intelligent.

Mankind has achieved incredible feats, particularly in the field of modern medicine. The first heart transplant is a comparatively recent event. Understandably, we still regard it as an incredible achievement. Compare it to a teenager who has learned to replace the defective engine of his motorbike. To him that would also be a great achievement. But no way could he manufacture the steel and other materials that make up the engine and shape the components. It is only after generations of accumulated knowledge and technology that mankind can create the engine for the motorbike. But the greatest achievements of mankind are equivalent to the crudest caveman's axe, compared to the sophistication of a single cell. For all his knowledge and achievements, mankind cannot create a single living cell.

Don't be confused by the recent developments in cloning. That is not creation. Man has been cloning flowers, plants and vegetables for thousands of years. It's called 'taking cuttings'. It shouldn't surprise us that animal cells can produce the same results.

The problem is that we cannot speak directly to Mother Nature. So we have to rely on the experts of our own species for guidance. That's fine if you need guidance on your car or your computer. Expert man created the computer. But you surely wouldn't dream of allowing your pet gorilla to mend your computer; the result is certain to be disastrous. Don't you think the same principle applies when mankind interferes with something as complicated and sophisticated as the human body? Exercise great caution before you accept advice about altering the functioning of the human body. If that advice contradicts Mother Nature's, accept the advice of the real expert!

"But you've just said that we can't speak to Mother Nature!"

True, but we can listen. She has been speaking to us from the moment we were born. So overawed are we by our own intelligence and technology, we have stopped listening to her. Our eyes and our minds are closed. It is true that modern science has learned a great deal about the functioning of the human body. An eminent scientist recently described it as like creating a clearing in a huge forest. The larger the clearing gets, the greater the perimeter left to investigate. The existence of DNA is a comparatively recent discovery. It may have answered one mystery, but it has created thousands of others. Each gene is now a separate mystery to be solved.

As I write, I'm privileged to be sitting at a window with a picturesque view. This view is dominated by a magnificent oak tree. An oak tree is a thing of great beauty and strength. 'Heart of oak are our ships.' However, like most of the miracles of nature,

I've just taken it for granted. It is difficult to imagine that it was the result of a tiny acorn falling to the earth. No one watered it or fed it, yet it has grown into a magnificent cathedral, stronger, more beautiful and more enduring than anything made by man. It has stood for a thousand years and each year it has not only produced thousands of acorns to guarantee the perpetuation of its species, but has provided a home and sustenance to thousands of creatures. It is truly a miracle!

Strangely, my dictionary defines a miracle as 'a supernatural event', and supernatural as 'being beyond the powers or laws of nature'. To me the process by which an acorn becomes an oak tree is truly miraculous. That is because I'm a mere mortal. But there is nothing supernatural about it, and it is certainly not beyond the powers or laws of nature. On the contrary, it is one of the classic examples of the laws of nature. And did I say no one watered it or fed it? I've got the blinkers on again. Mother Nature provided the sun, the rain and the necessary minerals – a miracle to us, but a routine task for her. What better illustrates the message that I am trying to convey than that dictionary definition? Surely a miracle is an event that is not beyond the powers or laws of nature, but beyond the comprehension of mankind. An event that mankind is not knowledgeable or intelligent enough to explain.

I've said I regard this as the most important chapter of the book. It is probably not coincidence that I'm finding it the most difficult to write. I've also said that Easyway has much in common with AA teaching. Part of that teaching is that alcoholics do not possess the power to fight the demon drink alone, and need the help of a higher power. So am I saying that this higher intelligence that created us is God and that you should pray to him in gratitude and for help? If that is your faith, by all means do so. But that is not my message. You do not need faith. The process that created you is nature. It doesn't matter whether nature is the result of coincidence or is itself the creation of a higher intelligence.

These days I find it difficult to believe that I was so blind and arrogant for so long. For years I was surrounded by the miracles of nature, yet denied the existence of the intelligence that created those miracles. How could I have regarded myself as scientific and intelligent whilst flouting the advice of the intelligence that created me? The most valuable source of advice and information that we possess is our own natural instinct. I am exceedingly grateful to Mother Nature, for the simple reason that she has already provided us with everything we need to survive and to enjoy life. I'm talking about the greatest of all her creations:

THAT INCREDIBLE MACHINE

Drug addiction is actually on the increase in this enlightened age. This baffles society in general, and parents in particular. The prohibition experiment proved that you don't cure the problem by attempting to dry up the supply. Prostitution had already amply shown that you don't remove the supply by making it illegal. Some so-called experts have concluded that by making a drug illegal, you actually increase its demand. It becomes forbidden fruit.

Not only have we not absorbed the lesson provided by the prohibition experiment, but it would appear that we have learned nothing since the Garden of Eden. Some experts even advocate legalizing drugs like cannabis and heroin. They actually believe that youngsters fall into the drugs trap just to rebel against their parents and the simple answer is to make hard drugs legal. It's so obvious! Why didn't I think of that? If we legalized heroin, for example, the situation would be the way it is with alcohol: only 90 percent of them would fall for the heroin trap! Why don't we take it a stage further? Why don't we not only make cannabis and heroin legal, but openly encourage our children to take them, just as we used to with nicotine, and still do with alcohol?

Of course we try to deter our children from falling into the drugs trap. I also taught my children the Green Cross Code. If only I had realized that would cause them to rebel against me and give them an irresistible desire to jump under the nearest bus. The reason the so-called experts come out with such drivel is because they haven't the slightest idea how to stop youngsters from falling into the drugs trap, and that's because they don't understand how the trap works. The reality is that nothing has changed. The alcohol trap is identical today as it was when you and I first fell into it. It consists of three separate pieces of brainwashing. The first is that the human mind and body are physically weak and deficient and need outside help in order to enjoy life and to cope with stress. This creates the belief that we need outside chemicals to compensate for the deficiencies. The second piece of brainwashing is that alcohol will compensate for the illusory weakness and deficiency. Ironically, it actually creates weakness and deficiencies. The third is that we have been brainwashed to believe that we are more intelligent than the intelligence that created us. That is indeed arrogance!

This is why this chapter is the most important. Any businessman knows that if the demand dries up, you can advertise until the cows come home but you can't even give the product away. It is the belief that we are weak and incomplete that creates our desire for alcohol, and the illusion that alcohol compensates for that makes us feel dependent on it. The ingredients for most successful confidence tricks are a genuine need or greed and an illusory supply. Remove the need or greed and the victim will not fall for the trick. In the case of alcoholism, both the need and the solution are illusory. It's like selling a crutch that is riddled with woodworm to someone who hasn't got a broken leg. But if we don't remove the need, the void will remain – it's the difference between cure and recovery.

My state-of-the-art laptop is an extremely ingenious and sophisticated machine. It is also rather fragile. The first day I had it someone spilt a glass of liqueur and some of it splashed over the keyboard. It was immediately mopped up. Even so the machine seized up and had to be repaired. Obviously a machine such as the human body, which is infinitely more sophisticated, must be incredibly fragile. We are brainwashed to believe that. But look at the facts. For over a third of a century, I deliberately poured the same sticky poison down my throat, together with other poisons, in much larger quantities. Not only did I survive, I didn't even need to go in for repairs. OK I was lucky, many aren't. You must be one of the lucky ones too, otherwise you wouldn't be reading this book.

Read the opening paragraph of this chapter again.

That isn't evangelism or exaggeration. Wouldn't you like to feel like that? Your body is incredibly strong and so are you. You are also self-contained. The human brain in control of the human body is the most sophisticated machine on the planet. We already possess within us every drug, every instinct, every agent we need to live long, healthy, happy lives.

We possess an incredibly sophisticated early warning system. If the oil-warning light of your car started to flash, would you feel you had solved the problem by removing the bulb? If your lighting repeatedly fused, would you substitute a nail for fuse wire? Of course you wouldn't. Such actions might appear to solve the problem in the short term, but the bulb and the fuse were safety warnings; far from solving the problem such behaviour would guarantee disaster. But so much of modern medicine is based on pills or medicines that remove the symptoms of the disease and not the cause.

As a youngster I suffered regularly from constipation, which in turn developed into haemorrhoids. It was the source of considerable pain and concern for most of my life. My doctor prescribed opening medicine for the constipation and various concoctions for the piles. Why didn't he tell me that my constipation was caused by eating foods recommended by intelligent man, rather than the fuel designed for me by Mother Nature? After all, we wouldn't dream of putting diesel oil into an engine that was designed to run on petrol.

I'm sure we have all used pain-killers from time to time. In fact many people are hooked on them. But pain itself is not a disease. It is a symptom. It's your body telling you that something is wrong. Removing symptoms in your body can be much more disastrous than removing the oil-warning light in your car. Any doctor worth his salt will tell you that the most powerful and effective weapon you possess, for both the prevention and cure of disease, is your immune system. By removing the symptoms you negate your immune system. You can't expect the fire brigade to turn out if you don't sound the alarm.

I also wish that my doctor had explained that my body wasn't designed to be diseased, and that most of the complaints I consulted him about could have been removed by changing my lifestyle. Perhaps the worst effect of the progressive poisoning of our bodies is not on the liver but the immune system, which can no longer function properly. It's virtually equivalent to deliberately contracting AIDS.

If you've ever been compelled to drive a car in thick fog during daylight you will be aware that it is a frightening experience even at the slowest speed. Can you imagine how much more frightening it would be to fly an aeroplane over mountains at night in thick fog? Even with instruments which tell you height, speed and bearing, it would still be an horrendous experience. Obviously you would have to fly fast enough not to stall. If your altimeter registered your altitude at 2,000 feet, flying over a mountain range in which the peaks reached a height of 4,000 feet, would you quickly adjust the calibration of the altimeter to read 5,000 feet? Of course you wouldn't. The biggest idiot on earth wouldn't do that.

But that is exactly what we do when we take alcohol and similar drugs. I cannot over-emphasize that our bodies controlled by our brains are the most sophisticated survival machines on the planet. Mother Nature has equipped us with senses and instincts, the sole purpose of which is to make sure we survive, whether we like it or not. Just like the rabbit, we possess adrenalin and other drugs which our bodies will supply automatically when we need them and in the quantities we need. To interfere with our own senses and instincts is to court disaster and misery: it is about as sensible as the pilot altering the calibration of his instruments. Later I will explain how alcohol affects our senses to create the illusion of pleasure or of being a crutch.

Perhaps you think the comparison to flying in fog is an exaggeration. But there is a reason that our language contains the expressions 'blind drunk' and 'legless'. Look at it another way. Imagine you were born completely blind and stone deaf; with no sense of taste, touch or smell. How would you cross the road safely? Even if someone took your arm to guide you, you wouldn't even know it. Do you not think that would be akin to flying in fog with no instruments? Without our senses we would be flying through life in a permanent blanket fog. Our senses are the instruments on which we are completely dependent. To consume chemicals that affect the accurate functioning of any of our senses is foolish. To do so with addictive poisons is abject stupidity.

The alcohol trap is like a youngster wandering into a beautiful garden, having no desire to leave it, spending many years in it; then discovering that not only are the fruit and vegetables slowly poisoning him, but that the garden is an elaborate maze from which the only escape is the way he came in. It would obviously help if he could retrace his steps. Let's do just that:

HOW DID WE FALL INTO THE TRAP?

9 *How Did We Fall Into The Trap?*

The circumstances vary with each individual, but the principle is the same. Many of us sneak a little tipple at parties during childhood, but most of us start to dabble more seriously during that period of great upheaval in every youngster's life, when we are expected to change from happy, cheerful children into serious, responsible adults. Early childhood is generally more stressful than adolescence. But we survive it without the need to resort to drugs. Observe young children when they arrive at a birthday party. They are shy and inhibited. Half an hour later they are screaming with delight. They are on a complete high and they don't need alcohol, nicotine or any other outside drugs to achieve it. That is a true high: just feeling great to be alive. In fact, there are few greater pleasures in life than hearing the unadulterated laughter of others, be they babies, children or adults. You don't even have to know why they are laughing: laughter is infectious.

By the time they reach adolescence, the brainwashing has taken effect. I find it frightening nowadays. Youngsters seem to be searching for some crutch or prop, as if Mother Nature had provided for every creature on the planet, with the exception of the most powerful and sophisticated of all; as if she had omitted some vital ingredient. They are hardly to blame in a quick-fix culture that trusts technology over nature. The vision of the industrial revolution was that science would set man free but, like Frankenstein and his monster, there has been a reversal of roles, and we have become slaves to the technology we created. We are victims of our own intelligence: the intelligence that separates us from all other animals. The intelligence that invents an exercise-bike to burn all the energy we didn't use sitting at our desk-jobs, so that we can earn lots of money to spend on energy saving devices like TV remote controls, which turn us into sedentary sloths who have to go to the gym on sunny days to ride a bicycle that doesn't go anywhere.

Nowadays we cannot eat anything without worrying whether it is genetically modified or poisoned with insecticides. We are discovering new diseases for which we have no cure. TB and malaria have again reared their ugly heads. We are polluting our rivers, lakes, land, seas and even the very atmosphere we breathe. We are responsible for holes in the ozone layer and global warming; we are over-fishing and over-cultivating; transforming arable land into desert; destroying the rain forests; exhausting fossil fuels and essential minerals and chemicals; forcing other creatures into extinction and over-populating the planet at an alarming rate.

We inherited a magnificent planet which took three billion years to mature, with an eco-system that has enabled an incredible variety of species to live and procreate in perpetuity. We seem hell-bent on converting it into a concrete and barren wasteland in less than 200 years. For all our great progress in technology, we haven't eradicated disease or starvation. We haven't eradicated war. On the contrary, we've produced weapons so powerful and dangerous that we dare not even use them on our enemies. Such is the legacy we pass on to our children: a world of drug addiction and violence. Western civilized man has little to be arrogant about. It is true that we have rid the world of many evils. A high rate of infant mortality is a thing of the past, at least in the West. But the sum of human suffering seems to be constant, for the march of progress which removed these evils has brought its own problems in its wake. The excessive use of antibiotics has led to increasingly powerful strains of the very diseases they were meant to cure.

Yes we do have many things our ancestors lacked: psychiatrists, bigger and better police forces. We've got these things because we need them. And we created that need. Modern man threw a brick through his own window in order to sell himself a burglar alarm. More of us live in larger and more crowded cities than ever before, yet become more isolated, so we have invented pills to try to fight the blues and the stress of living the fast life in the big city. Not content with pushing ourselves to the limit, we push our children to it. Education has become an end in itself rather than a means to an end. Why else would we tolerate an exam system which tests three years of learning in three hours, and guarantees that the pupil will never have practical use of 90 percent of that knowledge? That is if he makes it to the exam hall without suffering a nervous breakdown.

And all for what? So that our children can afford to become more dependent on technology than we are? Even those who pass their exams with honours aren't guaranteed employment fit for their attributes. For all our intelligence, we are the only species that has learned to cry; and the only species to make our lives so miserable that we deliberately sacrifice the most powerful instinct that Mother Nature gave us, by taking our own lives.

We've also been brainwashed from birth to believe that we are weak and fragile and dependent on pills, and that alcohol will provide us with both a pleasure and a crutch. As youngsters, why on earth should we even question the brainwashing? It must be true. Why else would the rest of the population be taking pills for their nerves, or to relax, or sleep; and why would 90 percent of them be drinking if it didn't help? OK, they might also tell us the dangers of drinking alcohol. So what: they tell us that motorbikes are dangerous but does that stop us from riding them?

In any case, the dangers haven't stopped them drinking, and there's no way they could describe their intake as moderate! Nevertheless, they tell us that alcohol's OK in moderation and that a little of what you fancy does you good. Have you noticed that the people who say that always indulge in a great deal of what they fancy?

It would be a miracle if we didn't try that first experimental drink at some point in our lives. The occasion on which we take it doesn't matter one iota, nor does the reason we take it. But that first alcoholic drink is the most ingenious aspect of the trap: it tastes awful. A teenager tasting their first pint of bitter will secretly be thinking, "Have I really got to drink this muck? I'd much rather have lemonade!" But lemonade is for kids. Beer is for adults. And it tastes foul. Which removes the teenager's fear that he might get hooked on the stuff.

This is what springs the trap. The fly wouldn't continue to eat the nectar if it tasted awful. That's because the fly acts on instinct. But we are intelligent, rational human beings. We have been brainwashed to believe that adults drink because they enjoy the taste. Why should we dispute it? You've only got to ask them. It's obvious that Uncle Ted doesn't drink to make himself throw up and pass out every night; that's just an unfortunate side effect that he's prepared to put up with because the drink tastes so good. Why else would our parents have a bottle of wine with their meal when they eat out? Obviously, a bottle of wine is a special luxury and must taste marvellous. If that first alcoholic drink tasted like nectar, alarm bells would ring: it would confirm why Uncle Ted has sunk so low. But no way could we actually become hooked or dependent on this foul-tasting, foul-smelling concoction! Any fears we might have had of going the same way as Uncle Ted are immediately removed.

Perhaps the most pathetic aspect of alcoholism is how hard we work to get hooked. Fortunately, we can ease ourselves into it by starting off with sweeter tasting drinks like shandy, cider, port and sweet sherries. But we soon progress to beers, wines and spirits. It is not long before the beer tastes so normal that we wonder how we could have drunk kid's stuff like lemonade. Of course we have to dilute the spirits with mixers to start with, but we soon learn to drink them neat. We feel really tough then, particularly if we can down it in a single shot, like John Wayne or Clint Eastwood, and if you can do it without even shuddering you feel even tougher. I heard of a student at Oxford who could down a pint in two seconds without swallowing, and another who could drink a yard of ale inside two minutes and not throw up. No wonder Oxford is respected world-wide as a seat of learning. In vino veritas? Like hell! The more vino the less veritas.

Before you know it, and without making a conscious decision for it to be this way, drinking has become a normal part of your social life. You wouldn't dream of holding a party or going to a disco without drinking. Unless, of course, you were driving. But have you noticed how, just as you tend to favour stronger and stronger drinks, and the volume you take tends to increase, so you tend to drink at a greater variety of social occasions? Of course, it's never we ourselves who are responsible for the progression.

In my early golfing days, after the game I would go straight home to the Sunday roast. Until one day: "Aren't you going to buy me a drink? Come on, don't be unsociable. After all you've won my money."

I could barely afford to play golf, let alone treat the old fogey. But how could a new member ignore a request like that, especially as this particular old fogey happened to be captain of the club? Then, of course, he would be embarrassed if I didn't allow him to reciprocate. I can't remember making a conscious decision to do so, but it soon became normal to stay for a drink after every match. Then it became two or three. Occasionally, I would stay on for a frame or two of snooker. After all, what was the point of going home? The dinner would be dried up and not worth eating, and I could do without all the nagging after a hard week at the office. Perhaps my Uncle Ted wasn't so bad as I had pictured him. It's quite possible, indeed probable, in fact there's no doubt: Aunt Mabel had obviously driven him to drink.

In the winter, before teeing off, I began to join some of the other members for a brandy or two, just to get the blood circulating, you understand; and yes, they were large ones, and naturally we continued the habit in the summer. If I was having a particularly bad round, I would look forward to having another brandy, or two, at the half-way house. For some reason I always seemed to be having a bad round lately. I can't think why. I used to win quite a few competitions when I first joined the club.

Some of the lads used to carry a flask around with them. I promised myself that I would never have a flask. To me, a flask was the first step to alcoholism. But one of my children gave me one for my birthday. It was a beautiful silver one with my initials on it. I couldn't offend her by not using it. Actually, it turned out to be very useful, a bit like my computer really. I don't know how I managed without it. Lovely as it was, my flask was a bit on the small side. Naturally, it was polite to offer it around. Amazingly, some of the younger members didn't have a flask, and those that did weren't so free with theirs as I was with mine. I wasn't drinking more, you understand, I was just naturally generous. That must have been the reason why my flask was always the first to be empty. I solved the problem by buying a larger one.

I used to despise those old fogies when I first joined the golf club. They were rude, irritable, bad-tempered old men, with large red noses and bleary red eyes to match, sitting around sipping their whisky and water. The high point of their year was if they could catch the steward topping up their glass with Teacher's instead of Bell's, or vice versa. They'd make so much fuss that you'd think he had topped them up with poison. Come to think of it, he had.

It didn't dawn on me that I was slowly but surely turning into an old fogey myself.

While all this was going on, drink had of course become a normal part of so much of my life, not just social events. I used to take lunch in a comfortable cafe that provided excellent food at very reasonable prices. I can't remember taking a positive decision to switch to standing up in a crowded, smoke-filled bar, with a pint in one hand and a dried up sandwich in the other, but that is what I did. I can't remember the first time I had a drink with a colleague before going home after work, or how and when it became a daily ritual.

My first marriage couldn't stand the strain. Did I drink because my wife nagged me, or did she nag me because I drank? I can see it so clearly now that I've escaped from the pit. But at that stage I was in no doubt who was to blame. After all, I was no different from any other normal drinker. I wasn't drinking in the office, although lunch had tended to start earlier and last longer. And occasionally I would have a small one, or two, before I left for the office, but only if I anticipated that the day would be a particularly bad one. But no way could anyone describe me as an alcoholic. If I'd drunk more than usual my voice might be slightly slurred, but you'd never find me paralytic or rolling on the floor. In fact, just the opposite was the case. I could drink quite a lot without it even affecting me. I hadn't lost my job or smashed up my car.

The above is my story. But it doesn't matter whether your favoured pastime is darts, football, snooker, or just an evening at the pub with the lads. Nor does it matter whether your job is stressful or mundane, because alcohol seems to relieve both stress and boredom. Whatever your story, it moves in one direction only. Like the fly in the pitcher plant, there *is* only one direction: downwards. The accumulative effects of the poisoning – together with our increased consumption and the fact that we are getting older and are not as fit as we used to be – all these factors combine to bring us to what I call:

THE CRITICAL POINT

What is the critical point? It is equivalent to the stage that the fly reaches when it has sated itself, when the nectar is beginning to make him feel sick and all he wants to do is to fly away, but finds out that he can't. You reach the stage when you are getting hints from your family and friends that you are drinking too much. Perhaps your boss has hinted that the quality of your work after lunch falls somewhat short of that of the morning. Perhaps you notice someone wince when they smell your breath. Perhaps you've smashed up your car. You still can't accept that you are an alcoholic, but you cannot deny that you are drinking too much. So now you are going to prove what you have always told your family, your friends and yourself: that you are in control? How will you prove it? By cutting down.

It doesn't really matter whether you cut down on the number of occasions that you drink, or the volume that you drink, or a combination of the two. Something critical has now happened. Up to now you have been in the habit of drinking as much as you want to and whenever you what to. Logically, you might think that if your level of drinking was causing you problems, you would automatically not want to drink as often or as much as you used to. Obviously, part of your brain doesn't. That's why you decided to cut down. And so it was with me. But did that mean that I no longer wanted to play golf on Sunday? Of course not! Golf was the only pleasure I had left: except for smoking and drinking.

So why didn't I just not drink when I played golf? Because I couldn't imagine golf without drink. That would be like playing darts without a pint, or Ascot without champagne, or a party without booze. So why didn't I just drink less on these occasions? I tried on more than one occasion, as you probably have, but it didn't work. After a couple of drinks it didn't seem to matter anyway. I'd say to myself: "I need a drink; only one and it'll make a new man of me." And it did. And the new man needed just one drink. In any event, I didn't want to sit there worrying about how much I'd had to drink. How can you enjoy yourself if you have to do that?

Do you see the point? The part of your brain that made you want to drink as often and as much as you wanted to; that doesn't change just because another part of your brain now sees your drinking as a problem. Everyone knows that dieting makes food ten times more precious, not less. And alcohol is a drug. As I will explain later, the natural tendency with drugs is to take more and more, not less and less. Before you reached the critical point, your drinking was no problem, or at least you didn't see it as a problem. Now you do see it as a problem. Problems create stress. What do we do to help relieve stress? That's right, we have a drink.

When a doctor tells a drinker he'll not see another birthday unless he quits the booze, the drinker does two things: the first is to make a solemn vow that he will quit, and the second is to have a drink in the nearest pub to help him over the shock. If a doctor makes the statement to a chronic alcoholic who has tried and failed to quit many times, he is actually telling that alcoholic that he is going to die, so the alcoholic will go to the nearest pub to get blind drunk.

Once the drinker recognizes that his drinking is causing him a problem, he has not one new problem but two. When he is drinking he feels guilty and miserable, and when he is not drinking he feels deprived and miserable. I call this the 'critical point' because at one and the same time he is drinking too much and can't get enough to drink. I couldn't put it better than AA:

'It is compounded by an overwhelming craving for the very thing that can only worsen the effects of physical suffering, irrational behaviour and increasing isolation.'

Just as the more the fly struggles, the more trapped it becomes, so the more the alcoholic tries to exercise control the more precious the pleasure and crutch appears to him, so the more dependent he feels. In order to control his intake, he has to exercise willpower and discipline. No matter how strong-willed he is, eventually he finds himself drinking more than he did before he decided to cut down. After several failed attempts to cut down, the alcoholic comes to the conclusion that the only solution is to quit completely. Unfortunately for him, he attempts to do so by using:

THE WILLPOWER METHOD

10 *The Willpower Method*

Like cutting down, the willpower method of stopping, far from achieving its objective, just helps to ingrain into our minds that we can never be cured. You need to understand why.

Before we took the bait we were brainwashed to believe that drinking was a pleasure and a crutch. When we took those first experimental drinks, there was certainly no pleasure. But for some strange reason we persisted and, surprise surprise, alcohol did indeed seem to become a pleasure and a crutch. But now we've reached the stage where it has also become a problem, and the problem itself has become so serious that the apparent pleasure and crutch are not sufficient to compensate for it. We've tried to cut down or control it like normal drinkers, but we must be abnormal because we don't seem to be able to do that.

So there is now only one solution: to give up completely. But this isn't a very pleasant thing to contemplate. The mere fact that we use the expression 'give up', as opposed to 'quit' or 'stop', implies that we are making a sacrifice. Even the word 'abstain' has the same effect. My thesaurus includes such alternatives as 'deny', 'forbear', 'forgo', 'give up' and 'withhold', all of which imply a sacrifice. And why not? We do believe that the sacrifice is genuine. In addition to the brainwashing we have been subjected to from birth, which is reinforced by our experience in the trap, there is the even more frightening brainwashing of how difficult it is to quit.

It is blatantly obvious that the residents of skid row are getting no pleasure or crutch whatsoever. It is equally obvious that it is alcohol that has reduced them to their present state and that, far from being happy, their lives are completely miserable. So why do they continue to drink? It's little wonder that AA conclude that they must have some chemical defect. There certainly appears to be no rational explanation. And if you've already attempted to cut down or 'give up' by using willpower, you already know how difficult and depressing it can be. It's not surprising that we put off our attempts to escape for as long as possible.

So instead of starting our attempt with a feeling of elation, of excitement and challenge, we start with a feeling of doom and gloom as if we are about to attempt to scale Everest without the benefit of ropes or oxygen. And what is the first thing we reach for if we are feeling miserable? That's right: our friend and crutch. So before we even start, we are hit with a double misfortune: because we can no longer have a drink to cheer ourselves up about the fact that we can no longer have a drink! This makes us feel even more depressed, which in turn makes the need for the drink even greater, and so it goes on. We hope that time will solve the problem and that, provided we can endure the misery for long enough, one day we'll wake up and shout "Eureka! I've kicked it! I don't want to drink any more!"

But why should that ever happen? To use two more clichés:

'Forbidden fruit tastes sweeter.'

Only if you believed it tasted sweet in the first place. And:

'Absence makes the heart grow fonder.'

But only if it was fond in the first place. If you believed that drink gave you a genuine pleasure or crutch before you quit, how on earth can you prove that it doesn't once you are not allowed to drink? This is another reason that I want you to continue to drink until you've completed the book. I need you to be able to prove to yourself that there is no genuine pleasure or crutch. But not yet.

Back to the willpower attempt to quit. Let us suppose that you do have the willpower to survive a few hours, days, months or even years of the misery. Something else is happening that on first examination you might think is helping your attempt to quit, but in fact makes it harder. The moment you stop taking alcohol, all the powerful and valid reasons that made you want to quit begin to disappear. Your health begins to recover, and so does your financial situation. Your personal relationships and your job prospects start to improve. It's rather like witnessing a horrific accident when you are driving. It will slow you down for a few miles, but the next time you are late for an appointment, you've forgotten about the accident and you step on the gas.

One of the kindnesses of Mother Nature is that we tend to forget bad experiences in our lives. But if we ignore her advice such kindnesses tend to backfire. The fact is that the longer we abstain the less we remember about the misery of drinking, and the less reason we have to resist the other side of the tug-of-war, increasing the temptation to have:

JUST ONE DRINK

Eventually, our resistance is exhausted and, with the ingenuity typical of our species in general, and of drug addicts in particular, we find an excuse that will enable us to have just one drink. But of course alcohol dehydrates us, which makes us want another drink. It also removes our inhibitions, which makes it easier for us to have the second drink; and so on, ad infinitum, ad nauseam, ad mortem.

You fall straight back into the trap again. It makes no difference whether you slide down helter-skelter as many people do, or whether it's gradual like the first time.

And why shouldn't you fall back in? The trap hasn't changed and neither has your conception of alcohol. If it were possible to communicate with flies, so that they could completely understand how the pitcher plant worked, do you think they would fall for the trap? If a mouse could understand the mechanics of a mouse-trap, do you think he would be stupid enough to attempt to eat that piece of cheese? He might do if he were hungry enough. But would he then run the risk if he knew the cheese itself was poisoned? Of course not. Unfortunately for mice and flies, no one can explain the ingenuity of the traps.

Some people do manage to abstain and recover for long periods on the willpower method, but very few manage to escape completely. Those that do manage to abstain permanently have no greater expectation other than to recover, or for life to be satisfactory. Fortunately, you and I can communicate and you don't have to use the willpower method. But let's remove some more of the brainwashing. Let's establish once and for all that there are no advantages whatsoever to drinking alcohol. Ask anyone why they drink and they'll give you:

EXCUSES NOT REASONS

11 *Excuses Not Reasons*

What makes us want to start drinking in the first place? That's pretty obvious. It is because 90 percent of the adult population drink; and surely they wouldn't drink unless they got some pleasure or crutch from it? When we decide to quit, why is it so difficult? The reasons are equally obvious: it is the terrible physical withdrawal pains combined with the fact that we have got into the habit of drinking, and habits are difficult to break. Wrong! These are excuses not reasons. As I will explain later, the actual physical withdrawal symptoms from alcohol are so mild as to be almost imperceptible. And habits are easy to break, provided you really want to break them.

As I explained earlier, the true reason that this particular practice can be so difficult to break is because of the schizophrenia. We believe we are making a genuine sacrifice. The booze might be ruining our lives, but our whole lifestyle is now dependent upon it. We believe we can't enjoy social occasions without it, we think we can't handle stress without it, and we have nothing to take its place. Life seems utterly miserable without it and that is why it can be so difficult to quit.

It wouldn't be so bad if the other 90 percent didn't drink either. But not only do they drink, they sit there at the meal enthusing over the quality of the wine:

"It's satisfyingly full-bodied but not the least bit pretentious. Are you sure you won't have some old chap? No? Surely one glass can't do any harm."

Your dinner companion is trying to convey the impression that he is a connoisseur and that the wine is a special vintage that the restaurant stocks just for him. You are fooled by the ploy because you are distracted by the thought of how you explain to this idiot that if you had just one sip, you would end up drinking three bottles and pour the fourth over his head. What you actually say is:

"No, I don't think I will. I have a big day tomorrow and I need to keep a clear head."

What he is actually drinking is the house wine with which the restaurateur tops up the vinegar bottles. It's little wonder that recovering alcoholics tend to keep their own company. The object of this chapter and the following few chapters is to get three facts clearly into your mind:

- DRINKING ALCOHOL GIVES NO ADVANTAGES TO YOU WHATSOEVER!

- THE SAME APPLIES TO OTHER DRINKERS! YOU WON'T BE MISSING OUT!

- ALL DRINKERS TELL LIES!

Nowadays, most youngsters are introduced to the dubious joys of alcohol before they leave school. Even our universities are prolific breeding grounds for alcohol and other drug addiction. If you approach a group of students who have only recently started drinking, and ask them why they are doing it, I guarantee that not a single one will reply:

"I might be a student but I am no longer a child. I'd feel stupid drinking lemonade when all the others are drinking beer."

What the student will actually reply is:

"Because I enjoy a drink."

He will say it in a tone that implies that you have asked a very stupid question: surely the answer is obvious. But it is as clear as day to you that he is not enjoying that drink. He has told you a deliberate lie. You cannot prove it was a lie, but you know it was and so does he.

So when you ask someone why they drink, how can you tell whether they are lying or telling you the truth? Is the answer they give the true reason or merely an excuse? You use your common sense. A good guide is to ask yourself whether the reply seems rational. In the example I've just given, the student's reply sounds quite rational, but he is betrayed by the fact that he takes infrequent little sips at it, with a barely concealed look of disgust on his face. It is quite obvious that he is not enjoying that drink.

Sometimes it is difficult to tell whether the answer is a lie or the truth. If you were to ask the same student the same question three months later, you would probably get the same answer, but this time it might contain a grain of truth. By now he might have acquired the taste, and genuinely believe that he is quenching his thirst with that particular drink because he enjoys that taste. If so, he is not deliberately lying to you. Nevertheless, he is still giving you an excuse not a reason. If you put the question "What is it you actually enjoy about drinking?" and he replies "It quenches my thirst", you can be pretty sure that he is lying. He might well drink alcohol when he is thirsty. Most drinkers do. But most drinkers also know that alcohol dehydrates you. Even if they don't, water is cheaper and does the job far better.

"Ah, but I like the taste of beer. I can't stand the taste of water."

This one is more difficult to prove. You can argue that water hardly has a taste, but is the best thirst-quencher in the world, whereas beer tastes bitter and creates thirst.

You might go on to argue that alcohol cannot possibly quench thirst, otherwise you wouldn't have to go on drinking. The student replies that they don't go on drinking it because of thirst but because they enjoy the taste so much. We'll talk about taste in some detail later, but for the moment just imagine you were Mother Nature. You have spent millions of years creating this myriad of different creatures. In order to survive, they need food and water. We are intelligent human beings and are fully aware that we will die if we don't eat and drink. But other animals don't know that. How would you ensure that other creatures ate and drank?

One clever way would be to make them feel thirsty whenever the water content of their body fell below a certain level, and hungry when they needed energy or were deficient in vital minerals. And that, of course, is exactly what she did. But how do these creatures distinguish between food and poison? After all, our parents ensure that poisons are safely locked up out of harm's way, until we are old enough to learn the difference. Mother Nature's solution was far more ingenious. She made poisons smell and taste foul and food smell and taste nice. Thirst, hunger, smell and taste are just four of the essential attributes with which Mother Nature has equipped the incredible machine, to ensure that we survive whether we like it or not.

Consider the ingenuity of the system. When food turns to poison, such as when fruit putrefies, it will smell awful and taste awful. It will also feel awful and look awful. Touch and sight are two other senses essential to our survival. Man didn't invent 'sell by' dates. Mother Nature has been using them for millions of years and they are far more sophisticated and reliable than man's. Incidentally, alcohol is the product of vegetable matter that has gone past the putrefaction or rotting stage and started to ferment.

IT IS A POWERFUL POISON
AND TASTES AWFUL!

This is a good moment to address the bane of my life. I'm referring to the person who rings up in the middle of a phone-in, when I'm in full flight and can sense that I'm beginning to get through to the audience, when I've managed to stop the interviewer asking questions like:

"Does alcohol really destroy the liver?"

Yes, of course it does, but alcoholics know this, and if we bore them with what they already know they'll switch to another programme.

The bane of my life says something like:

"How can you possibly say that alcohol provides no advantages whatsoever, when my doctor categorically states that a glass of wine actually reduces tension and the risk of heart attacks. He happens to be a Harley Street specialist and the top man in his field."

Yes, he would be, wouldn't he? He always is. I seem to be the only person in the world who has a middle of the road GP for a doctor. How can you counteract statements like that? What the caller doesn't tell you is that his doctor's specialized field is chronic hallucinations. I've even come across a doctor who, in this relatively enlightened age, still claims that smoking is good for you. He is, of course, a smoker. He also happens to be a member of the magic circle. Delusion rather than doctoring is obviously *his* speciality. Half a century of hard medical fact up in smoke!

The bane goes on to cite an even higher authority: the Almighty himself. Apparently, everything on this planet has been put there for a purpose: to benefit mankind. Alcohol must be a benefit because every undiscovered tribe in the world has learned to brew its own concoction. Having opened the call by confounding you with the indisputable statements of a brilliant scientist, he finishes it by advising you to let pygmies be your guide. Fortunately, the closing point is quite easy to counter. You can merely ask how he found out, if the tribes are undiscovered. But the preposterous claims of such people does amply illustrate how ingenious addicts are in searching for reasons to justify their addiction. Perhaps the Almighty has supplied everything for the exclusive benefit of mankind. Man himself seems to think so: witness the manner in which we generally treat other species. Alcohol has its uses. It is a powerful detergent and can be burnt as a fuel. (Just think what it does to your insides!) Alcohol can be of benefit to mankind. So can streams. But to conclude that the Almighty supplied us with alcohol so that we could poison ourselves with it, is about as logical as claiming that the sole purpose of streams is for us to drown ourselves in them.

Note that the bane also conveniently overlooks all the disadvantages of drinking alcohol. This merely emphasizes my point that drinkers offer you excuses not reasons.

One of the sad aspects of all drug addiction is that when you do manage to abstain using the willpower method, you will probably be envying those friends who still drink. It doesn't occur to you that those friends might be envying you. You can get involved in a sort of war of poker in which you are trying to bluff them about how nice it is not to have to drink, and they are trying to kid you that you are being deprived of a genuine pleasure or crutch. With Easyway you won't need to bluff. You'll have four aces and they won't even have a pair of twos. But some of the points they'll come up with, although specious, can be difficult to counteract. This is why your own common sense is so vital. If you ever start to doubt yourself, whether it be before you finish reading this book, or after you have escaped, always remember that it doesn't matter what anyone else thinks: you are reading this book because you have a problem and this book will show you an easy way to solve that problem. That is fact! It will also help to re-read the opening paragraphs of Chapters 6 and 8. It might be a good idea to do that now.

Back to the subject of whether any one actually takes alcoholic drinks because they taste good. Having made the point that alcohol tastes foul, the next counter is usually:

"Ah, but blended with other drinks or substances, alcohol can be very tasty indeed. Classic examples are gin and lime, vodka and orange, whisky and lemonade, rum and blackcurrant and port and lemon."

This is another point that can be difficult to counter: that a liquid that has a foul taste can be more acceptable if blended with another liquid that has a pleasant flavour. That is undoubtedly true. I find I cannot refute that point. But that doesn't explain why we should want to mix a foul-tasting liquid with a drink that tastes pleasant, especially when the foul-tasting liquid happens to be a very expensive and powerful poison. I fail to see the logic in that.

"But I definitely enjoy the taste of a glass of wine with my meal and I don't need any mixers in that."

But wine is alcohol diluted with water and other additives to sweeten it and make it taste good.

"Yes, but I like dry white wine."

But didn't you switch to dry white wine because you heard sweet wine tends to make you gain weight?

"That's true, but I'm positively revolted by the taste of sweet wine nowadays. I can't think how I ever used to enjoy it now that I've acquired the taste for dry wine."

It had to come up sooner or later. Let us address the subject which creates more confusion than any other:

THE ACQUIRED TASTE

12 *The Acquired Taste*

Many of us were weaned onto alcohol with sweet drinks like shandy, cider, sweet sherry or port, drinks we don't have to acquire a taste for. Our impression of taste can be confused by the occasion. Some smokers believe they enjoyed the taste of their first cigarette in spite of the fact that they didn't actually eat it. If your first experience of alcohol was champagne at Royal Ascot, even if you didn't particularly enjoy the taste, or the effect of the bubbles backfiring down your nose, at such an excitable and happy occasion it wouldn't be surprising if you formed the impression that you did. In any event your senses, including your memory, would be distorted and unreliable after just one glass.

Fortunately, if you are blessed with a good memory, you will remember taking drinks that actually tasted foul. The vast majority of people, when asked how the first pint of beer tasted, will reply something like:

"I was thinking: have I really got to drink this muck for the rest of my life?"

The foul taste is your body ringing an alarm bell:

"WARNING! WARNING! YOU ARE TAKING POISON! PLEASE STOP!"

But alcohol has the dual effect of making you thirsty and deadening your senses to the unpleasant taste, so the tendency is to have another pint and another, and another. Does the incredible machine give up on you and allow you to kill yourself? No.

Instead it brings into play another ingenious survival technique with which Mother Nature has equipped us: vomiting! Throwing up isn't a particularly pleasant experience, but don't knock it, it literally saves your life. It is also about as loud and as clear a warning as you are going to get that you are doing something to your body that you shouldn't.

If we had suffered a similar experience through eating too many green apples, we would have heeded nature's warning and learned our lesson. But because 90 percent of adults drink, including our role models and our parents, we ignore the real expert and follow the example of intelligent mankind, and persist in learning to take alcohol on a regular basis. You could hardly blame Mother Nature for giving up on us at that point. But she doesn't. So ingenious is the system that the incredible machine starts to build an immunity to the poison. Rasputin deliberately built up an immunity to arsenic. He could take 20 times the dose that would kill a normal man.

"Why would he do a stupid thing like that?"

It wasn't stupid. It was common practice to poison your fellow man in those days. Come to think of it, nothing has changed much, except today we call it being sociable rather than murder. One of the ingenious aspects of the immunity process is that it not only partially negates the poisonous effects, but the taste gradually begins to seem less foul. In fact, if you persist long enough, you actually start to believe that you enjoy the taste.

"Wouldn't it have been more ingenious if the taste had got worse rather than better?"

Very likely. But you can't blame Mother Nature for that. She can't believe that any creature would be stupid enough to deliberately poison itself on a regular basis.

So she assumes that you have no choice. In any case, the foul taste didn't prevent you from persisting, and she is helping by making the taste seem pleasant. It is a typical example of the rules of Mother Nature backfiring on you if you flout them.

But let this not distract us from our purpose. The alcohol itself doesn't change. It remains a powerful poison. Neither does the taste of alcohol change: it always tastes foul. Just because our brains and bodies become immune to the foul taste, that doesn't mean that the taste itself changes. It is our perception of that taste that alters. A man working on a pig farm can become immune to the smell to such an extent that he is no longer aware of it. But if he goes home in work-soiled clothes he'll get a sharp reminder from his wife. Another very common example is the different effect that stale tobacco has on non-smokers compared to smokers. In fact, many alcoholic drinks taste so unpleasant that even regular drinkers cannot bear them without adding mixers and sweeteners. This the case with all spirits. It is true that some people drink spirits neat. But they didn't start drinking them that way. What happened is that as they became immune to the drug, they needed more and more to achieve the same effect, and it became boring to have to drink a litre of orange juice in order to get that effect. So they acquired a taste for neat gin.

You'll find that the products that we have to acquire a taste for are invariably drugs and poisons, such as nicotine, caffeine and alcohol. Acquiring a taste is merely building an immunity to a foul-tasting poison. No doubt someone who persevered and acquired the taste for dry white wine will say he is pleased that he did so, because now he can enjoy a glass with his meals for the rest of his life. It is a difficult argument to counter, but it is a specious one.

You must know someone who used to take two spoonfuls of sugar in their tea and then decided to cut it out completely. You inadvertently spill no more than two grains of sugar in their cup before you remember they no longer take sugar. You say nothing, thinking they won't even notice. Won't notice? They spit it out as if you've just handed them a cup of arsenic. This proves two things. One is that lifetime habits are easy to break provided you want to break them.

"So why isn't it easy to quit smoking or drinking?"

They are not habits, they are drug addiction; and, besides, they are easy to kick if you know how. But let's tackle one thing at a time. The other thing the no-sugar-in-the tea example proves is that our taste-buds are flexible and we don't have to be slaves to them. Most drinkers do acquire a taste for their particular tipple. You've no doubt heard someone say:

"I love the taste of a pint of bitter!"

What further proof do you need? My dictionary defines bitter as: 'a foul and unpleasant taste'. This is a classic example of how addicts lie to themselves and to other people. The problem is that such statements are so commonplace we take their validity for granted. "I love the taste of a pint of bitter!" is quite clearly a contradiction in terms. But have you ever heard anyone point that out to the person making the statement?

There is not a single drug addict, living or dead, who planned to end up a junkie. There is not a single drinker, living or dead, who planned to become an alcoholic. It follows that there is not a single youngster, living or dead, who made the conscious and deliberate decision to persevere with the foul taste of alcohol, merely to acquire that taste. Surely it worked the other way around: we only acquired the taste because we persevered for some other reason. We have already established that one of the ingenious aspects of the trap is that the first drink generally tastes awful. This helps to reassure us that we won't get hooked. Many smokers and drinkers believe they are stupid. In fact, they are not. The drug trap is ingenious. But would any of us be stupid enough to say: "I'll persevere with the foul taste until I learn to enjoy it?" Wouldn't that be tantamount to saying:

"I WANT TO GET HOOKED"?

Back to the person that enjoys a bottle of white wine with a meal.

Are they saying that there are no non-alcoholic drinks that taste as good?

"Of course there are. I'll often have a soft drink if I'm driving."

Does it taste just as good?

"Yes, but I find after a couple of soft drinks they become sickly and I don't want to drink any more."

Ah, so it isn't just for the taste. But if you've quenched your thirst, why would you want to drink any more?

"Because I enjoy drinking with a meal."

We've come full circle. However, this question of soft drinks quickly becoming sickly is a valid one. It ceases to be a problem whilst you are drinking because you merely switch to alcoholic drinks. But recovering alcoholics can find it a real problem. I will address this in due course.

One thing we have established is that whether they are youngsters just starting out, normal drinkers, or alcoholics, people do not drink alcohol because it tastes good. When drinkers tell you they drink because they enjoy the taste, they are trying to deceive both you and themselves. Therefore, if people don't drink alcohol for the taste, or to quench their thirst, they must do it for some other reason. Let us address another common misconception:

DOES ALCOHOL GIVE YOU COURAGE?

13 *Does Alcohol Give You Courage?*

We've certainly been brainwashed to believe it does. Why else would it be a tradition in the British navy to issue rum before a battle? For many years I was convinced that alcohol gave me both courage and confidence. That is until the discovery of Easyway. This caused me to open my mind and to question lifelong beliefs that I had previously accepted as facts. The whole process turned my life upside down. Correction: it was upside down in the first place. But because I was used to it that way, it seemed quite normal to me. Not until I had opened my mind could I see matters in their true perspective.

No doubt you understand the meaning of the word 'courage', and associated words like 'bravery' and 'cowardice'. But remember I asked you to take nothing for granted. Before we can understand the effect that alcohol has on courage, we need to fully understand courage itself. We also need to examine another word closely associated with the subject: FEAR!

Imagine I make a toast on the occasion of the christening of your son:

> "May he grow up to be as fearless as his father."

You might think I was being somewhat over-dramatic. Nevertheless, you would feel flattered; and you might also hope that he would become a fearless individual. If you got your wish, you would be condemning him to an early death. We tend to regard fear as an evil. It might be an unpleasant experience, but it is in fact an ally and a friend. It is another essential ingredient with which Mother Nature has equipped us to ensure our survival. It is our fear of heights that guarantees we take the necessary precautions when climbing ladders; our fear of fire that prevents us from exposing petrol to a naked flame; our fear of drowning that makes us wear a life jacket, and a fear of injury or death which prevents us from taking unnecessary risks in battle. Fear is not an evil, any more than a fire alarm is an evil. It is Mother Nature's ingenious device to warn us that danger threatens, and thus it enables us to take remedial action.

Ideals such as bravery and cowardice do not exist for wild animals. But fear does, and when they experience it, they just act on the instincts with which Mother Nature has equipped them. Let me use my cat to illustrate. True she is a domesticated animal, but when she is chasing a mouse or a bird, she reverts back to the wild.

On this particular occasion, I was watching her stalking a mouse in the garden. She was clearly having a marvellous time and there didn't seem to be any evil intent on her part. To her the mouse might just as well have been some paper tied to a length of cotton. For the mouse, it was no game but clearly a matter of life or death. For several minutes the poor little chap tried to run or hide but to no avail. Eventually she had him trapped in the corner of an outhouse. To my utter amazement he stood up on his hind-legs and faced up to her as if he was going to attack her. My cat was even more amazed than I was. She actually jumped back and allowed him to escape.

How would we assess that scene by human standards? We wouldn't regard the mouse as either brave or cowardly for initially running away. Bear in mind that the cat to him would be the equivalent of a Tyrannosaurus Rex to us. I thought he was incredibly brave when he faced up to her. In fact it wasn't bravery but instinct. His first natural instinct was to run. When he could no longer do that, he followed another natural instinct and tried to defend himself by attacking. And it saved his life.

I was thoroughly ashamed of my cat for backing off. You couldn't find better proof of the notion that bullies are cowards. But, in fact, she was being no more cowardly than the mouse was being brave. She was well fed and wasn't going to starve if she didn't catch the mouse. So why should she risk injury, no matter how slight the risk? Her actions were no more cowardly than ours are when we try to avoid being stung by a wasp or a bee. It's just common sense to get out of the way.

We use expressions like 'brave as a lion'. Lions aren't brave. They instinctively prey on the species least likely to cause them injury, and target the feeblest member of the herd. And they have no qualms about the whole pride ganging up on the victim. It is only during times of scarcity that a lion will stalk more dangerous prey like giraffe or buffalo, when the fear of starvation overrides the fear of injury.

There is no such thing as cowardice or bravery in the animal kingdom. There is only the instinct to survive. Perhaps you would maintain that an animal risking its life to defend its offspring is a form of bravery. It might appear that way if we judge the situation by our own confused standards. But just as Mother Nature ensures that we survive individually, whether we like it or not, so she has equipped us with instincts to ensure the survival of the species. The instinct to protect our families is an example. Another example is the sex drive. Pleasant as it can be to satisfy, its purpose is to make sure we propagate. In some cases, the instinct to reproduce takes preference over individual survival. The death of salmon after spawning is an example, and the next time you complain that your wife has bitten your head off, be grateful that you aren't a praying mantis. The female literally bites off her partner's head after mating.

Perhaps you feel somewhat indignant, because you believe that the human race has progressed beyond wild animals and that the ideals to which we aspire are self-evidently noble and consistent, and therefore unquestionable. I also suffered from this misconception for most of my life. But let's look at the facts. Allow me to use myself as an example.

For most of my life I was haunted by the belief that I was a coward. I'm sure my school friends and work colleagues would find that difficult to believe. After all, how could someone who was a boxing champion, and a fearless tackler on the rugby pitch, be a coward? That's just the point. I wasn't fearless; on the contrary I was terrified. As a child I was brainwashed to believe that boys should be fearless and that it was natural for them to be aggressive and to enjoy fisticuffs. After all, every Hollywood western or war epic includes a punch-up in a bar, and the combatants are depicted as finding the experience immensely enjoyable. It would be understandable if they were fighting the enemy, but usually it's the navy versus the marines. In British war films the young flying officer can't wait to 'get a crack at Jerry'. The average life expectancy of a Battle of Britain pilot was about three weeks. At the time I felt quite certain that I would gladly forgo the opportunity to get 'a crack at Jerry' if it meant that Jerry couldn't get a crack at me. Fortunately I was only seven so I wasn't required to do my bit. If another boy picked on me, far from wanting to fight him, my instinct was identical to that of the mouse: I wanted to run, and it didn't matter if the other boy was smaller than me. It was clear to me that I was both abnormal and cowardly.

So why did I become a boxing champion? I assure you it wasn't due to natural aggression. It was merely to hide my shame. I hated boxing, but my fear of being hurt was overridden by the fear of my friends finding out that I was a coward. Why did I become a fearless tackler? I never did. The fear never went. Every time I dived head first at those flying knees, I fully expected to break my neck. The first time I was selected to play for the school was in a derby match against our arch-rivals. I funked a tackle which lost us the match. My cowardly act was apparent to players and spectators alike. No one mentioned it. In fact no one spoke a word to me. That silence was more painful than any physical injury I ever received in the ring or on the pitch. They say: 'A hero dies but once, but a coward suffers a thousand deaths.'

The incident taught me the truth of that statement and I never had the courage to funk another tackle. Hence I got the reputation for being a fearless tackler. You might contend that, far from being a coward, I was acting very bravely to continue boxing and tackling when I was so terrified. At one time I agreed with that view. After all, surely the very essence of bravery involves is surmounting fear? If someone commits what appears to be a brave act but has no fear, it can hardly be described as bravery. "Fools rush in where angels fear to tread." But was I really being brave? I had a choice of two evils: the fear of suffering physical injury and the fear of being revealed as the coward I believed myself to be. Was I being brave because I chose the lesser of the two fears? Not at all: I was being rational. Many would also challenge my statement: 'I never had the courage to funk another tackle.' Surely that's a contradiction in terms. How can it take courage to funk a tackle? I will explain in a moment. I now realize that I was being neither brave nor cowardly. The real problem was the brainwashing created by 'intelligent' mankind's phony principles, which went against my natural instincts and created doubt and confusion. To this day children are regularly taunted and condemned as a 'scaredy-cats', as if being scared is a crime, rather than a natural instinct, essential for survival.

Does this mean that I believe that there are no such things as bravery or cowardice for humans? Am I saying that we are no different from wild animals? No, we do have highly developed brains which enable us to remember and thus learn by our mistakes. Therefore we can adapt past experiences to solve new problems. But that intelligence should be used to enhance our natural instincts, not to confuse and contradict them with double standards. I'll use an example.

Imagine someone dared me to walk across a narrow steel girder bridging two tall buildings. I would have no hesitation in refusing and there would be no feeling of cowardice or self-recrimination whatsoever. The only effect taunts like 'scaredy-cat' would have on me would be to make me regard that person as a complete idiot. But if there was a child in danger of falling and the only way to save it was for me to cross that girder, my conscience would tell me that I must make the attempt. If I were able to overcome my fear and make the attempt I would regard it as a courageous act. If I couldn't, I would regard myself as a coward.

I would define cowardice as: failure to act as my conscience dictates, because of fear of physical injury or ridicule. Does this mean that I would go into a burning building to rescue someone? Not necessarily, I would assess the risk and if I didn't think it was worth taking, I wouldn't take it. I would expect to take greater risks for my own family than for strangers.

My confusion and doubt disappeared after discovering Easyway, and today I could never suffer a similar dilemma to the one I went through as a youngster. If my natural instincts hadn't been confused and distorted by 'intelligent' mankind's phony principles, I would no more have participated in boxing or rugby than I would cross the steel girder just for a dare. I had no more desire to inflict pain and injury on another boy than I had for him to do so to me! The confusion was the cause of much physical injury in the ring and on the pitch; many hours of fear anticipating serious injury; and many years of believing that I was a coward. All completely unnecessary! It would have taken courage as a child to have stood up to authority and the generally accepted standards of the day, just as it takes courage for a genuine conscientious objector to stand up to the abuse. But without the confusion, I believe I would have had the courage. This is why it would have taken courage to funk future tackles. Had I done so, I would have needed the courage to bear the abuse I would have received from my schoolmasters and friends.

If we were at war again, would I have the courage to do my bit? Who can tell? But I have every reason to believe so. Do I live in apprehension wondering whether I will one day be put to the test and found wanting? Not in the least. I have already been put to the test on several occasions since I discovered Easyway. Perhaps they were not quite as dramatic as the steel girder or the fire. But they did involve a certain amount of courage on my part. Despite the fact that I now know that I wasn't a coward at school, I can well remember what it was like to feel like one, and for me the easier option is to face the fear.

We are now in a position to address the main object of this chapter: does alcohol give you courage? I've no doubt that the majority of the sailors were grateful for that tot of rum, and that many of them genuinely believed that it made them *feel* braver. But how could alcohol possibly make you feel truly brave? Bravery involves surmounting fear. So if you reduce the level of fear, doesn't it follow that it takes less bravery to surmount it? It is an established fact that alcohol inebriates you, and that the process of inebriation reduces all your faculties, including your faculty to feel fear. Would you not agree that the tot of rum not so much gave the sailors more courage, but helped to remove some of the fear?

Let's use an everyday example to help see the situation more clearly. It is common practice for people who suffer from a fear of flying to get themselves plastered before a flight. No way do they delude themselves that alcohol makes them feel braver, because they don't feel brave even after they've taken the alcohol! There is no doubt they are taking it to remove the fear. It's more difficult to see with the tot of rum because the sailors are being truly brave. In both cases the effects of the alcohol is exactly the same. Alcohol reduces fears:

ALCOHOL DOES NOT GIVE YOU COURAGE!

You might ask what difference it makes whether it reduces fear or increases courage? Perhaps that tot of rum made the difference between the sailors doing their duty and mutinying. Perhaps the alcohol allowed the passenger to get on the plane. That may well be so. But it is essential to realize that it didn't give him courage, but removed a sufficient part of his fear to enable him to board the plane. You also need to understand the effect of using alcohol in this manner. Let's refer back to Mother Nature.

An ostrich will put its head in the sand when it sees danger. It does so because it believes that if it cannot see the danger, it no longer exists. Now, an ostrich is a comparatively large animal, equipped with two powerful legs which are formidable weapons in their own right. Those legs are also capable of conveying their owner at speeds which would outpace most predators. Quite apart from adopting a posture that looks ridiculous, by sticking its head in the sand it deprives itself of three attributes essential to its survival: sight, fight and flight. It renders itself effectively 'legless'. I'm sure I've heard that expression somewhere before.

All birds have very small brains, hence the expression 'birdbrain'. An ostrich is no exception. We are fortunate to be equipped with considerably larger brains. Therefore such a strategy would not work for us. With our superior intelligence we would be fully aware that far from removing danger, putting our heads in the sand would render us completely defenceless to it. In our case it wouldn't even remove the fear. On the contrary, it would increase it. We would be fully aware that even if we couldn't see the hungry lion, he could still see us.

The ostrich analogy is a very valuable one in that it helps us to see our own instincts more clearly. By sticking its head in the sand the ostrich removes its fear, and as a result greatly increases the danger. Was that an intelligent thing to do? Obviously not. Fear itself is an asset in exactly the same way that a burglar alarm is an asset. Fear is a warning of danger, a warning which, as in the case of the burglar alarm, could either prove to be real or unfounded. To remove fear through any means other than removing the *cause* of the fear, is like believing that you put out the fire merely by turning off the alarm. In fact by doing so you've also prevented a solution to the problem: the fire brigade won't come if the alarm doesn't sound. Turning off the alarm is exactly what you do when you use alcohol to remove fear. You negate any possibility of dealing with the source of the fear and thus removing it permanently.

Perhaps you believe that all this is obvious. In the case of the ostrich it is, for the simple reason that wild animals act on instinct alone. For them the matter is not confused by such man-made concepts as courage or cowardice; or ideals such as duty to friend, family or country. We have no right to ridicule the ostrich for adopting this simple technique to remove its fear, because we are acting just as stupidly every time we deliberately inebriate ourselves in order to lessen or remove a fear. What's the difference between making yourself 'blind' drunk and sticking your head in the sand? Either way you have rendered yourself defenceless! Would you describe sticking your head in the sand in the face of danger as an act of courage? Of course not, it's more like cowardice. So how can we possibly claim that inebriating ourselves in the face of danger gives us courage?

I have been informed on more than one occasion that ostriches do not in fact adopt this ploy of burying their head in the sand during times of danger. If this is so, you might feel that I should not use this analogy. But it doesn't matter whether ostriches do it or not, my point is that it would clearly be a stupid thing to do. In fact I was very relieved to learn that ostriches do not do it. It is directly opposed to the laws of Mother Nature and it is very doubtful that a species that adopted such a ruse could survive. It also means that, in spite of our huge brains and advanced technology, we are even more stupid than the ostrich!

Let's go back to our analogy of flying an aircraft over the Alps in blanket fog. This would be a scary experience for a competent pilot with all his instruments functioning properly. Just imagine how many times more scary it would be if you couldn't rely on any of your instruments: not your radar, your altimeter, your petrol gauge, your radio or your compass. Imagine that on top of this you are gradually losing your senses of sight, hearing and touch. But worst of all, your brain – the computer that controls your mind and body – ceases to function properly. That is real fear. That is what alcohol does to you and the more you take the more it does it. Take enough and it will literally render you 'legless'. I knew I'd heard that expression before. Take any more and you will become completely senseless. That's certainly no way to fly in fog. Can it really be sensible to go through life with your head in the sand?

If you still find this point difficult to grasp, imagine being a passenger on that flight, and watching the pilot taking regular swigs from his flask. What would your response be? I'll wager it would be exactly the same as the airline company's. If one of their pilots had just one swig he'd be sacked! Your brain and body are extremely ingenious devices. Do you really believe that you can improve their operation by taking chemicals that will distort their functioning? LSD makes some people believe they can fly. Does that mean they really can fly on LSD? Well no one has managed it yet, but several have died in the attempt! Perhaps the tot of rum did prevent the sailors from mutinying. Unfortunately it also affected their ability to make strategic decisions, their eyesight, their coordination, and their reactions.

This might be one of the times when you begin to doubt; when you think ignorance is bliss and that you are better off believing that alcohol gives you courage. Please don't fall for that trap. Let me remind you that I have nothing but good news for you. In any event, we don't completely fool ourselves when we inebriate ourselves during times of danger or stress. We know deep down that it isn't real courage. That why we call it 'Dutch courage'. We sense that we are making ourselves more vulnerable; and just as the pilot's fear would be many times greater if he knew his instruments were faulty, so our fear increases with this awareness of increased vulnerability. And just as reducing fear by drinking alcohol at times of danger creates the illusion of giving you courage, so creating fear by drinking alcohol at such times creates the illusion of removing courage.

Don't worry if you find the last statement somewhat confusing. Let's consider it without the illusions. It is obvious that alcohol does not give you courage. It is equally obvious that drinking alcohol during times of danger will increase your fear, because you know that by doing so you are removing your defences. The effect is to make you feel less courageous. That doesn't necessarily mean that you genuinely lack courage. It just means that the alcohol prevented you from using it. You might find this point difficult to accept, but I assure you it is true. In fact we know it all our lives. Do we see a drunk as someone bravely facing up to the trials and tribulations of life? On the contrary, he is clearly someone who feels that he cannot face life on its own terms, and is trying to block it out, unsuccessfully I might add. It is equally obvious that his predicament is caused by alcohol! Alcohol doesn't give you courage:

ALCOHOL DESTROYS COURAGE!

If it's so obvious, why can't the drunk see it? Because he has been brainwashed from birth to believe that alcohol gives you courage;

and because his slide down the pitcher plant has been so gradual that each day he felt no different to the day before. He's forgotten what it feels like to wake up bursting with energy and full of confidence. He blames his depleted state on old age and the sort of problems that normal drinkers cope with in their stride. He doesn't realize that alcohol is the villain. On the contrary, he now believes it's his only friend. The more poison he drinks, the more it knocks him down, so the greater his need for another drink. The sides of the pitcher plant get steeper and steeper.

Alcohol doesn't give you confidence or courage; on the contrary it convinces you and everyone else that you possess neither quality! Fortunately that is an illusion! You'll soon be amazed by the amount of courage and confidence that you actually possess.

Another effect closely associated with the illusion that alcohol gives courage is that:

ALCOHOL REMOVES INHIBITIONS

14 *Alcohol Removes Inhibitions*

It is an illusion that alcohol gives courage. It does however remove inhibitions. The illusion in this case is that the removal of inhibitions is advantageous. At one time I was convinced that the key to a successful party was to pour as much alcohol as I could down the throat of each guest, as quickly as possible. I believed this would help the guests to get beyond that embarrassing stage when they just stand around shy and inhibited. Once the drink starts to take effect, the guests begin to lose their shyness and their inhibitions. That is also an illusion. Bear in mind that most of those guests have found it necessary to have a little 'Dutch courage' before they even arrive at the party, and no matter how much and how quickly you encourage them to drink, every social gathering involving strangers will start off with separate little groups holding polite conversation.

Just like fear, our inhibitions are there to protect us. In a way our inhibitions are a form of fear. Not necessarily a fear of physical danger, but a fear of looking silly or being seen in an unfavourable light, in other words a shyness or lack of confidence. I agree that shyness and lack of confidence can be very unpleasant. It is usually blatantly obvious when someone suffers from shyness, particularly if the victim is a child. And their discomfort is clearly increased tenfold when a 'helpful' parent says:

'Come on, don't be shy, show everybody how nicely you sing.'

Why do we do that to children? If you suffer from shyness, the very last thing you need is to be forcibly made the centre of attention. Does that cure their shyness? Of course not. All it does is to convince the youngster that what is in fact a perfectly natural feeling is a serious and debilitating fault, which in turn makes them feel inferior. Little wonder that the majority of us go through life feeling guilty because we never completely get over our shyness, no matter how successfully we are able to hide it. Again I never solved my personal shyness problem until I discovered Easyway.

How did Easyway help me to do that? By enabling me to realize that shyness and inhibitions were quite normal and a vital part of my protection. You cannot gain the trust of a wild animal until you have convinced it that you won't harm it physically. Likewise it is only natural that children should be wary of strangers until they are convinced that person will do them no harm, be it physical or mental.

It was nice to learn that my shyness was quite normal and as a result I stopped worrying about it. It also helped me to realize that what I had always assumed to be stand-offishness by other people at social gatherings was really due to their own shyness. By concentrating on helping them to get over their shyness, I become oblivious to my own and get a great pleasure from breaking the ice. It's rather like helping a bud blossom into a beautiful flower.

So what's wrong with taking a couple of drinks to help remove your inhibitions? Because it does just that. Let's look at a few examples. My lack of aggression as a boy is a typical one. Have you noticed that when two youths are about to fight over some real or imaginary slight, rather like stags during the rut, the actual fisticuffs are preceded by a ritual of puffing up the chest and issuing verbal threats. The effect of the brainwashing is incredibly powerful. I've described how I believed myself to be abnormal, because the prospect of causing pain and injury to another boy promised no joy whatsoever, and the prospect of him doing the same to me was anathema. It never occurred to me that the other boy had also been subjected to the same brainwashing and was just as apprehensive as me. We were like two stags each hoping that the other would back down so that we wouldn't have to fight. This is why the vast majority of confrontations between two normal males rarely end in actual physical violence. As we grow older and hopefully wiser, the physical confrontations tend to die out completely. But if two youths have been drinking, they lose their fear of being injured. They also lose their inhibitions, including their inhibitions about hurting and being hurt. A normal physical confrontation between stags or boys will cease automatically, once superiority has been established; but a youth affected by alcohol will go on punching or kicking his opponent senseless. All too often the victim is rendered permanently senseless. What a happy, sociable, enjoyable pastime drinking is!

Another classic example is drinking and driving. I have to confess that before the 'Don't drink and drive!' campaigns, I was one of those idiots who actually boasted that he was a better driver if he had had a couple of drinks. I regard myself as a reasonably intelligent man. How could I have been so stupid? Probably because I had been drinking when I made the boast. Now I knew from certain teenage experiences that a large amount of alcohol would render me completely senseless. It is logical to assume therefore that a little alcohol would slightly distort my senses. So how come I believed that alcohol made me a better driver? It was because it removed my fear of injury, which in turn enabled me to drive faster than I normally would, without any feeling of apprehension. In other words, the alcohol lulled me into a false sense of security when driving. Did that make me a better driver? On the contrary.

But the worst aspect of drinking and driving is not that you lose the fear of injury to yourself, but that you lose your inhibitions. You become insensible to the fact that alcohol has not only diminished your faculties but your responsibilities. Can you imagine the horror of killing another human being because you were drinking and driving? Can you imagine killing your own child and having to live the rest of your life with that knowledge?

No doubt you are one of the sensible ones who never drink and drive or become aggressive, so what harm is there in you having a few sociable drinks at a party? You must have met one of those people who never seem to stop talking. Their brain seems to have a direct line to their mouth. Whatever thought enters their head is immediately transmitted to all and sundry. Some people describe the condition, crudely but aptly, as verbal diarrhoea. Its practitioners whet your appetite by telling you how fascinated you will be by an experience which happened to them the previous Monday, or was it the Tuesday? This is followed by a seemingly endless monologue designed to establish the correct day. After ten minutes, you know you are being rude but can stand it no longer, so you politely ask whether the actual day is crucial to the story? You are admonished rather sharply: "Of course it matters, that was the day I caught the bus." You just manage to prevent yourself from pointing out that it doesn't matter what day the bus was caught, because you realize that would only prolong matters. So you politely and patiently listen to the entire experience only to find that the discussion about whether it was Monday or Tuesday was by far the most interesting part.

Most of us have one or more check-points between our brains and our mouths. I have just one. Its purpose is to edit the thoughts that enter my brain before I transmit them through my mouth. It is an exceedingly useful device. It prevents me from transmitting many statements that might be stupid, boring or offensive to other people. It would be correct to describe such a device as an inhibition. Some people have several check-points. So many in fact that you never hear them say anything that could be regarded as remotely controversial. Such people we tend to regard as somewhat inhibited and this doesn't make for lively conversation. I don't know what the ideal number of check-points is, possibly two; what I do know is that I am occasionally embarrassed and ashamed because my check-point didn't pick up a boob.

Alcohol removes these inhibitions. This is why a happy social occasion can suddenly erupt into violence: someone has said or done something offensive that they wouldn't dream of had they not been under the influence. You might argue that someone who is inhibited would be a more interesting person if they lost some of those inhibitions, but not enough to cause offence. But it's impossible to gauge that point. Alcohol inebriates you: if you are progressively losing control of all of your faculties, how will you be able to judge the point beyond which you musn't go? But even if that were possible there's still a flaw in the argument. Normally inhibited people don't become more interesting when they are inebriated; on the contrary they become over-emotional, repetitive, incoherent and boring. It wouldn't be so bad if the inhibited person felt better for it, but they don't; they are in a stupor and you cannot appreciate a situation unless you have your senses to appreciate it with.

What impression do the other people at the party form? If they are equally sloshed, their opinion doesn't matter one way or the other, they aren't themselves anyway. Effectively, they are not even there. How many times have you heard someone say: "I must have had a good time last night, I was so drunk I can't even remember it." Why on earth should you remember it if you were semi-conscious at the time? How can you enjoy yourself if you are unconscious? The problem is that we are usually sloshed ourselves when a normally inhibited person lets their hair down, and therefore cannot assess the true situation accurately. But it is easy to check it out. Just observe two normally inhibited people who are both inebriated and having one of those 'interesting' conversations when you yourself are sober. You'll find out exactly how interesting they are. You'll also know just how 'interesting' you become when inebriated.

I forget which comedian said: "I've been to bed with some of the most beautiful women in the world and woken up with some of the ugliest." What's wrong with that? Isn't that the pleasure that a few drinks can give, to make the world appear to be a happier and more beautiful place? But the reality is that if he was so sloshed that he couldn't see her face, I doubt whether his other faculties were working any better. It's common knowledge that a one-night stand with a drunk invariably ends up as a one night-flop in every sense of the term. And I don't suppose those ladies were over-enamoured by the sweaty impotent with the foul-smelling breath whose snoring kept them awake all night.

But how would the usually inhibited person be viewed by the people at the party who remained reasonably sober? We are all familiar with the expression:

TAKE NO NOTICE – IT'S THE DRINK TALKING!

I can remember when I was financial director of Triang Toys. The annual reps' dinner would start off with the usual polite, respectful and phoney conversations. By the end of the evening one of them, who was as meek as a lamb when he came to get his expenses signed, would always have his arm round my neck, breathing foul fumes into my face, whilst he harangued me about where we were going wrong and what he would do if he were in charge. Did he impress me? Did I think: "Now there's a dynamic type. We must mark him down for bigger things?" On the contrary, it was so obvious that it was just the drink talking, that all I did was to make a mental note not to get stuck next to him the following year.

Did I never make a fool of myself when I'd had too much to drink? Of course I did. More times than I care to remember: and that's one of the problems, when you are sloshed you don't remember. But I can well remember feeling ashamed and guilty the next day. Just look back on your life. Is anyone ever fooled or impressed by a drunk? Do we really get pleasure from being 'out of it'? Are we genuinely proud to have been so afterwards? Are drunks good role models, the sort of people we look up to? Of course not: we regard them as we would a little man who wouldn't say 'boo!' to a goose normally, but can't keep his hand off the horn once he's cocooned in the safety of his big car.

It is an illusion that alcohol gives courage. It does remove fear and inhibitions: the illusion in this case is that this is a good thing. An unaccompanied girl on her way home from a nightclub is meant to be somewhat fearful. If she is drunk, this natural fear is removed and she lays herself open to all sorts of dangers.

We will now address a similar illusion:

ALCOHOL STEADIES MY NERVES

15 *Alcohol Steadies My Nerves*

It was one of those very hot days that we pray for during winter and curse in the summer. The ventilation system wasn't used to coping with such weather and neither were the clients in the group, so the door and windows were wide open. Suddenly the door slammed and the lady who sat opposite me jumped two feet in the air. She was clearly at rock-bottom and began to sob, "You can see the state of my nerves. I've got so many problems at the moment. If I'm like this with my crutch, how do you expect me to cope without it?"

She hadn't noticed that I myself had been startled by the sudden slamming of the door, as had the rest of the group. Fortunately for us, her tears distracted us from our own reactions and the embarrassment we would have felt. I asked her if she'd ever noticed how nervous birds appear to be when feeding, and how the slightest sound will send them back to the safety of the trees. I pointed out that to them the slightest sound meant a cat, and that it is not only natural for birds to react like that, it is absolutely essential to their survival.

This is yet another classic example of the brainwashing we are subjected to from birth. We are brought up to believe that a perfectly natural fearful reaction is some form of deficiency or weakness in our physical or mental make-up, when in reality our nerves are just another facet of our incredible machines, designed to help us survive. In fact the incident proved to be very fortunate. The lady had been so low that she hadn't been taking much in up to that point. But she could suddenly see that her jump, far from being abnormal, was a sign that her body was functioning normally. The effect was quite remarkable. The tears immediately turned into a big smile. She was able to discuss all the other terrible problems that were weighing her down. They turned out to be the typical annoyances with which everyone is afflicted in Western society, and she admitted that none of them was particularly tragic. I pointed out that I had exactly the same problems but that they no longer worried me. The incident did help her, and the rest of the group, to realize that the only reason that these concerns appeared to be greater to them was because they were regularly administering a powerful poison to their own bodies, a poison that was debilitating their health and energy and destroying their courage and confidence. It's so obvious really, if you feel physically and mentally low, molehills become mountains.

We tend to confuse stress and responsibility. And we tend to think of nerves as a bad thing. It is essential that we understand each of these terms clearly. Our nervous system is an asset, a vital part of our protection. Responsibility can be good or bad. If you like responsibility, then you will thrive on it. A boring or mundane job would be stressful to you. Someone who is not equipped to take on responsibility would find a responsible job stressful.

Just as we are brainwashed to regard fear and pain as evils, so we tend to regard stress as an evil in itself. It isn't. Just like fear and pain it is merely a warning sign, an indication that something is wrong. If the oil-warning light in your car started to blink, it would obviously be rank stupidity to remove it and assume that you have solved the problem. By doing so you would guarantee that a slight problem became a disaster. Isn't it blatantly obvious that it would be just as stupid to remove fear, pain or stress, without removing the cause of these symptoms?

Have you noticed that nowadays doctors are reluctant to prescribe relaxants like Valium? That's because Valium works rather like alcohol. If someone is distressed, the only cure is to remove the cause of the stress. Valium doesn't do that. It merely removes the warning light. When the effect of the drug wears off, the patient is back where they started and needs another dose of the drug. And another and another. As far as your body is concerned, the drug is an unwanted invader affecting the efficient working of all systems. So the incredible machine starts to build an immunity to it. The result is that the drug doesn't appear to be as effective as it was, and the tendency is to take larger and more frequent doses, until it becomes completely ineffective. What do we do then? We start taking a stronger drug and continue our inevitable descent. In the meantime, unless we have removed the original source of stress, the victim's life is now infinitely more stressful. All drugs have physical and mental side effects, not least of which is that the victim is now completely dependent upon the drug.

If that's the effect of a drug prescribed by a qualified doctor, then how much more stupid to resort to a drug like alcohol: a drug that happens to be a powerful poison and gradually debilitates every one of your senses. Get it clearly into your head that alcohol does not remove stress. On the contrary it is a major cause of stress.

Am I implying that we should never take pain-killers for physical pain, or relaxants for mental anguish? No, I'm not. When I'm having a tooth extracted, I for one am grateful to be rendered senseless by Valium. In this case Valium is a valuable asset that enables the cause of my stress to be removed painlessly. Nor am I saying that Valium and similar drugs should not be used as a short-term measure in the case of severe stress, provided of course that the cause of the stress is removed or alleviated in the meantime. But if you are permanently relying on pills to relieve headaches or to sleep, they are obviously not curing the problem.

"But wouldn't you resort to pain-killers if you were permanently in pain?"

Yes, I probably would, but I would also ask my doctor to find the cause of the pain in the meantime.

"But if alcohol can be used as a short-term pain-killer, then surely it is incorrect to say that it has no advantages whatsoever?"

Not so. You could use your head to hammer in a nail but you would hardly describe that as one of its advantages. To use alcohol to relieve physical or mental stress is about as sensible as chopping off your foot to remove a painful corn. If you need a genuine pain-killer your doctor will prescribe one that is more effective and far less dangerous.

"But surely alcohol in moderation does help you to relax after a hard day's work?"

An excellent example! It will help us to see the true situation clearly. We talk about something relaxing us, finding certain situations or activities relaxing. But if you are already completely relaxed, how could a drink, or anything else for that matter, relax you? In order for anything to relax you, you must first be unrelaxed. When we come in from a hard day's work, there might be several factors causing us to feel unrelaxed. Perhaps our minds are still occupied with problems at work, in which case we might switch on the television, read a book, or discuss the problems with our partner. If we feel hot and sweaty, we'll take a shower, and if we feel physically tired and unclean, we will relax in a bath. If our feet are aching we'll put on some slippers. We'll change into more comfortable clothes. If we are hungry, we will eat. If we are thirsty, we will drink. In each case we are either removing an aggravation or distracting our minds from one. Why do we find a hot bath relaxing? Because it helps to soothe the aches and to remove the grime and the cold. But on a very warm and humid day, a hot bath would tend to increase your discomfort and a cold shower would be preferable. Lounging in a comfortable armchair is relaxing if you are physically tired, but to a child bursting with energy it would be the opposite. The point is that none of these activities is intrinsically relaxing. They are only relaxing if they remove an aggravation, and it is equally obvious that the remedy must be related directly to the particular aggravation. For example, eating will remove your hunger but it won't solve the problem of your aching feet. So how can a drink containing alcohol relax you, given that it doesn't remove the source of the aggravation that caused you to feel unrelaxed in the first place? The beautiful truth is that it can't. It won't even cure your thirst.

So why are drinkers so convinced that alcohol does relax them? There are two main reasons. The first we have already addressed: alcohol deadens all your senses. It doesn't remove any of the above aggravations, it merely makes you oblivious to them. That is why chronic alcoholics don't bother to wash or shave or eat. When the effect of the drug has worn off, far from removing a single one of the aggravations, alcohol has actually made each one worse! Now the alcoholic has an even greater need to inebriate himself and so the never-ending downward spiral continues.

It is wrong to describe any drug as a relaxant. Complete relaxation is indeed a blissful state and consists of having no distress whatsoever. It is a state that someone dependent on a drug can never achieve. Just think about it. Why would anyone want to inebriate themselves if they felt completely happy? Suicide is permanent oblivion and proof positive that the person is very unhappy indeed. Inebriation is temporary and partial oblivion, the degree depending on the level of inebriation. Doesn't it follow that people who need to inebriate themselves are unhappy? And if alcohol solved the problem and actually made them happy, they wouldn't need to inebriate themselves repeatedly. In order to understand the second reason why drinkers believe that alcohol relaxes them, we need to take a closer look at:

DRUG ADDICTION

16 Drug Addiction

For most of my adult life I was a chain-smoker. I would often refer to myself as a nicotine addict. But I never thought of myself as a drug addict. It was just an expression I used. I would also refer to myself as a golf addict. They were just expressions I used. I knew that tobacco contained nicotine but I didn't perceive it as an addictive drug. Nicotine was just something that left an unpleasant brown stain on my fingers and teeth: just a rather distasteful side effect to the pleasure of smoking. Likewise, I couldn't think of alcohol as an addictive drug, in the same way that heroin is an addictive drug. This was in spite of the fact that I had been rendered paralytic by it more times than I care to remember, and a social function without alcohol would have been a contradiction in terms. Like the rest of the population, I just accepted the brainwashing.

But what does addiction actually mean? In relation to drugs, my Oxford dictionary defines it as:

'Doing or using something as a habit or compulsively.'

Now I find that definition rather confusing and misleading. People who take drugs often refer to themselves as 'users'. To me this implies that they are not addicted, but are in complete control of their intake. Such people refer to their 'habit' rather than to their 'addiction'.

At what stage do they start referring to themselves as addicts rather than users? I would suggest that it is at exactly the same stage that heavy drinkers refer to themselves as alcoholics: i.e. when they realize that they have lost control.

I would suggest that a more realistic definition of addiction is:

'Doing something repeatedly, which you wish you didn't do at all but can't stop doing, or that you wish you did less, but cannot.'

So how do you tell whether you are addicted to something? There are useful indicators. I made a positive decision to take up golf rather than drifting into it. The pleasure was immediate and I didn't have to struggle to acquire it. That was because I genuinely enjoyed it and it caused me no problems. From the very start I always wished I had the opportunity to play *more*. Now you could argue that a drinker always wants to consume more. He doesn't! Our definition of an addict is the complete opposite. He wishes he could quit or cut down, but is compelled to drink more.

Cast your mind back to the learning stage, when you smoked five cigarettes and drank three pints over the weekend. Can you ever remember thinking: "I really envy these people who can smoke a whole pack and drink ten pints in an evening"? Isn't it always the other way around? Isn't it the heavy smokers and drinkers who envy the people who only need to smoke and drink on social occasions? I bet there's not a golfer in the world who doesn't envy Tiger Woods! But can you imagine a man who smokes twenty cigarettes a day and enjoys a bottle of wine with his evening meal thinking: "I wish I smoked sixty a day and needed two bottles"?

Do not confuse this with a situation in which someone *does* need sixty cigarettes and two bottles of wine, but only smokes twenty and drinks one because of health, financial or other restrictions.

Although golf was an expensive pastime, I never felt that I was wasting my money. With golf there was no sinister black shadow at the back of my mind, and much as I loved playing golf, I didn't feel that I was being deprived or that there was something missing when I wasn't doing it. I wouldn't dread a holiday that didn't involve golf. In fact, I could go on holiday and not play golf without feeling the slightest bit deprived. And when I decided that I no longer wished to play golf, I didn't have to go through some terrible trauma. I just quit.

I can say in all honesty that I never had a feeling of dread about going on a fortnight's holiday that didn't involve alcohol or tobacco. That's because it wasn't remotely conceivable that I would go on a holiday where I couldn't smoke and drink. It's quite obvious that I was already dependent upon both poisons long before I reached the stage of regarding myself as addicted. You might argue: why should I deprive myself of the pleasure of drinking or smoking on holiday? If so you've missed the point: that is the answer that every 'user' gives to show that he is in control. The point is that I could and did go on holidays during which I didn't once indulge in a pastime that gave me far more pleasure than smoking or drinking: golf. But I couldn't have gone on a holiday without alcohol or nicotine:

I WAS ALREADY DEPENDENT!

This is the real difference between addiction and genuine pleasure: with golf I was in control. There was no schizophrenia. Half my brain wasn't thinking "Why do I waste my hard-earned money on this activity?" and the other half wasn't thinking "But how will you be able to enjoy life or cope with stress if you don't play golf?"

Much of the confusion about terms like 'addiction', 'habit' and 'user' is due to the fact that even the so-called experts do not understand the mysteries of addiction. This is why they often refer to drug taking as a 'habit', as if the only reason that we do it, is that we got into the habit. But are we as simple-minded as that? Don't we normally have a reason for habitual behaviour? When in England, I'm in the habit of driving on the left side of the road. When I cross to the Continent, I immediately break that life-long habit without any hassle whatsoever. I confound the platitude that habits are difficult to break. I don't even have to insult your intelligence by explaining why I was in the habit of driving on the left side of the road, and why I broke it. If I try to justify a course of behaviour by saying that I do it out of mere habit, what I am really telling you is that:

I DON'T UNDERSTAND WHY I DO IT!

You need to understand why you drink. It's very easy to see that someone who injects heroin into a vein is an addict. It's not so easy to see our sociable pastimes of smoking and drinking in the same light. But society's attitude towards smokers has undergone a drastic change in recent years. Practically all adult smokers in the West will now admit that they wished that they had never started, and they sense that they have fallen into a trap rather than chosen to be in it. People who have never smoked cannot understand why anyone would actually pay good money just to set light to dried vegetable matter and breathe the filthy and lethal fumes into their lungs. Incidentally, smokers themselves don't understand why they do it. Non-smokers regard smokers in rather the same way that a smoker or drinker would regard a heroin addict. We cannot imagine how someone could possibly get pleasure from pushing a hypodermic syringe into a vein. But can you understand why they do it?

"That's obvious, it's because they are addicted."

But that doesn't explain anything. Like habit, addiction is just a word, it doesn't explain why they do it. I will help you to understand why they do it. Like most of the population, I was brainwashed to believe that heroin addicts took heroin because of the wonderful highs they receive. Try to picture a heroin addict with no heroin. Imagine the panic they go through, the fear, the terrible craving. Now imagine the utter relief when they finally get their shot. Do you really believe they are injecting themselves to get a wonderful high? Christmas can be a wonderful high, but do we get into a terrible panic because there is no Christmas for the rest of the year? The heroin addict has to go through that terrible ritual to try to end the awful lows that the first dose created and the following doses perpetuated.

Drug addicts are under the illusion that they only suffer withdrawal when they try to quit. They suffer it throughout their addicted lives and it is in fact the only reason they take the next dose. Non-heroin addicts don't get this panic feeling of being without heroin: the fear, the craving. The heroin doesn't relieve those symptoms. It creates them. It takes away with one hand to give back with the other. Why isn't this obvious to the heroin addict? For exactly the same reason that it isn't obvious to a smoker, drinker or any other person who is unfortunate enough to fall for the drugs trap. The trap varies slightly according to the poison you become addicted to. But the following factors are common to all:

1. We are brainwashed to believe that we are incomplete, that we possess an inherent void.

2. We are brainwashed to believe that we will receive some pleasure and/or crutch from the poison, that will help to fill that void.

3. The initial doses taste foul and provide no pleasure or crutch whatsoever, real or illusory. This removes any fear that we might become addicted. After all, why would we want to continue taking something that tastes foul and does nothing for us? However, in the case of drugs like alcohol and caffeine, the foul taste is often partially or completely obliterated by mixers or sweet-tasting additives. We sugar the pill.

4. When the drug leaves our body we suffer withdrawal: an almost imperceptible, empty, insecure feeling, very similar to a hunger for food. Because we cannot separate it from hunger or other causes of distress, and because we do not suffer it whilst we are actually taking the drug, we do not regard the drug as actually causing distress.

5. If you take another dose of the drug during the withdrawal period you will partially relieve that part of your distress which was caused by withdrawal. You will actually feel more confident and more relaxed than you did a moment before. That is not an illusion. But because you receive that actual pleasure or crutch

whilst you are taking the drug, your brain is fooled into believing that the drug is providing a genuine pleasure or crutch, which confirms all the brainwashing.

IT IS AN ILLUSION

In fact the most pathetic aspect of all drug addiction is that the true reason the addict continues to take the drug is to be rid of the insecure feeling that the drug has created. In other words to return to the state you knew the whole of your life before you began taking the drug. Since your body becomes immune to the drug, and you cannot therefore get back to that blissful state even whilst you are taking a dose, the drug cannot possibly help you to relax. In fact, it causes you to feel empty, insecure and unrelaxed.

6. As the accumulative effects of the drug drag you down both physically and mentally, so the feeling of dependence becomes greater and greater, and your intake increases accordingly: an endless downwards spiral. Ironically, just as a stale crust would seem like a banquet to a starving man, so the illusion of pleasure or crutch becomes ever more deceiving to the addict, and the reality more obvious to his family and friends. In fact, even the illusion of pleasure or crutch is almost imperceptible.

7. We have been brainwashed to believe that drugs are difficult to quit, and that the more dependent we feel the more deprived and miserable we will feel when we try to quit. And sure enough, if a drug addict is going through a period of trying to control the drug or to quit, the longer he craves the drug without giving into that craving, then the greater the feeling of deprivation and misery and the greater the feeling of pleasure or crutch when he finally gives in to the craving. Make no mistake, in such circumstances both the misery and the pleasure are genuine and intense. Hence the expressions, "The drinking wasn't so bad. It was the bits in between that were tough", and "It's as if I was born two Martinis below par."

Those miserable bits in between are caused by several factors:

1. The immediate hangover effects created by the previous binge.

2. The accumulative detrimental effects caused by regular heavy drinking: on your physical and mental health, and on your finances and personal relationships.

3. The other genuine stresses in your life which have nothing to do with your drinking problem, but which you would have addressed and solved, had you not chosen to block your mind from them by inebriating yourself.

4. The empty insecure feeling created by the 'little monster'.

5. The mental craving.

Alcoholics are fully aware that the first factor is caused by alcohol. They are less aware of the second factor because the effects are gradual and tend to be blamed on the ageing process and life in general. They choose not to think about the third factor, and in itself the fourth is barely perceptible, so they only know it as: "I rather fancy a drink!" This creates the fifth factor, which is more powerful than the other four put together.

During the bits in between the drinking, the alcoholic craves a drink. He knows a drink will temporarily satisfy that craving and take his mind off the other factors. However, during these in-between bits, for whatever reason, he has to suffer the craving rather than relieve it. That is real misery! But if the little monster is almost imperceptible, why is the craving such torture? For the same reason that an itch might be almost imperceptible but, once you become aware of it, becomes intolerable if you are unable to scratch it. It feels pretty good when you do scratch it, even though in itself the itch was barely noticeable. It's rather like that feeling you get when a distant burglar alarm has been ringing for so long that you only become aware of it when it stops. The silence is golden! What you are really enjoying is the ending of the irritation. Even though you hadn't been conscious of it, it was still an irritation. What you really enjoy in an alcoholic drink is not the drink itself, but the ending of the irritation of wanting that drink. Non-drinkers enjoy that all the time.

Now imagine that burglar alarm is much closer; blaring away just outside your window. No way could you block your mind to it. You could neither relax nor concentrate on your work. That noise would dominate your life until the alarm was switched off, and that's why the fifth factor – the mental craving – is more powerful than the rest put together. Once a drinker decides he must satisfy his craving for a drink, he will be utterly miserable until he is able to do so. And the longer that misery lasts, the greater will be the relief and the illusion of pleasure.

I don't need to tell you that the misery of the bits in between the drinking is perfectly real. And in itself so is the intense pleasure that alcoholics feel when they are allowed to satisfy the craving. The illusion is that alcohol itself provides the pleasure and that it satisfies the craving. Re-read the five factors that contribute to the misery of the bits in between. Every one of them is caused by drinking alcohol and this applies at whatever stage you have reached in your slide down the pitcher plant. Imagine not being allowed to remove a pair of tight shoes for a whole week, and at the same time being expected to function normally at both work and play. Of course you would experience a feeling of intense relief when you were finally allowed to remove those shoes. But to suggest that alcohol provides genuine pleasure is tantamount to claiming that wearing tight shoes is genuinely relaxing. No one would be stupid enough to deliberately wear tight shoes for a whole week, just to receive a few moments of pleasure after removing them. Far from satisfying the craving, alcohol is both the initial cause of it and the sole reason for its perpetuation.

Get it clear in your mind: the misery of the bits in between is caused by alcohol. Even more important: unlike the fly, you can escape, you don't have to suffer that misery. For now, forget about the misery of the times when you weren't allowed to drink. Let's take a closer look at all those glorious hours you spent when you could drink. But try to look back on them without the brainwashing. To do this, you need to discount those moments of illusory pleasure that I have just described above: the relief when ending a period of abstinence. Do not confuse the ending of the misery of craving with genuine pleasure. A pain-killing injection might well end the misery of pain, but that doesn't make it a pleasure in itself. It would provide no pleasure if you weren't in pain. The period of abstinence always seems so long and miserable, and the moment of ending it so ridiculously brief. Why should those moments be discounted? Because they are not really part of the pleasure of drinking. Because we are miserable when we aren't allowed to drink, we assume that we must get tremendous pleasure when we can. This is one of the illusions of all drug addiction and we are now trying to find out whether it is true. The relief we feel when ending a period of abstinence is just that: relief. The real drinking starts from that point on, and that's what we are going to examine.

You must also exclude any occasion when you were satisfying a genuine thirst. That is a genuine pleasure but, as we have already established, alcohol creates thirst in the long run. Also omit any occasions that were happy, not because you happened to be drinking alcohol but for other reasons. This would exclude all parties, discos, weddings and meals; in fact, all social, sporting or entertaining occasions. Again you might be wondering why such occasions should be excluded. After all, aren't they the very occasions that we most enjoy a drink? Do we? Remember to keep an open mind. Perhaps it is just the occasion we enjoy, and the fact that we couldn't enjoy such occasions without them doesn't automatically mean that we enjoy the drink. After all, non-drinkers are perfectly capable of enjoying parties without alcohol.

For most smokers the most enjoyable cigarettes are at parties or after a meal. At our smoking clinics, we ask smokers who believe that they enjoy smoking to light up, and ask themselves what it is that they are actually enjoying. Invariably, they find it difficult to explain. In fact, most times they'll say something like:

*"I don't know. I'm not actually enjoying this one. In fact it tastes horrible.
But I do enjoy one after a meal."*

It never seems to occur to them that two cigarettes out of the
same packet cannot possibly be different. How can a cigarette at a
party be inherently more enjoyable than its identical twin from the
same packet? It can't. All cigarettes always taste horrible. So why
do cigarettes smoked at parties seem enjoyable? The explanation is
quite simple. If I can't jump over a ten foot wall, but can clear it
with the aid of a pole, the obvious conclusion is that the pole
deserves the credit. Smokers don't enjoy parties at which they
aren't allowed to smoke, but do enjoy parties at which they can.
Obvious conclusion: the cigarette made the difference. It did. Not
because cigarettes are enjoyable, but because smokers are miserable
without them.

We can't ask drinkers to consciously sample their favourite
tipple at an alcohol clinic, because we need them to be not only
sober, but clear-headed. However, one of the reasons that I have
asked you not to attempt to quit or to cut down until you have
completed the book is because the only way to find out just how
pleasurable drinking is, is to study it whilst you are drinking. It is
essential to remove the illusions, and you won't be able to do that
if you have already quit. Whatever the occasion at which you are
drinking might be, just pause at times and consciously savour the
poison. Ask yourself what is so enjoyable about it.

Look back on your life. Sure, you enjoyed hundreds of
occasions at which you were drinking, but try to separate the
occasion from the drink. Can you remember even one occasion
in your life when you got genuine pleasure not because of the
occasion, but from consuming a drink just because it contained
alcohol? Think back to the learning stage, when you were working
hard to acquire the taste. Drinking alcohol can't have been much
fun then. What about the in-between stage: after you had learned
to cope with the foul taste, but before your drinking became a
problem? Did alcohol seem so special to you then, or did you
more or less take it for granted? During that period, when you

were going out for a meal with friends, perhaps you can remember looking forward to the meal, or meeting those particular friends, or to the ambience of a special restaurant. But can you remember ever thinking: "How lovely it will be to drink that bottle of wine!"? Isn't it true that drinking alcohol only became so precious to you after it became a problem? Doesn't all the evidence suggest that it's not so much that we enjoy drinking alcohol, but that we feel miserable and deprived without it?

If you can open your mind, and accept that the good times were happy for reasons other than because you were drinking alcohol, you'll find that for most of your drinking life even the illusion of pleasure was hardly perceptible. And, of course, we musn't forget the times when your speech was slurred, when you were spouting gibberish, staggering around, being offensive and aggressive, when you were feeling queasy or throwing-up. And, even though you can't remember them, we must include the times you were paralytic. So it would appear that the times when we are drinking are no better than the miserable times in between. Indeed, they are often worse. Never forget that the misery at both times is caused by drinking alcohol, and that it provides no pleasure or crutch whatsoever.

However, if you believe that you possess a congenital flaw, in other words that you were born two Martinis below par, you might also believe that the true alcoholic has no choice but to crave alcohol. Not so. We only crave something if we believe it will provide us with a genuine crutch or pleasure. We only crave drugs because we are deluded into believing that they provide a genuine crutch or pleasure. Once the delusion is removed, so is the craving. I will address this matter in due course.

Smokers find it easier than drinkers to relate to heroin addicts for two reasons. The first is that just as it seems completely unnatural to stick needles into a vein, so we sense that it is unnatural to breathe lethal fumes into our lungs. Drinking, however, is a completely natural function that is not only a genuine pleasure but also vital to survival. Drinking alcohol isn't any of these things, but our perception of it is clouded by the brainwashing we have all received from birth: the hammering home that drinking alcohol in moderation is both pleasurable and natural.

The second reason is that because of the nature of nicotine, we soon reach the stage where we smoke all day and get in a panic if we run out of cigarettes. In fact the casual smoker who can go all day without a cigarette is regarded by 'normal' smokers as an abnormal but lucky freak. With alcohol it is the reverse, the morning drink and the permanent flask are viewed as abnormal: sure signs of alcoholism.

The difference can be explained by the fact that nicotine is a very fast-acting drug: within an hour of extinguishing a cigarette most of the nicotine has left your body. This is why most smokers soon reach 20 a day. Although this feeling is real and physical, it is so imperceptible that we only know it as a feeling of needing something to do with our hands, or just as: "I want a cigarette." When we light the next cigarette the nicotine is restored, the insecure feeling goes and the illusion that smoking relaxes and gives confidence is reinforced.

With alcohol, there is no physical withdrawal pain from the drug itself. However, drinking alcohol does cause several undesirable physical effects. We have already addressed inebriation and dehydration, and the first time we get drunk it doesn't require an Einstein to deduce that the vomiting and next morning's hangover are a direct result of drinking alcohol. Far from needing 'a hair of the dog that bit us', the thought of more alcohol is anathema. In fact this is usually the first of several occasions when we make the pledge never to let alcohol soil our lips again. This is why it can take from 2 to 60 years to become an alcoholic and why most drinkers never reach the flask stage: our natural revulsion for the unpleasant effects acts as a check on our inevitable descent.

However, if you reach the early stages of inebriating yourself in order to block your mind from stress, it is a completely different story. Many such people learn to limit their intake so they take enough to hide from the source of the stress, but not so much that they are aware of it seriously affecting their lives. So when the physical effects of the inebriation wear off, a 'hair of the dog' ceases to be anathema. You haven't solved any of your problems, and you know it. But there is a simple solution. Another dose of the drug can get you back to the same stage of inebriation, so your problems don't weigh so heavily on your mind.

"Is that so bad? Aren't you 'using' and controlling the drug?"

No! It is ingeniously controlling you! You are aware of some of the bad physical effects, but at this stage they don't seem to present a serious problem, so any instinctive desire you might have to quit or to control your intake is curtailed. But no matter how gradual and imperceptible it might be, you are on a perpetual downwards spiral. Because as your body becomes immune to alcohol, you'll need to take larger doses to reach the same level of inebriation. This tends to happen so gradually that you are hardly aware it *is* happening. And because you take more and more, your problems – mental, physical and financial – get worse and worse. Again, this tends to happen relatively slowly, so that day-by-day you don't even notice it happening. The worse your problems become, the greater your need for the illusory friend or crutch. So even if you've reached the stage where you begin to suspect that you might have a drink problem, now is never the right time to do something about it. Better wait until life is less stressful. But if you are caught in the drugs trap, life is guaranteed to get increasingly stressful. More about that later.

The point I want you to get clearly into your mind is this: because we seem to need to take a chemical that is also a poison on a regular basis, it is logical to assume that there is some physical property in the chemical itself which compels us to do so, and that we must suffer physical withdrawal symptoms when we stop taking it.

It is all illusion. We are never addicted to the chemical itself. What addicts us is the belief that we get some genuine benefit from taking it, which in turn creates a false belief that you cannot enjoy certain occasions or cope with others without it. What addicts us in the case of alcohol is the inebriation! Or rather the illusion that the inebriated state makes social occasions happier, and helps to relax you and relieve stress. I repeat: it is an illusion. The solution is entirely mental. Once the illusion goes:

SO DOES THE ADDICTION

So let's continue removing the cobwebs. Another subtle ingenuity of the trap is:

THE SIMILARITY BETWEEN ALCOHOL AND FOOD

17 *The Similarity Between Alcohol And Food*

We have considered how Mother Nature has equipped all creatures with a device called hunger, to ensure that we remember to eat. But have you ever considered what an incredibly ingenious device hunger is? There is no physical pain when you are hungry. OK, your stomach might be rumbling and you might be feeling empty and irritable, but there is no actual pain. I should make it quite clear that I am not talking about starvation. That is quite another matter on which I am not qualified to comment. I am one of those fortunates who has never gone a single day without at least one decent meal. I'm not talking about starvation but this everyday business of eating three meals a day.

Why is hunger so ingenious? Because not only does it involve no actual pain – we only know the feeling as: "I'd like something to eat" – but for most of our lives we aren't even aware of it. Now, it is pretty obvious that Mother Nature's intention was to make sure that we supply our bodies with sufficient energy and nutrients in order to be fit and healthy and survive. The moment I finish breakfast, I begin to burn up that energy and use the minerals. Yet here I sit eight hours later, actually writing about food, but I don't feel in the least bit hungry. It will be another two hours before I eat and I won't get hungry in the meantime. Now I realize that this is because that has been my regular eating habit for years. But what I can't understand is why I don't begin to get hungry the moment I stop eating, or why in two hours' time I will suddenly have a ravenous appetite. Fortunately I don't need to understand it. I'm nowhere near as clever as Mother Nature but I do feel very grateful to her, because I can enjoy the immense pleasure of satisfying that appetite twice a day for the rest of my life.

One of the ingenious aspects of drug addiction is that it is almost identical to a hunger for food. When we need a drink, and I remind you that I mean a drink containing alcohol, we only know that feeling as: "I want a drink." As in the case of food, there is no physical pain, it is almost imperceptible. In the early stages we can go long periods without getting the feeling, and only associate it with certain activities, such as social occasions. But once we do get that feeling of wanting a drink, providing we can have one, we do get a feeling of satisfaction or relaxation similar to satisfying a hunger for food, even if the drink itself doesn't taste very good. So what's the difference? There appears to be very little: in reality there are several differences and they are important. In fact drinking alcohol and eating food are exact opposites:

1. Good food genuinely tastes good if you are hungry. Alcohol itself will always taste foul.

2. Food is essential to your health, enjoyment, well-being and survival. Alcohol is a poison that will systematically and progressively destroy you physically and mentally.

3. Eating is a genuine pleasure. Drinking is a confidence trick.

4. Alcohol inebriates you and debilitates every one of your senses. Food does neither.

5. Eating doesn't create hunger but will genuinely satisfy it; not forever, but so much the better, you can continue to enjoy the pleasures of eating for the rest of your life. Alcohol actually creates the craving for alcohol. It doesn't even quench your thirst. Far from satisfying the need for alcohol, it ensures that you'll suffer it, and the other undesirable effects that go with it, for the rest of your life.

It's so obvious if you think about it: even alcoholics didn't need alcohol before they started taking it. We didn't even need it to quench our thirst! So all we achieve by taking it is to create a need, not for food, but for a poison that will destroy us.

You might have noticed that I referred earlier to my regular eating 'habit'. This might imply that eating is merely a habit. If you believe that try breaking it! Eating is not a habit but essential to survival. It is true that different people are in the habit of satisfying their hunger at different times with different types of food. It is also true that many of us get into a habit of over-eating. Different addicts are in the habit of trying to satisfy their craving at different times, with different drugs, but drinking alcohol is not a habit either. It is simple drug addiction.

It is this great variety in the habits of drinkers that send certain 'experts' delving into the different types of drinker. It's about as sensible as trying to analyse the different types of mice that fall into a mousetrap. All it achieves is to make the mysteries of drug addiction infinitely more confusing. It doesn't seem to deter these 'experts' in the least that, having categorized the various types, they don't know how to cure any of them. The type of drinker doesn't affect the matter one iota, they are all in the same prison and the key is the same for all of them. This is an appropriate time to explode another illusion that keeps many people in the trap, as it did me for many years:

THE MYTH OF THE ADDICTIVE PERSONALITY

18 *The Myth Of The Addictive Personality*

Like most of my generation, I began drinking and smoking regularly when I started work. If there were such a thing as a smokaholic, I would have had to accept that I was one in my early twenties. Because I became a chain-smoker so quickly, I truly believed I had an addictive personality. And just as AA conclude that alcoholics have a different chemical make-up to 'normal' drinkers, so I believed I was different to 'normal smokers'. I believed that there was either some flaw in my chemical make-up that 'normal' smokers didn't suffer from, or that tobacco contained some chemical ingredient which I couldn't survive without, but 'normal' smokers could take or leave as the mood took them. I had no idea which of the two alternatives applied and to me the effect was the same.

These days even smokers themselves regard smoking as abnormal and antisocial. But when I was a boy over 90 percent of adult males smoked. You were abnormal if you didn't smoke, and regarded by many as a 'sissy'. Because over 90 percent of adults in Western society drink on a regular basis, drinking is still regarded as normal. But just as you could argue that it is extremely abnormal to inhale cancerous fumes, so you could argue that there is nothing normal about adding a foul-tasting poison to an otherwise pleasant and nutritious drink.

For convenience I will continue to use the expressions 'normal drinker' and 'normal smoker'. In order to avoid confusion, I would define 'normal drinkers' as:

"People who believe they get a genuine pleasure and/or crutch from drinking alcohol; people who are aware that there are health risks, but believe that the benefits outweigh them."

These people do not see drinking as a problem and believe that, if ever it became a problem, they would simply cut down or quit. In other words, by my definition 'normal drinkers' are 'people who believe that they are in control of their drinking'.

Although this might seem to contradict the last sentence, 'normal drinkers' would include people who occasionally get drunk. For my definition of a 'normal smoker', just substitute smoking for drinking. I should also make it clear that at no time in my life did I relate either my 'addictive personality' or my 'chemical flaw' to drinking. I didn't even suspect that I might have a drinking problem until my mid-fifties, and didn't accept that I did indeed have one until my early sixties. By that time I had already discovered Easyway and had realized that no one, including me, had ever been forced to take a poison because they had an addictive personality or a congenital flaw.

Most people who have never smoked suffer the illusion that people who smoke heavily do so because they find cigarettes more pleasurable than casual smokers. It seems logical, but like practically every other aspect of drug addiction, the reality is the exact opposite to the general belief. If you chain-smoke, no way can you kid yourself that you are deriving some pleasure from it. If you've reached the stage where you cannot even contemplate the simplest of mental or physical tasks without a cigarette, you might conclude that it was something of a crutch! But what possible 'magic' could a cigarette contain, that I couldn't press a button on a TV remote control without first lighting one?

From the first filthy cigarette to the last I loathed every single one. 'Normal' smokers don't so much accept the health risks as close their minds to them. I'd already watched my father and my sister die through smoking, and with the state my lungs were in, the only mystery was why it hadn't already happened to me. So why did I go on smoking? Because I was utterly miserable whenever I tried to quit! I was between the devil and the deep blue sea. I hated being a smoker, but without nicotine I didn't seem to be able to enjoy life or cope with stress.

Quite clearly I was different from the vast majority of 'normal' smokers. There was another factor which mystified me. I had been brainwashed to believe that a bit of willpower was all that was required to quit smoking. But I also knew that I was a very strong-willed person. I hated being a smoker. I desperately wanted to quit, no one but me was forcing me to smoke, and I knew I was very strong-willed. So I assumed that I must have an addictive personality and a congenital flaw in my make-up. What other possible explanation could there be? But if smokaholics and alcoholics really did have a congenital flaw in their physical make-up, surely a doctor could examine them, X-ray them, take samples of their urine and blood ... or do whatever it is that doctors do to diagnose physical diseases. With the miracles of modern science, particularly in the field of genetics, surely it would be possible to detect the flaw and warn addicts before they took their first cigarette or drink?

If alcoholism was due to a chemical flaw, it wouldn't take from two to sixty years to become one: you would become one immediately. In fact you could be an alcoholic without ever drinking alcohol! Have you ever met a drug addict who had never, ever taken the drug to which he was supposedly addicted? No, the congenital flaw theory itself has too many flaws to be viable. In any event, a physical flaw could only prevent you from achieving some physical act. It cannot prevent you from doing nothing. Lockjaw might stop you drinking alcohol, but with alcoholism your only problem is not to drink alcohol. How can a physical flaw possibly prevent you from not doing something? It just doesn't make sense!

We use the word 'addict' to describe someone who would dearly love to quit a drug but cannot. But the word does nothing to explain why that person has to go on taking the drug, when no one but themselves forces them to. The expression 'addictive personality' is equally meaningless. It doesn't explain the anomaly, but is merely a red herring used by people who do not understand drug addiction. It just piles further confusion onto an already confused subject. In any event, it is a contradiction in terms. If I had a gregarious personality I would want to mix with other people. Doesn't it follow that if I have an addictive personality, I actually want to be an addict? I've yet to meet anyone that actually wanted to become addicted to a drug.

The addictive personality theory suffers from similar defects to the physical defect theory. If you were born with a mental and/or physical defect, whereby just one drink would compel you to go on drinking, it would become obvious the moment you started drinking. Why would some people have to wait sixty years? If I'd truly had an addictive personality, I would have soon become addicted to everything that was going: cannabis, heroin, cocaine, the lot. So would you if you genuinely had an addictive personality. The only people I have ever met who claimed to have an addictive personality also happened to be addicted to a drug, or were at one point. Do you not think that is an incredible coincidence? Have you ever met someone with an addictive personality who never became an addict?

It is blatantly obvious that Mother Nature has gone to enormous lengths to ensure we survive. Is it logical that she would give some of us a physical or mental defect which gave us the desire to systematically destroy ourselves? Even if she were that stupid and cruel, it still doesn't explain our behaviour. I am grateful to have been equipped with a sex drive, which I regard as normal. I'm also convinced that my sex drive is both physical and mental. But I would have no difficulty whatsoever in resisting that natural desire if I was aware that my partner had a sexually transmitted disease. So even if alcoholics were that way because they were born with an addictive personality or a physical defect, why, when they know that alcohol is destroying their lives, should they have such problems resisting temptation?

Just think for a moment about these distinctions the so-called experts make: between drug 'users' and addicts; between people who are in control of their intake and people who are not; between 'normal drinkers' and alcoholics; between addictive personalities and non-addictive personalities. If any of these distinctions really did exist (apart from in the minds of these so-called 'experts'), that would mean that the drug itself is irrelevant, there would be no such thing as an addictive drug!

Why did I once believe that I had an addictive personality or a flaw in my chemical make-up? Because I didn't understand the true reason why smokers, alcoholics and other drug addicts continue to destroy themselves, when they are clearly receiving no benefit from the drug whatsoever. When I discovered Easyway I discovered the true explanation: which has no flaws or contradictions whatsoever and which doesn't fly in the face of basic common sense.

Unfortunately, I can't prove to you that this explanation is correct, because I can't prove that the addictive personality doesn't exist. Let me illustrate by using the legend of the Loch Ness Monster as an example. It adds a little colour to our lives and attracts tourists, so I have no intention of trying to disprove it. But I couldn't even if I wanted to. You can prove that something does exist by producing it, but it's impossible to prove that something doesn't exist. So how do you decide? You check out the probabilities and use your common sense. OK, Loch Ness is very deep and contains a large volume of water. But 'Nessie' herself is reputed to be a very large animal, and in order for any species to survive it must contain sufficient numbers to avoid extinction by interbreeding. With modern technology, if 'Nessie' did exist, wouldn't it have been proved beyond doubt?

Imagine a famous beauty spot viewed from a sandy beach. But as you stand admiring the view, your feet sink into the soft sand. Most people can stand for hours on end and seem to be able to just walk away whenever they choose. But a small minority find that they are trapped, some having stood for a few minutes only, and no matter how hard they try they cannot escape, not even when the tide comes in.

Various theories are put forward to explain the anomaly. Several people suggest that it is quicksand. One person suggests that the people who cannot escape have a chemical flaw in their make-up. Another suggests that it is not so much a chemical flaw as a flaw in their personality. I won't insult your intelligence by asking which explanation you would find the most viable. However, if your choice was other than the first, I would suggest that you have failed to open your mind. If you do not believe me, put the scenario to other people, but without relating it to alcoholism.

You might ask why some people don't sink in the quicksand? What if I told you that they *were* sinking, but so slowly that they didn't realize it, and nor did anyone else? After all, think about one of these so-called 'normal drinkers' that you know. I bet you they drink more than they did ten years ago. They certainly drink more than they once did. They must do, because at one point they didn't drink at all. And in ten years time they'll be drinking more than they do today.

The only reason that some people sink faster than others is that some people weigh more than others. It's like the bloated fly in the pitcher plant. The weight of the person in the quicksand represents the degree of realization that they are trapped and the resulting feeling of panic – which makes them reach for the very poison they are panicking about, which in turn increases their feeling of being trapped and the illusion of dependence on the very thing that is destroying them. If you can accept this analogy you'll see that there can only be one explanation: the answer lies in the nature of quicksand itself, and everyone's sinking. Some people believe they are dependent on one whisky a day, some on thirty. In either case it is an illusion and both people are suffering from the same disease, and that *is* the disease: the belief that alcohol does something for you and that you are dependent on that so-called benefit. You are cured once you see alcohol for what it is: a poison that does nothing whatsoever for anyone. After all, if it does something for so-called 'normal drinkers', shouldn't it follow that it does a lot more for someone who drinks a lot more of it. If it really did bestow some sort of crutch or pleasure on 'normal' drinkers, then surely alcoholics would be the happiest, most confident and secure people on the planet! And by the same token, since it does in fact make alcoholics miserable and terrified, doesn't it also follow that it must make 'normal' drinkers sad and fearful?

AA state that the only person who can tell you whether you are an alcoholic or not is you. That doesn't sound very scientific to me. Bear in mind that there is not one single item of hard evidence to show that a chemical defect or an addictive personality is the cause of anyone becoming addicted to any drug. It is merely a theory offered up as an explanation by people who don't understand the true cause of addiction. However there is strong evidence to disprove the theory.

If alcoholism and other forms of drug addiction were due to an inherent physical or mental flaw, they would indeed be incurable. So how do people who believe in either theory explain how I was cured of drug addiction overnight, along with thousands of other people who have used Easyway? Do you not think that the only rational explanation is not that you have an addictive personality or some chemical defect in your nature, but that you have been taking

A HIGHLY ADDICTIVE DRUG?

Bear in mind that another of the ingenious subtleties of alcohol is to make us believe that the fault lies inherently within ourselves rather than the drug. This applies to all addictive drugs. After all, we know that it's affecting our health and our pocket, and when we consciously examine the actual pleasure or crutch we get, our reasons seem somewhat feeble. Our rational brains are telling us to cut down or quit. We know that no one but ourselves forces us to take the drug. And we believe that the majority of drinkers are in complete control. Because of all these factors it is logical to assume that we are part of a minority inflicted with a physical or mental flaw. But let's examine some of the ridiculous excuses that drinkers and smokers offer as reasons for taking their respective drugs, including the majority who believe they are in control:

"Traffic fumes are as harmful as smoking."

Possibly, but you wouldn't dream of deliberately putting your mouth over an exhaust pipe and breathing the fumes into your lungs, and you certainly wouldn't pay for the privilege.

"I don't smoke so why shouldn't I have a drink?"

That's equivalent to saying: "I haven't cut off my leg so why shouldn't I cut off my arm?"

"Life's too short, I could step under a bus tomorrow."

But would you deliberately step under a bus? And we can't leave out the old favourite:

"The occasional drink is the only pleasure I've got left!"

It's incredible that the last brief statement can contain so many misconceptions. To begin with, it is never made by people who drink occasionally, but only by people who have become completely dependent upon alcohol. To most people the statement might appear to be a gross distortion of the truth and therefore just another ridiculous excuse. Is life really that gloomy a business? Unfortunately to the alcoholic, it seems to be true. And it is true in the sense that he no longer has other pleasures. But it doesn't seem to occur to him that it is his drinking that has robbed him of those pleasures. When you feel physically and mentally low, life is depressing. Another misconception is that there is genuine pleasure in consuming alcohol for anyone. The so-called pleasure that occasional drinkers believe they get from alcohol is an illusion. And the final misconception in the statement is that for the person making it, even the illusion of pleasure has gone!

This is an excellent illustration of another ingenious aspect of drug addiction: the more it drags you down, the greater the illusion of pleasure and/or crutch. Are genuine pleasures that rare? You'll soon be discovering that when you feel physically and mentally strong, life itself becomes a pleasure. Have you forgotten expressions like 'joie de vivre', 'it's great to be alive' and 'the sheer joy of living'?

Isn't it obvious? If our every natural instinct is to ensure that we survive, doesn't it follow that life is precious and meant to be enjoyed? Alcohol is a chemical depressant and a powerful poison. It destroys us both physically and mentally. By inebriating us, it destroys every survival instinct that we possess and takes the joy of life with it. In short: it makes us feel suicidal. And that's what it amounts to:

SLOW AGONIZING SUICIDE

Like any other poison, the more you consume, the greater those effects will be. Alcohol doesn't suddenly change from being one type of thing when consumed by a so-called normal drinker to another type of thing when consumed by a so-called alcoholic!

Do you still find it difficult to believe that our life-long pleasure and crutch is a highly addictive drug? If so, open your mind: why else do you think 90 percent of the population are drinking DEVASTATION? Why do you think you are reading this book? The problem with these flimsy excuses is that because generations of drinkers have been using them for years, we never question them, we just take them for granted.

We fully understand the nature of quicksand. So we don't get into convoluted debates as to why certain people get stuck in it, and conjure up highly improbable explanations; we know that the answer lies in the very nature of quicksand itself. So why, when analysing the difference between a 'normal drinker' and an alcoholic, do some people advocate that the alcoholic suffers with a physical or mental flaw that 'normal drinkers' don't possess? Why don't they plump for the more obvious explanation: that alcoholics are merely at a more advanced stage of the same disease? After all, they are both consuming exactly the same poison. It is an accepted fact that alcohol both dehydrates and inebriates and that the combined effect is to make you want to consume more and more. And the reality confirms the theory. It's not just alcoholics who increase their intake; 'normal drinkers' start their drinking careers with a few experimental drinks and find that they are soon drinking on a regular basis. It is a fact that all alcoholics start off as 'normal drinkers', that it usually takes years for them to cross the line that divides one from the other, and that where that line actually lies is a matter of much rather vague debate by the so-called experts. AA cop out of the debate altogether by saying that no one but you can decide. And there are usually many years between suspecting you have a problem and accepting the fact. You might remember grandma from Chapter 3, who hardly ever drank alcohol; and Uncle Ted, who hardly ever did anything else. Somewhere between them lie the billions of other drinkers in the world. Isn't it blatantly obvious that the only difference between 'alcoholics' and so-called 'normal drinkers' lies not in a physical or mental defect but in the stage they have reached in their downward slide?

AA's booklet 'Who Me?' states:

'Not all drinkers are alcoholics. Many people can drink normally and suffer no physical, mental or social ill-effects. For them, alcohol is not a problem and we can only say "May it always stay that way".'

But if AA are correct, how could it do anything but stay that way? If alcohol is not a problem, and the reason that it is not a problem is that this divide exists, and exists from birth, and they are the right side of this divide, how could they do anything but stay the right side of it?

Let us not forget that apparently the real difference between a 'normal drinker' and an alcoholic is that the 'normal drinker' can control his intake and the alcoholic can't.

The statement begs the question: what is 'normal drinking'? The passage infers that it is drinking at such a level that you suffer no physical, mental or social ill-effects. But how many 'normal' drinkers do you know who have never thrown up; or been drunk or hung-over; or been offensive or acted stupidly through drinking alcohol? So what happens to them when they are like this? Do they temporarily acquire this inherent mental or physical defect, and does it disappear again, as if by magic, when the effects of the drug wear off? And is AA implying that alcoholics never drink moderately and are never in control of their drinking? Surely they were exactly the same as 'normal drinkers' before they degenerated. And what is a recovering alcoholic if he is not exercising control (at least some of the time)? So if 'normal drinkers' occasionally lose control and alcoholics occasionally gain it, the difference is surely not in an inherent physical or mental defect, but one of degree. Which would indicate what I've been saying all along: that an alcoholic is at an advanced stage of the same disease.

If it is so obvious, why doesn't society generally see it that way? Because it only becomes obvious once you open your mind, remove all the misconceptions, the myths and the brainwashing; when you use your common sense and accept the facts. But don't under-estimate the power of the brainwashing.

You would expect an ex-alcoholic to jump at the chance to see no longer having to poison themselves in its true light: as a heaven-sent release from an awful disease, rather than being deluded into feeling permanently deprived because they can no longer enjoy the pleasures of 'normal' drinking. But as much as they might wish to see it in its true light, no one is going to believe me just because I say so. I have to prove it them. It is easy for any drinker to solve their problem, when they can see drinking alcohol the way it really is. But it is not necessarily easy to enable every drinker to see it that way.

No one would dispute that alcoholism is a disease. But to accept that there is no inherent distinction between 'normal drinkers' and alcoholics, and that alcoholism is simply an advanced stage of the same disease, you must first accept that 'normal drinkers' also have the disease. But we've been brainwashed to believe that far from being a disease, drinking alcohol is a pleasure and a crutch and that's the only reason we choose to do it. 90 percent of adults drink alcohol and the majority of them believe they are in control. But if alcoholics themselves confirm that they are inherently different from 'normal drinkers', what do you think the chances are of convincing just one 'normal drinker', who enjoys a glass of wine with his meal, that he is not actually drinking it because he enjoys it, but because he is being controlled by a drug?

Even if you present that drinker with all the evidence and facts, it will get you nowhere. Why not? Because no matter how intelligent and open-minded that drinker might be about other matters, the nature of the drug is to make you close your mind to the facts even when they are jumping up and biting you on the nose. Don't waste your time even attempting to do it. It will only cause you frustration. Probably the most common comment in the thousands of letters I receive is something like: "Why can't I make so-and-so see how easy and wonderful it is to be free?"

Perhaps you still find it difficult to believe that these 'normal drinkers' are already hooked. But is the concept so unacceptable? After all, it is not a million years since we regarded 'normal smokers' as being in control of their pleasure and/or crutch. Is that how we view them today? Nowadays even smokers themselves know deep down that they aren't smoking because they choose to or because they genuinely enjoy it. Why else would smokers so vehemently try to persuade their children not to fall into the trap? And when we do see a youngster puffing away, do we envy him, or do we shake our heads knowingly thinking, 'You poor sap, if only I could make you see what you've already let yourself in for!'?

I soon learned that it is a waste of time discussing the subject with a drinker who doesn't suspect that he has a problem. I'm only interested in helping someone like you, who knows that they have a problem and is looking for a solution to it. All I can ask you to do is to open your mind, look at the facts and use your common sense. However there is an important aspect which you might think I have conveniently overlooked. Perhaps there is an inherent difference between 'normal drinkers' and alcoholics: perhaps the so-called experts are right when they say that 'normal drinkers' have the willpower to control their drinking and alcoholics do not. I have promised to address this matter and I will explain in the next chapter:

WHY WILLPOWER IS JUST ANOTHER RED HERRING

19 *Why Willpower Is Just Another Red Herring*

We first need to reverse the brainwashing created by the Hollywood image of a typical alcoholic as the down-and-out, meths-drinking tramp, occupying the gutters of Skid Row. That might well be how many alcoholics end up, but the reality is that alcoholism knows no bounds of class, race, gender, religion, education or intelligence. The fact is that the majority of 'normal' drinkers who degenerate into alcoholism do so *because* they were highly intelligent, strong-willed and successful people.

You might find this difficult to believe, but fortunately it is easy to prove. If you attend AA meetings you will discover that the majority of members are educated, intelligent and articulate and either are, or were, successful. This tends to be true of all drug addiction, even with heroin. The popular image is of young girls being tricked into addiction by evil men, in order to force them into prostitution. I'm not saying that doesn't happen. What I am saying is that my profession and vocation is to cure drug addiction; and the vast majority of the heroin addicts and ex-addicts I have met were highly intelligent, educated and strong-willed people. In fact, they represented the cream of our youth, if somewhat soured, and the vast majority of them fell into the trap at university.

Just look at the facts. People who are destroyed by drugs – whether it's alcohol, nicotine, cocaine or heroin – tend to be highly successful, strong people who have fought long and hard to reach the top of their professions. The Richard Burtons, the Elizabeth Taylors, the George Bests of this world. The list is endless. You could argue that because people in the entertainment and sporting worlds receive a lot of publicity, this distorts the overall impression. But if you scratch the surface you will discover the same is true in all professions. Drug addiction is particularly rife among the professionals that you would think would be put off by the fact that in their working lives they come face to face with the very worst effects of drugs: like doctors, nurses, lawyers and police.

In the old days men were regarded as sissies if they didn't drink or smoke. The reason some didn't get hooked was either because they weren't physically strong enough to cope with the poison, or because they hadn't got the willpower to go through the learning process of acquiring a taste for it. The Hollywood heroes like John Wayne and Humphrey Bogart were all hard drinkers and heavy smokers. So were the sophisticated leading ladies like Marlene Dietrich and Bette Davis.

I must be careful – perhaps I'm giving the impression that drinking and smoking made them tough and sophisticated. Just the reverse, these people were tough and sophisticated in spite of drinking and smoking. Marlene Dietrich would have looked sophisticated with a turnip sticking out of her mouth! These stars were selling alcohol and nicotine. The drugs did nothing for them; on the contrary, they were the direct ruin of many of them. But let us accept the fact that only strong-willed people can survive in highly competitive professions such as entertainment and sport. Likewise, weak-willed people do not choose to become doctors, nurses, lawyers or police officers. To reach the pinnacle of these professions, you must be incredibly strong-willed.

I knew from other aspects of my life that I was a very strong-willed person. If you are now worrying that Easyway will only work if you are very strong-willed, rest assured. The truth is that it is only your willpower that makes you drink. Difficult to believe but, again, look at the facts. Think back to one of those times when part of your brain was saying "Don't have another drink: you've had enough"; and another part was saying "I know I've already had too much and that I'll regret it tomorrow, but I still want another drink." Who were you actually arguing with? Your real problem is that you are schizophrenic. I regret that I need to digress for a moment. I have recently been chastised for using this word in this context. I'm fully aware that schizophrenia is a serious psychotic disorder. So is alcoholism. Schizophrenia could not be a more appropriate word to describe alcoholism.

The real problem is indecision. Part of your brain says you don't want to drink and part says you do. Remember that no one is forcing you to drink. . .but you. Willpower involves the overcoming of hardship in order to achieve an object. A classic example of willpower was my aim to become a chartered accountant. I hated the job, and I spent night after night studying subjects I loathed, earning a pittance, whilst my friends were out enjoying themselves. You could argue that part of my brain wanted to qualify, and another part wanted to go out and enjoy myself. That is true, but there was no indecision and therefore no schizophrenia, no real conflict of wills. I made my decision and accepted that I would have to make sacrifices. I never doubted my decision.

Now it might well be that in the past you've made a vow that you will never drink again, or that you will cut down on your drinking: a vow that you weren't able to keep. In fact you might have done so several times. The logical conclusion is that you didn't have the willpower to see it through. Not true. All indecision is unpleasant. It can be extremely frustrating if you cannot decide which car to buy. Your choice might flit from one model to another. But as soon as you have made your decision and bought the car, the indecision is ended. But a decision to quit drinking or control it can be reversed at any time in your life. And as I have already explained in Chapter 10, one of the problems when using the willpower method is that you begin to question your decision immediately, and part of your brain starts to say:

I WANT A DRINK!

But your rational brain is still saying: "Please don't give in and take that drink!" You can't understand why one part of your brain is saying one thing, and another is saying the exact opposite. It's very confusing, and not at all pleasant. No one likes being told what to do, least of all by themselves. So what are your alternatives? One is to try to resist the temptation and to have to go through the rest of your life resisting it. Some 'experts' try to help you by saying: "It's not so bad really, you only have to refuse one drink: the next one." They forget to tell you that you will have to go on refusing that next drink for the rest of your life. Another alternative is to end the misery and have the drink. That doesn't solve the dilemma: you are out of the frying pan and back into the fire.

I once survived the misery of the willpower method for six months. It was six months of sheer hell. Eventually my resistance ran out and I was back in the trap. I was crying like a baby because I thought I would never be free. I knew I hadn't got the willpower to abstain for longer than six months. I cursed myself for being so weak: perhaps I might have made it if I could have held out for another day, or week, or month. Ironically I felt a tremendous sense of relief because I didn't have to go on fighting.

I realize now that it wasn't lack of willpower. It's the schizophrenia, the conflict of wills, that causes the problem. Trying to quit or cut down on alcohol, without the true facts at your command, is like a child having a tantrum because it can't have its sweets. A weak-willed child will soon get over the tantrum. A strong-willed child will keep it going until the parent gives in. When the connection between smoking and lung cancer was first made, many smokers quit. Was it because they were strong-willed? No, it was because their fear of contracting lung cancer was greater than their fear of stopping smoking. It takes a strong-willed person to block their minds to the health risks of smoking. It also takes a strong-willed person to resist the anti-social pressures to which smokers are subjected today.

The idea behind National No Smoking Day is that on at least one day in the year smokers will face up to their problem and try to cut down or quit. The reality is it's the one day in the year when most smokers will smoke twice as much and twice as blatantly, because we don't like being told what to do, particularly by people who haven't a clue why we do it. Smokers and drinkers aren't weak-willed. A smoker who has run out of cigarettes will swim the channel to get a packet, and I don't have to tell you what an alcoholic will do to get alcohol.

I couldn't understand why my friends could limit their smoking to five or ten a day. I knew that I was just as strong-willed as they were but that nonetheless I had to chain-smoke. I was completely dominated by nicotine. It never occurred to me that it's not just when we attempt to cut down or quit that we suffer from the schizophrenia. We suffer it throughout our smoking and drinking lives. Some people can't afford to drink or smoke as much as they would like to. Some don't have the same opportunities because of their lifestyle, jobs, families, hobbies or friends. Others permanently restrict their intake, either because they are aware of the harmful effects, or because they sense that something evil has taken possession of them. Of course we try to block our minds to the bad effects! If we had to think about them every time we had a drink or a smoke, even the illusion of pleasure would go. You won't find this hard to believe if you have followed my advice and consciously tested the taste when drinking your favourite tipple. Some people can only drink or smoke a little because their physical constitution doesn't allow them to cope with the poisonous effects of more. You need a good pair of lungs to chain-smoke and you need a strong liver to drink a bottle of whisky a day.

I was lucky that I gave up that willpower attempt after only six months. I admit that at the time the last thing I felt was strong-willed. That's because I had been brainwashed to believe that my failure was due to lack of willpower. Now that I fully understand the trap, I realize that I had no cause to admonish myself. In fact, it took considerable willpower to survive six months of misery. Am I not contradicting myself now? Surely if it took considerable willpower to abstain for six months, it would have taken even more willpower to abstain for longer! True, but that is just my point, it wouldn't have solved the problem. That's why I was lucky; all it would have done was to prolong the misery until my willpower inevitably ran out.

How can I tell that I wouldn't have succeeded if I'd had the willpower to hold out longer? At the time I couldn't. But because

I now understand drug addiction, I know that I would never have been free, no matter how long I'd hung on. The schizophrenia was still there. I believed that I was making a genuine sacrifice and that I couldn't enjoy life without the drug. Time wasn't altering that belief. On the contrary, it was ingraining it. I took the attitude that I'd rather have the shorter, sweeter life of the addict rather than the longer and more miserable alternative. And if that really were the choice, I would still have a drink problem. I'm pleased to inform you that your life will be infinitely more enjoyable once you have solved your problem.

We have helped to make one important point perfectly clear. When drinkers try to quit or to cut down, they make the mistake of trying to do just that: their aim is to never drink alcohol again, or to take less of it. It is completely the wrong approach and to succeed they would have to exercise willpower and discipline for the rest of their lives. Doesn't that mean that drug addicts can quit with the use of willpower? This is exactly the point I'm trying to make. How do they know if they have quit for good if they have to use willpower to resist temptation? Don't alcoholics talk about how long they've been dry? Don't they make statements like "I'm just one drink away from being a drunk!" and recommendations such as 'take each day as it comes!' or 'take one day at a time!'? Don't they say that there is no cure to alcoholism and that they are still alcoholics, even when no alcohol has touched their lips for twenty years? How will they know whether they have indeed kicked it, until they die? And how will they know once they are dead?

Make no mistake, I have nothing but admiration for their willpower, but do you really want to go through that misery? Perhaps you still believe that there is no alternative. A conversation that I once had, with an officer of the Advertising Standards Authority or ASA, might help you to see why it is possible to control your drinking, immediately and permanently, without the use of any willpower whatsoever.

I should point out that the object of the ASA is to protect the public from misleading adverts. Unfortunately it is financed by the advertisers themselves which creates an undesirable conflict of interests. Any advert for a product that claims to help smokers quit must include a statement to the effect that it will only do so in conjunction with the smoker's willpower. This presented a problem because one of the cornerstones of Easyway is that it doesn't require any willpower.

The officer couldn't see what my problem was. All I had to do was to state in the advert that it did require willpower. I pointed out that he was actually encouraging me to tell a deliberate lie, and that surely his sole function was to make sure I didn't lie. But he was adamant that there were only two options. Either I lied or I couldn't advertise.

I asked them why they had a rule to prevent smokers from learning about a method that didn't require the use of willpower. Was it to aid their main advertiser at the time: the tobacco industry? No, it was because their medical 'expert' had decreed that you cannot quit smoking without the use of willpower. I pointed out that I had been helping people to do just that for years, and asked if I could allowed to discuss the matter with the 'expert'.

I was told that there was no need because everyone knew that it took willpower to quit smoking. Undaunted, I asked him if it would take willpower not to get on a Number 9 bus, if you had no desire to get on a Number 9 bus. He failed to see the connection. I explained that the only reason that a smoker lights a cigarette is because he has a desire to light a cigarette. And that Easyway permanently removes that desire before the smoker extinguishes his final cigarette. If the ex-smoker never has the desire to smoke again, why on earth should it take willpower not to smoke again?

Needless to say, I got nowhere with that officer, but I hope you can see the principle. It is quite clearly the schizophrenia that causes the problem. If no one but yourself forces you to drink, part of your brain must have a desire to drink at certain times. That is indisputable! Otherwise you would never drink. It is equally indisputable that part of your brain wishes that you didn't want to drink as much as you do want to drink. If that were not so, you wouldn't have a problem, and you wouldn't be reading this book.

It is also indisputable that although alcohol is a chemical, the problem itself is mental, and so is its solution. The answer is to end the schizophrenia, which is entirely mental. It is also indisputable that this schizophrenia didn't exist before you started consuming alcohol. We haven't removed all the brainwashing yet, but is it entirely beyond the realms of your imagination that you can return to the blissful state you enjoyed before you fell into the trap?

I would remind you of one more indisputable fact: thousands of people have already done just that with the help of Easyway, and there is nothing to prevent you from joining them.

Let's explode another myth:

I ONLY DRINK TO BE SOCIABLE

20 *I Only Drink To Be Sociable*

Could any one really dispute the assertion that drinking is a highly friendly and sociable pastime? Well, I suppose you might question it when some normally inoffensive individual finally plucks up enough Dutch courage to tell a friend what he really thinks of him, and the glasses start to fly and the bottles are being smashed. And when a drunken friend reaches the over-emotional stage while you are still sober, and starts slurring embarrassing compliments with his breath about an inch from your nose. You would not describe such behaviour as being sociable. Especially when you suspect that it's only the drink talking, and that he is not being entirely truthful with those compliments. Your other guests know exactly how truthful he is being. While you've been kind enough to nip out and buy yet another bottle of whisky, he has been complaining about how you never buy enough. He overlooks the fact that he is the only person at the party that drinks whisky. When he starts to throw up over your new living room carpet, you begin to regard drinking as definitely anti-social. But perhaps you regard such experiences as unfortunate rarities and not really worth consideration. So let us concentrate on normal parties, or a visit to your local. Could anyone deny that they are sociable pastimes?

I wouldn't for one moment. What I do claim is that no one drinks to be sociable. Why is any pastime regarded as being sociable? No one would deny that theatrical or choral societies are genuinely sociable institutions. The same can be said of golf, tennis, bridge or chess clubs. No doubt members enjoy the friendship and companionship that joining a club can provide. But people do not generally join clubs for that reason. Their prime reason is because they enjoy that particular activity.

My current sporting activity is lawn bowling. Yes I know it's an old man's game, but it also happens to be a very enjoyable, healthy and sociable pastime. If I suspect that a friend or acquaintance who has lost their partner is lonely, I recommend that they join a bowls club. In this case their prime motive for joining the bowls club might well be to seek companionship and friendship. But they wouldn't continue to play bowls unless they enjoyed it, particularly when there are dozens of other equally sociable activities which they could enjoy.

However I must confess that I continued to go through the routine many months after I became utterly sick of playing golf. The reason that I persevered so long was because so much of my social life was based around the golf club, and some of my best friends had become friends only because we were members of the same club. I was frightened of the void that giving up golf would leave in my social life, and of losing many friends. You could argue that during those months I was playing golf purely for sociable reasons. Even that isn't strictly true. I could have stopped playing golf while continuing to enjoy the social side. In fact, though my visits are now very rare, I'm still a social member of the club. As it turned out I needn't have been frightened of the void. The social side of golf was immediately replaced by the social side of bowls, and of course I didn't lose any real friends. I don't see my golfing friends as often as I would like, but that makes their company even more enjoyable when I do.

It is fear of the void that will be left that makes alcoholics frightened to quit or cut down. No doubt part of that fear is that there will be a void in their social life. My only regret is that I wasted those months playing golf when I could have been partaking in an activity that I did enjoy. I don't doubt that you might have been exceedingly miserable when you tried to quit or cut down on the booze in the past. But you were using the willpower method. With Easyway you'll soon be putting the past behind you and enjoying a fresh, happy and exciting future.

People don't take up drinking to be sociable. Why then do we believe that drinking is a sociable pastime? Because we've been brainwashed from birth to believe it: alcohol is considered essential at practically all genuinely social gatherings like parties, weddings and even wakes. In fact, at some social gatherings, like the Oberfest, it would appear to be the only reason for the event. But like any other activity, people don't do it to be sociable. "I only drink to be sociable" is not a reason but an excuse.

The first social gatherings I attended as a teenager, I did so with but one purpose in mind: to meet girls. My intentions were neither sociable nor to drink. No doubt most of us start drinking at parties, dances or discos. But that does not mean we drink to be sociable. If I was on holiday with three others who wanted me to make up a four at bridge, they could justifiably accuse me of being anti-social if I said I'd prefer to read. You might argue that a youngster who refuses to drink with his friends is being equally anti-social. It is completely different. The bridge players need an extra player and bridge is a genuinely pleasant pastime. But the youngsters can all 'enjoy' their drinks without their friend drinking. Surely they are being exceedingly anti-social by pressurizing him to do something he doesn't want to do, especially if the pressure causes him to end up an alcoholic?

Why do drinkers pressurize non-drinkers to drink? It happens with all drug addiction. If the drug is illegal it's called pushing and if it's legal it's just being sociable. I pride myself that I have never been a pusher. When I first started courting Joyce she was one of those people that could sit all evening in a pub, happily sipping one or two drinks, and she still is. I used to feel somewhat uncomfortable that she didn't match me drink for drink, and it wasn't because she never bought a round. So I would encourage her to drink more than she did. I wasn't pushing, just being polite you understand. One of my friends accused her of being anti-social because she wouldn't drink more, and Joyce has since admitted that she was often made to feel like a party-pooper, not just by this particular friend, but by other heavy drinkers. Ironic that the friend was accusing Joyce of being unsociable and was in fact being exceedingly unsociable himself; whereas Joyce was made to feel unsociable, when she was actually being sociable. She was choosing to be mentally present for her friends or, to be more accurate, she was not choosing to be mentally absent. In today's pop psychobabble she was 'there for them'; and good for her.

Smokers and drinkers find that even the illusion of pleasure goes if they are the only one doing it in a given situation. This is particularly so at a party, when it is patently obvious that everyone else is perfectly capable of having a good time without having to continually choke themselves and/or pour a poison down their throats. Such behaviour seems much less absurd if everyone around you is doing the same thing: you blend chameleon-like into the background, your addiction camouflaged against everyone else's. This is why all drug addicts have a tendency to group together. Such behaviour is often explained as "being sociable". The reality is that, no matter how much they try to convince themselves and other people that they are in control, all drug addicts sense that something evil has taken possession of them. Just as persecuted minorities, and other people with similar problems to each other, find comfort in banding together, so drug addicts feel safer amongst their own kind. It is difficult for non-heroin addicts to see the ritual of 'sharing a needle' as sociable behaviour.

Being sociable means being friendly and companionable. It is natural for civilized people to be sociable, whether it is to celebrate happy occasions like birthdays or weddings, or to mourn and pay respects on sad ones like funerals. People not only form clubs to enhance the pleasure of their chosen sport or activity, but to support each other during trials and tribulations such as cot deaths or disabilities. In the case of drug addiction the tendency to flock together is always for the latter reason, to try and reduce the sum of human misery, whether it is during the period of drug-taking, or after it. Alcoholics Anonymous, Nicotine Anonymous and Narcotics Anonymous do not exist to enhance the consumption of alcohol, nicotine and heroin. They exist solely to help rid the world of the DEVASTATION that these drugs cause; not just to the victims themselves, but to their families and friends. People who drink alcohol cling together for exactly the same reason that all drug addicts cling together: because they sense that they have been trapped by something evil, and a problem shared is a problem halved.

But have I never heard of a drinking club or the local? Of course, but you can be sociable at the local without drinking alcohol; and if anyone joins a club purely to drink, their next club is likely to be AA, and I don't mean the Automobile Association. The same applies to people who join bowling clubs, not to play bowls but to get cheap drinks. Opium dens were regarded as sociable establishments in China. And why not, what better way to spend your time than to share your stupor with people of similar tastes? I hope you don't need me to tell you. If the only purpose of your local is to drink, then you might just as well be in an opium den, and your local pub can be a lot more violent and unfriendly. We have an extremely distorted view of the friendly local. It is true that a bunch of friends will be laughing and joking, but that is because they are friends, not because they are consuming alcohol! You get exactly the same atmosphere in the changing room before a football or rugby match when no alcohol has been consumed. Next time you are in a pub, note how many people are sitting drinking alone, just staring into space. Your friendly local originated as a welcoming establishment in which the weary traveller could obtain food, rest and sustenance, and be brought up to date with the local gossip. It didn't exist solely for people to drink ale and certainly not so they could be rendered paralytic.

Why did my friend accuse Joyce of being anti-social? For the same reason that all drug addicts feel uncomfortable in the presence of people who aren't addicted: they know that what they are doing is stupid and people who aren't in the same prison remind them of their stupidity. For this reason alone drinking is an anti-social pastime. It creates barriers between drinkers and non-drinkers, at parties and other social functions. If someone were to ask you why you play football, you might think that the answer was pretty obvious: because you enjoy it! If you replied: "I only play football to be sociable", you would be telling that person that there are no other reasons that you play, and that therefore you don't actually enjoy playing football. So if someone says: "I only drink to be sociable", they might not realize it but they are telling you that they do not actually enjoy drinking. They are not giving you a truthful reason but an excuse. Why do they need an excuse? Because they sense they have no valid reason. People might do things that they don't particularly enjoy doing, if they think it will improve their health or give them some other benefit. But nobody does something which they don't enjoy for no reason at all, particularly if it ruins their health and finances. Unless of course:

THEY ARE ADDICTED TO A DRUG

The youth that is not strong enough to resist the peer pressure might claim that he is only drinking to be sociable. Even so, it's not a reason but an excuse. It's the same when they say "I'm a rebel" or "I like to be different". Rather than attempting to explain the dangers of drinking to them, ask them if they think they'll ever have the courage to be a true rebel; instead of just copying their friends. Of course the true reason that they are drinking is not to be sociable or rebellious or different, it is that they aren't yet confident enough to resist the peer pressure. We can't blame them. All we can do is to try to help them.

But fashions do change. Not so long ago smoking was regarded as a sociable pastime. But did we think that a non-smoker at a party was being anti-social? I must admit that I used to feel somewhat uncomfortable in the presence of non-smokers, particularly at parties. But it wasn't that I felt there was some failing in them, more that they might find the smell on my breath or clothes offensive; or that they perceived me as being as stupid as I regarded myself. Of course, after I'd had a few drinks I couldn't have cared less how stupid they thought I was, or how I smelled for that matter. That was sociable of me, wasn't it? Nowadays smokers at parties are regarded as social pariahs. A smoky atmosphere is about as popular as a fart in a lift.

There is no doubt that the "Don't drink and drive!" campaigns have had an effect on our attitude to drinking. Most of us have now desisted from this ridiculous practice of trying to force one for the road down someone who can hardly stand up. The change has proved that it's not just these non-drinking weirdos that can enjoy parties without alcohol. Even drinkers can do it; if they have to.

You might accurately describe yourself as 'a social drinker', not because you drink just to be sociable, but because you believe you only drink on social occasions. If you are in the practice of visiting your club or local everyday just for a drink, you are no longer just a social drinker. Your only motive is to drink. Let us address the next illusion:

DRINKING MAKES ME HAPPY

21 *Drinking Makes Me Happy*

Although smoking kills more people, alcohol is the No.1 cause of unhappiness in our society. But you would be hard put to convince a 'normal drinker' that alcohol doesn't make them happy. But use your common sense. How can alcohol possibly make people happy? It is a depressant. Let's put it to the test. When some dubious-looking stranger accosts you in the street, what is your reaction? Probably fear. Has he escaped from some institution? The slurred speech indicates that he is only a drunk. My father taught me never to hit a woman, a blind man or a drunk. The first two seemed pretty obvious, but he never explained why you should never hit a drunk. I was only six at the time so I didn't give the matter much thought. It might have been self-preservation since he was often drunk himself. More probably it was because a drunk is less capable of defending himself than a blind man. They say that a drunk has the strength of ten men. The reality is that every single faculty of a drunk has been rendered a hundred times less efficient, if not removed altogether.

Have you experienced that situation in the park, where a huge dog rushes up to you and barks, fangs bared and evil intent in its eye? The owner laughs and tells you not to worry because he doesn't bite. You stand there frightened and embarrassed, thinking, "There's always a first time." It's exactly the same when you are accosted by a drunk. Drunks have a tendency to turn violent for no apparent reason. Perhaps he isn't going to attack you. Perhaps he just wants someone to talk to, or a few pence for a beer or a sandwich. In such circumstances we are naturally more concerned with our own fear and embarrassment. But on reflection, does the drunk strike you as being a particularly happy person? If you are in any doubt as to his state of mind, it is soon removed by the departing obscenities when you finally manage to extricate yourself. When you are literally legless, the room spinning as you repeatedly throw up, is that happiness? Is having no home, job, family or friends happiness?

"That's obvious, but surely drinking in moderation makes people happy?"

Does it? Let's examine that statement. Alcohol is a chemical. It tastes awful and doesn't quench our thirst, so we must be taking it for the effect it has on us. If that effect is to genuinely make us happy, it follows that the more we take the happier we should be. Now we know for a fact that a giggling group of drinkers can suddenly erupt into violence. We explain the incident by blaming it on some individual who is violent by nature. But what has really happened? Let us assume that the individual is indeed violent by nature. What purpose did the alcohol serve? By removing his inhibitions it gave him Dutch courage and was directly responsible for him releasing his pent-up violence. If you have ever attended a wedding or party which has been ruined in this way, you will know that the Hollywood image of everyone enjoying a good punch-up is a complete myth. Do you really believe that having a broken glass pushed into your face can make you or anyone else happy? Imagine being the person who was responsible for the affray. Once you recovered from your stupor, do you really believe it would make you happy to have to accept that it was you that transformed a wonderful occasion into a nightmare? If alcohol genuinely did make people happy, there would be no such thing as a violent or unhappy drinker.

Have you noticed how, when these incidents happen, the violence is often not just restricted to the two individuals involved, but every other 'happy' drinker can't wait to pile in? Sometimes even the women join in! It's not so long ago that football was our most popular spectator sport; not just entertaining but a genuinely happy, sociable day out for family and friends. Alcohol has turned it into a war.

So why do people laugh and look happy when they've had just a few drinks? It's nothing to do with the alcohol: we tend to drink on occasions that are happy anyway. Weddings and parties are happy occasions: that's why people laugh and enjoy themselves. It's not the drink that's making them giggle and horse around. If alcohol really did have that effect, people would never drink at funerals: after all the last thing you want to do at a funeral is to start giggling. Funerals tend to be solemn affairs, in England at least, and most of us wish our mood, or at least our outward demeanour, to reflect that solemnity. But we do drink at funerals. If people maintain that it is drink that makes them frivolous and giggly at weddings and parties, shouldn't they also claim that they drink at funerals because drink makes them solemn and serious?

The problem is that we never get the opportunity to compare the atmosphere at a party where there is no alcohol. If you arranged such a party for drinkers, it would be a miserable affair, not because alcohol makes people happy, but because people hooked on alcohol would be miserable without it.

I believe that the truth lies in the expression "drown our sorrows". Anyone who has fallen into the alcohol trap has done it. No one would dispute that the effect of drinking alcohol is to inebriate you. I'm not denying that this inebriation has the effect of temporarily blocking your mind to a problem. Some would claim that as an advantage. But, as we have already established, in reality it is about as advantageous as an ostrich sticking its head in the sand in the face of danger.

Does drowning your sorrows make you happy? If drinking a little alcohol has the effect of making you happy, drinking a lot of alcohol should make you very happy indeed. Have you ever tried drinking to excess to end the misery of a broken relationship, or any other problem for that matter? Did you find after a few drinks that you felt incredibly happy? Or did you just render yourself paralytic? And was the problem miraculously solved when you came out of the stupor? Were you happy then? Or did the hangover make everything appear twice as bad as it really was.

In any event, you don't need to take my word for it. Test it out for yourself. Separate the alcohol from the occasion so that the issue is not confused by extraneous matters. Pick a moment when you are neither particularly happy or morose. Arm yourself with sufficient quantities of your favourite tipple. As best you can, eliminate any factors that might distort the results of the experiment. Shut yourself alone in a room with no distractions such as TV, phone or radio, and sample drink after drink concentrating on the taste and the effect. The more you do this, the harder you will find it to concentrate. You might even find yourself giggling. If so, that is the exact moment to ask yourself: "Am I really happy in this situation? Do I want to spend the rest of my life in this frightening fog?" You'll find that with each drink you have you are less able to pin down the effect. That's because the chief effect of alcohol is to deaden you to everything you are going through, and indeed to impair your critical faculties. That is why alcohol seriously compromises your ability to enjoy genuine pleasures.

In fact you don't even need to carry out the experiment. If drink made you happy or solved any problems you wouldn't be reading this book. Never forget that alcohol itself never changes. It is a destructive poison, not just for you, but for any other person who has been unfortunate enough to fall into the trap! We all know that heavy drinkers are irritable people. Doesn't it follow that casual drinkers become slightly irritable?

But the main reason that we think alcohol makes people happy at parties is that so many of the "I enjoy a bottle of wine with a meal" brigade couldn't enjoy that meal or party without it. This is the enigma of all drug addiction: because we know that we could enjoy social occasions and cope with stress before we got hooked, we sense that alcohol does nothing for us. But because we also know that we cannot enjoy certain occasions without it, we tend to close our minds to the fact.

There are two other ways to test it out. One is just to look at the facts. How could a drug like DEVASTATION cause you anything but abject misery? The second is observation. Check out your friends and assess whether the truly happy ones are the drinkers or the non-drinkers. Attend a children's birthday party and see what a great time social events can be without any drugs whatsoever.

Try going to an AA disco, or another social event where non-drinkers are celebrating. There's just as much laughter, if not more. And there's never this spectre looming in the background: that someone's going to drink too much and ruin the occasion. My collaborator Crispin Hay tells me he was once at a restaurant on the occasion of an AA member celebrating *not* drinking for X number of years. The atmosphere was so high that the owners assumed it must be due to the amount of alcohol that had been consumed. They also assumed that a few extra bottles on the bill would go unnoticed. In fact, not a drop of alcohol had been consumed.

The next time you are at a restaurant where a group of people are obviously having a marvellous time, bear in mind that in all probability some in the group will be non-drinkers. Without examining what each person is drinking, try to distinguish the drinkers from the non-drinkers, purely on the basis of whether they appear to be happy or not. The results will amaze you. Check the atmosphere in the winning team's changing room after the match. Do the players have to drink the celebratory bottle of champagne to be happy? Of course not. They will be on a high the moment the final whistle blows. In fact they usually *don't* drink the champagne, more often they'll squirt it over each other. Does the atmosphere in the losers' dressing room change from gloom to happiness when they have a drink? Or does alcohol, the depressant, make them even more depressed?

Just as complete relaxation is having no aggravations, so complete happiness is having no worries or fears: feeling physically and mentally healthy and just great to be alive. The losers might take a drink to drown their sorrows, but in no way will it make them feel happy. A real sorrow won't be drowned by a little alcohol. To render your mind oblivious to a real tragedy, you'll have to drink enough alcohol to render yourself senseless. When the effect of the alcohol wears off, the tragedy will still be there and will seem even more tragic than it really is.

If you use alcohol to give you confidence or remove inhibitions at social occasions – or to block your mind from whatever aggravation, worry or fear is causing you to be unhappy, unrelaxed or distressed – then you have embarked on a very dangerous course. Perhaps you feel that your problem is not just that you have an inferiority complex, but that you are genuinely inferior. Anyone in possession of the incredible machine regarding himself as inferior, is like a billionaire regarding himself as a pauper. If you lack confidence there is a reason for it that can be addressed. Taking alcohol to try and deal with a problem ensures that you will never treat the true cause of your unhappiness.

If you have to drink alcohol in order to enjoy a social event, or need a bottle of wine in order to enjoy a meal at a restaurant, you are already hooked. I don't mean that you have reached the chronic stage where you have become completely dependent. But just because physically and financially you are able to cope with the bad effects, that doesn't mean that you aren't hooked. Nor does the fact that you are able to enjoy the occasional meal or social function without alcohol. The question you should be asking yourself is: "Why would you want to take a drug like DEVASTATION at any time?" If you feel the need to do so, no matter how logical your excuses might sound, you are in the unfortunate position of believing that your happiness is dependent on a poisonous chemical depressant. It is an illusion, but if you believe that you cannot enjoy a social occasion without alcohol, it might just as well be true: you will be unhappy without it.

THAT DOESN'T MEAN ALCOHOL MAKES YOU HAPPY

How can anyone who feels dependent on a killer poison be happy? But you don't really need me to prove these things. You already have all the proof you need that alcohol doesn't make you happy: why else would you be reading this book?

Perhaps you are still convinced that you could not enjoy life without it. If so, you'll soon be discovering just how wrong you are. You are about to make a very important decision. Are you going to:

QUIT FOREVER OR CUT DOWN?

22 Quit Forever Or Cut Down?

You have probably noticed that up to now I have not categorically stated that, having completed the book, you must never ever drink alcohol again. But we have now reached the stage when you must decide one way or the other. Before doing so you should be armed with the facts. Does the thought of never, ever being able to drink alcohol again make you feel apprehensive? Perhaps it still fills you with panic; as it once did me. The most frequent conversation I have with people who have a drink problem, and the most important, is the following:

Client: "Do you occasionally crave a drink?"

Me: "Never!"

Client: "Could you have an occasional drink and not get hooked again?"

Me: "I could, but since I've no desire to drink alcohol, what would be the point?"

Client: "Could you teach me to have an occasional drink and not get hooked again?"

Me: "Of course I could. I could even teach you to take the occasional dose of arsenic."

Client: "Why on earth would I want you to do that?"

Me: "Exactly!"

Usually the penny begins to drop. Once you can see alcohol not as the pleasure, crutch or friend that we've been brainwashed to see it as, but as it really is DEVASTATION, then the fear about never, ever being allowed to drink again ceases to exist. I can remember this fear about never being able to drink again turning into the joy of never *having* to drink again. It was similar to the sensation you get when the sun breaks out from behind a huge cloud, and the cold and dark are suddenly replaced by warmth and light. But because I'd been dominated by alcohol for so long and had forgotten that a brighter world even existed, the feeling was magnified many times.

Why would anyone want to drink a poisonous, highly addictive drug that tastes foul; a drug that will shorten your life, debilitate your immune system and impede your concentration; a drug that will destroy your nervous system, your confidence, your courage and your ability to relax? Why would you want to take a drug that will cost you about £100,000/$142,000 in your lifetime and do absolutely nothing for you whatsoever?

Have you seen Hitchcock's classic suspense film *Notorious*? The heroine is poorly and is being nursed back to health by her husband. She discovers that she is not really sick, but that he is trying to murder her slowly by poisoning her food with a drug. As the effect of each dose wears off she tries to muster enough strength to escape, but her legs are becoming weaker and weaker, and her brain becomes more and more muddled. Does it put you in mind of something? Master as he is, Hitchcock makes you feel that it is you who is undergoing the nightmare. It was a frightening experience and you can imagine how relieved she was after Cary Grant had rescued her and she was no longer forced to take the drug.

The drug used in the film wasn't alcohol. But alcohol would have been just as effective. Casual drinkers do not find their situation frightening. Neither did the heroine whilst she believed she was taking medicine. But the nightmare of the alcoholic is that he is administering the poison to himself and seems powerless to stop. You need to stop thinking "I can never ever have another drink", and start thinking how wonderful it will be when you can stop poisoning yourself.

In all probability you have already made one or more attempts either to cut down or to control your intake, and come to the conclusion that it just doesn't work. It will help you to understand exactly why it didn't work. But you first need to understand why we believe it is possible to control our intake. The main reason is that the vast majority of drinkers are in control. You only have to ask them and they'll tell you so. You have no need to doubt their word, because for most of your drinking life, you yourself were in control. Surely you were? Let's take a closer look.

We have already looked at the similarities, and the differences, between taking alcohol and eating. When do we decide to eat? When the brain says "I'm hungry." When does it do that? When our stomachs are empty. So even with something as natural as eating we are not in fact in control; but are being controlled by the natural instincts that Mother Nature gave us. In the case of food, a very pleasant business it is too.

You could argue that you made a rational decision to try your first few drinks. I won't argue with that. But supposing a confidence trickster had persuaded you to buy shares in a company that didn't exist. You made a decision to invest in the company, a decision that was rational given what you knew at the time. But in retrospect you would hardly describe yourself as being in control of the situation. Likewise when you sampled alcohol for the first time you believed there was some benefit to doing so. But the so-called benefits are in fact illusions, and always have been. So the reason that you began sampling alcohol, whether it be brainwashing, peer pressure or whatever, is completely irrelevant.

YOU WERE CONNED!

But those first few drinks created the 'little monster' inside your body; and from that point on you have been controlled by that monster. It is true that in the early days that little monster might have only triggered the thought "I want a drink" at social functions. But how quickly did you decide that you wouldn't attend social functions if they didn't serve alcohol, or if there wasn't a convenient pub nearby? And when did you decide that you would drink more and more at social functions? You never did, any more than the fly decided to slide down the pitcher plant.

Fortunately for most drinkers they only get into the 'habit' of relieving their withdrawal pangs at social functions. But if you get into the 'habit' of drinking to relieve stress, or are 'lucky' enough to have a bar at home, it's quite easy to slip into the 'habit' of having one drink to relax you after a stressful day, or of popping into the local. And it's amazing how that one drink becomes two and then three and then five, and in no time at all every day seems to be stressful. You are poisoning your body daily, you are genuinely ill and permanently distressed. And what is your only solution: more poison!

AA states:

'We in the Fellowship of AA believe there is no such thing as a cure for alcoholism. We can never return to normal drinking ...'

So let us glance back at those halcyon days of 'normal drinking'. Can you remember how those first drinks tasted and how hard you had to work to acquire a taste for the poison? Can you remember the times you got drunk and made a fool of yourself and threw up? Do you remember the room spinning round and the lovely hangovers? Can you remember those happy social occasions that suddenly erupted into violence and were ruined by drink, whether they were Christmas or New Year's Eve parties, weddings, discos or dances; or what started out as just a friendly drink down the pub? Do you realize how many marriages have been ruined, even before the wedding, because of this most ridiculous of all rituals: the stag night?

Now try to remember just one social function that was truly superb not because you were with friendly, interesting people, or because the weather, decor, music or entertainment was great, but purely because the alcohol was so fantastic.

Let me explain why cutting down can never be a permanent solution or even a stepping stone towards quitting completely. Because of the nature of drug addiction, if you try to cut down or control your intake, certain terrible things happen. The first is that if you have just one drink, the dehydrating effect of alcohol will keep the evil little monster inside your body alive. The little monster will ensure the survival of the Big Monster inside your brain, and you will continue to crave alcohol the rest of your life. As your body becomes immune to the poison, so the number of occasions that you'll want to drink will increase, as will the volume you'll want to drink on each occasion.

You have got used to having a drink whenever you fancy one. Let's refer to this as your 'usual' level. If you cut down you can no longer do that. This means that you'll spend much of your life wanting a drink but not being allowed to have one, and this will make you feel deprived and miserable. This will not only cause you additional stress, but you will be actually wishing your life away just waiting for your next fix. The schizophrenia doesn't end when you try to cut down. There will be times when the part of your brain that wants to drink feels deprived and miserable. It is at those very same times that the part that didn't want to drink has that holier-than-thou feeling of being in control. But what is the true position? Now our lives are completely dominated by thoughts of when we will allow ourselves to have our next drink; and how many drinks we will allow ourselves to have. Being dominated and being in control are exact opposites.

We only decide to cut down when we realize that our 'usual' level has become a problem. Prior to that, because we weren't aware that we had a problem, we hadn't given the subject of our drinking much thought. In fact, we had just taken it for granted. We hadn't really enjoyed those drinks. They were just part of our lifestyle. But now, during those times that we are wishing our lives away, we are fully aware that the reason for our misery is the fact that part of our brain wants a drink, but we won't allow ourselves to have one. We will now be giving the subject of our drinking a lot of serious and conscious thought, and that is when we realize just how important drinking is to us. You could argue that exactly the same situation applies to good health or three square meals a day. When we have them, we take them for granted. Only when we are deprived of them do we appreciate their true value. But, as we have already discussed in Chapter 17, eating good food is a genuine pleasure and essential to survival, whereas consuming a foul-tasting poison is the complete opposite! The point is that, although we were brainwashed to believe that drinking alcohol provided some kind of pleasure and/or crutch, it was never really important to us when we were allowed to do it; it is only the process of cutting down that ingrains into our minds this belief that life without alcohol cannot be enjoyed.

Drinkers make the mistake of believing that they just got into the 'habit' of drinking too much, and that provided they discipline themselves to cut down, they will soon get back into the habit of not drinking so much. Get it clearly into your mind: it is not habit but drug addiction. It will never become habit to drink less. The nature of any drug is to make you want to take more and more, ad infinitum. You don't need me to tell you this. It is a known fact. I'm just explaining why, in order to cut down, you'll have to discipline yourself for the rest of your life. Eventually your willpower runs out, and you are left completely gutted. Less able to control your intake, and drinking more than before you attempted to do so. You are now even more convinced that there is some basic flaw in your make-up, and that there is no escape from this permanent, living nightmare. Can you see the similarity with the fly in the pitcher plant? The more it struggles, the more entrapped it becomes.

But the worst aspect of cutting down is this. Just as dieting makes food more and more precious, so the longer you crave a drink the more deprived and miserable you will feel, and the greater the illusory pleasure when you finally allow yourself to feed that craving.

So what are the effects of cutting down? On one side of the tug-of-war the illusion of crutch or pleasure is increasing, which in turn increases your desire to drink. On the other side you are drinking less poison and wasting less money. So you no longer feel it to the same extent in your body or your pocket. In other words, you forget why you wanted to cut down in the first place. It's not surprising that the vast majority of attempts to cut down end up with the drinker drinking more in the long run.

Ironically, it is during our attempts to cut down that we feel in control, but doesn't the mere fact that we are attempting to cut down prove that we are not in control? If we were in control, why would we even need to discipline ourselves to cut down? Supposing you could discipline yourself to cut down for the rest of your life: is that what you really want? Before you commit yourself completely, let's take a closer look at:

THOSE LUCKY NORMAL DRINKERS

23 *Those Lucky Normal Drinkers*

It is those lucky normal drinkers that get us hooked in the first place, and convince us that we are missing out when we try to quit. But when you see them free of your rose-coloured spectacles, they can be the most powerful reminder of all of just how lucky you are to escape from the trap. Before we examine them more closely, let's keep certain facts clearly in mind. They are taking exactly the same drug as you are. The drug is called:

DEVASTATION

They won't see it that way. If they did they would no longer be taking it. Remember that no matter who is taking that drug, and no matter what stage the victim has currently reached in his slide down the pitcher plant,

THE DRUG NEVER CHANGES

Since 90 percent of the population has fallen into the trap, I cannot deny that drinking is normal, but no way is it lucky! If 90 percent of the population were sinking in quicksand, and you were one of them, would you envy the people who hadn't yet sunk as deep as you? Would you envy people who didn't yet realize they were sinking? Drinking alcohol might be normal but don't let that fool you into believing that there is something natural about it. Just think how powerful and far-reaching the brainwashing is: the whole of society has been conned into believing there is something natural about administering regular doses of poison to our bodies. You would regard someone who administered regular doses of strychnine to their own body as decidedly abnormal, a candidate for the funny farm.

"But surely that would kill you quickly?"

Not if you took it in small enough doses. But in any case what difference does it make how strong the poison is or how long it will take to kill you? The point is: why the hell would you want to do it in the first place? Let me remind you of the AA statement:

'The unhappiest person in the world is the chronic alcoholic who has an insistent yearning to enjoy life as he once knew it, but cannot picture life without alcohol.
'He has a heart-breaking obsession that by some miracle of control he will be able to do so.'

What it amounts to is that he is miserable whether he drinks or not. It's not much of a choice is it? But can you imagine him being unhappy because he can't take doses of arsenic? AA also say:

'We in the Fellowship of AA believe there is no such thing as a cure for alcoholism. We can never return to normal drinking ...'

This is the crux of the whole problem: seeing the regular consumption of the same powerful poison in two completely opposing lights. There is the alcoholic, to whom the drug is absolute ruination. Amazingly this is the same person who "cannot picture life without alcohol". Then there is the 'normal' drinker: a person who drinks in moderation, is in complete control, and for whom the same poison miraculously provides numerous benefits.

There are two possible explanations for this paradox. The first is that alcoholics truly have a different chemical make-up to normal drinkers. The other is that they are at an advanced stage of the same disease. Why do we find the second explanation so difficult to accept? After all, with heroin, cocaine and other addictions it is widely accepted that the victims become addicted because of the addictive nature of the drug and not because they have some inherent physical flaw in their make-up. We are aware that millions of smokers, including thousands of self-confessed alcoholics, want to quit because they know that smoking is ruining their health, but find it impossible to do so. The reason for failure is widely regarded as lack of willpower, but the same situation with alcohol is attributed to a flaw in physical make-up!

Just like all addictive drugs, with alcohol there seems to be a period of several years during which we are not sure whether we are 'normal users' in full control, taking the drug as and when we choose for the so-called 'benefits'; or whether we are taking it because we are addicts and believe that we cannot live without it. And again, just like other addictive drugs, even when it is blatantly obvious to our family and friends, apparently it is only us who can decide that we are indeed addicts. Bearing in mind that, according to one of the so-called experts, alcoholics go through a period of between 2 and 60 years as 'happy normal' drinkers. Isn't it more logical to deduce that 'happy normal' drinkers are in the early stages of the same disease? After all, isn't this the usual pattern with other diseases apart from addiction to drugs? To begin with the symptoms are so imperceptible that we don't realise we have a disease. But can you think of another disease that provides benefits for all victims in the early stages, benefits that suddenly turn into complete disasters for a minority of sufferers in its later stages, and without the victim knowing the exact point at which the change occurs?

So when all the evidence would indicate that the problem is not with the alcoholic but with alcohol, why do both 'normal drinkers' and alcoholics prefer to believe the opposite? Because that is a characteristic of all addictive drugs. We never blame the drug, because it seems too valuable. Drugs fool you into believing that you obtain some genuine pleasure and/or crutch and that life won't be quite so enjoyable without them. In the early stages of casual or 'normal' drinking, when the drug is causing you no obvious harm, you have no reason to quit, so why should you deny yourself the 'pleasure' of a glass of wine with your meal? But do you think you would enjoy the illusion if you believed that you were in the early stages of alcoholism? Far better to believe that alcoholism is something that happens to other people. And why shouldn't you? After all many experts, and even self-confessed alcoholics themselves, tell you it's down to a physical flaw; and both categories ought to know. The experts have looked into the theory and the alcoholics have done the practice. And we have been brainwashed to believe that if an alcoholic has just one drink, he has no choice but to continue drinking until he becomes paralytic. Casual or 'normal' drinkers aren't like that so obviously they can't be alcoholics. We conveniently overlook the fact that every chronic alcoholic started off as a 'normal drinker'.

It's easy to see why casual drinkers prefer to believe that alcoholism is a disease from which only a minority suffer rather than a progressive disease suffered by anyone who has been fooled into taking poison on a regular basis, no matter how 'casual' the stage they are at. But why would chronic alcoholics choose to believe that they were born with a physical flaw that can never be cured? You would think that they would prefer to believe the exact opposite. In fact, their beliefs are not a matter of choice but of seeming logic and brainwashing. And bear in mind that most alcoholics don't seek the help of institutions like AA until they are near rock-bottom, and have already suffered considerable trauma trying to solve the problem on their own. To do this they used willpower, and lots of it. It is a fact that the majority of alcoholics are strong-willed people in other aspects of their lives. Yet it would seem that 'normal drinkers' can control their intake and alcoholics can't. Therefore isn't it logical to believe that the reason is not due to lack of willpower, but to a physical and/or mental flaw in the make-up of an alcoholic; and wouldn't it follow that if this were true there is no cure?

The appeal of this theory lies in the fact that there's something in it for both categories: the 'normal' drinker gets to keep his favourite tipple, and the alcoholic gets to salvage a morsel of pride. "It's not my fault: I'm an alcoholic." All too often this turns into an excuse to hang on to the bottle as well: "I'm an alcoholic, so I'll drink."

These are the doctrines AA members are taught. And if you truly believe that there is no cure for alcoholism, it is logical, honest and certainly preferable to believe that your unfortunate condition is due to an accident of birth for which you cannot be blamed; rather than lack of willpower, responsibility or control on your behalf, for which anyone can blame you, the biggest accuser being you. In fact, if alcoholism was caused by an inherent physical defect, a recovering alcoholic, far from being to blame, would be entitled to sympathy. And an alcoholic in recovery is worthy of our admiration. In spite of being inflicted with this terrible disease, they have managed to resist this insatiable urge to poison themselves. This would explain why, in recent years, it is quite common for the hero of a book or film to be a recovering alcoholic.

I have defined 'the willpower method' as any method other than Easyway. I have done this purely to avoid confusion in the book. This does not mean that other methods necessarily *advocate* the use of willpower. Indeed, one of the cornerstones of AA philosophy is that willpower is useless against addiction and that a higher power is doing for the alcoholic what he cannot achieve with his own will. But there are times when a person will find it very hard to harness that power, whatever that power might be for them, and at such times a person will tend to resort to willpower. So I believe my definition of the willpower method is accurate. In theory, AA members are supposed to use a higher power against alcohol. In practice many of them haven't got a clue what that means, so they are thrown back onto their own willpower. An atheist in AA is pretty much forced into using a certain amount of his own willpower.

There is a disease called alcoholism but there is nothing intrinsically or physically wrong with the alcoholic. Alcoholism is an entirely mental disease. There is nothing complicated about it. Remove all the confusion and hype and it is simplicity itself. I've stated that it is a logical conclusion for chronic alcoholics to believe that they are intrinsically different from 'normal' drinkers. But that logic is based on an incomplete knowledge of the true nature of alcoholism. It was quite logical to believe that the sun moved round the earth until Galileo proved otherwise. It is indeed unfortunate that this lack of knowledge has led thousands of alcoholics to believe that there is no cure, let alone an easy, immediate and permanent one.

Alcoholism is the disease you suffer from when you have an unnatural desire to consume the foul-tasting, powerful poison called alcohol. Alcohol itself is no more evil than arsenic or any other poison. However, just like any other poison, if you consume alcohol you will receive undesirable physical effects in proportion to the volume consumed. The real evil is the general ignorance about alcohol and in particular the false belief that its consumption provides certain benefits.

It is important to distinguish between the disease we refer to as alcoholism, i.e. 'the 'unnatural desire to consume alcohol', and the other discomforts that ensue if you give in to that desire. In case you are not absolutely clear about the distinction, a simple analogy will help. A tile has been missing from your roof for some time, which has led to internal damage due to rain penetration. The disease called alcoholism is equivalent to the missing tile. The moment you replace the tile you have cured your rain penetration problem, immediately and permanently. You cure your alcohol problem the moment the desire to consume alcohol is removed permanently. The cure is instant and complete. But just as it will take some time for the interior of your house to recover from the damage caused by rain penetration, so it will take a certain amount of time for you to recover from the effects of consuming alcohol. Fortunately the human mind and body are incredibly strong, particularly when they are not being poisoned on a regular basis, and it is possible to actually enjoy this recovery process. You might find this difficult to believe, particularly if you have previously abstained for long periods using a variation of the willpower method. Let's use another analogy.

Imagine you had a small spot on your face. I say, "Try this ointment, it's really marvellous!" You do so, and the spot disappears like magic, but returns again a week later, slightly larger. You apply more ointment and "Hey Presto!" the spot disappears again; only to return again in five days time. The process continues, and each time the spot returns it is larger, itchier, and more painful. The periods during which the spot disappears get shorter and shorter. It soon becomes a rash covering your whole face. Imagine the terror of your situation. Unless you can find a cure, the rash is going to spread over your whole body; and eventually the interval between using the ointment and the rash returning will disappear completely. Imagine how dependent you would be on that ointment. I'm now charging you a hundred pounds a tube and you have no choice but to pay it. Just the thought of running low on the ointment creates panic. You won't leave the house without it.

You then read an article in a newspaper and discover that this problem isn't unique to you. Thousands of other people have been afflicted by the same rash! But scientists have discovered that the ointment does not cure the sore; in fact it is the ointment itself which is preventing its cure. Indeed it is only the ointment that has caused the original spot to progress into the killer rash. Had you not used the ointment, the original spot would have disappeared in due course. The effect of the ointment was to make the spot disappear beneath the skin. Far from being cured by the ointment, the spot actually fed on it, then returned to the surface of the skin for further sustenance.

The article contains even better news. All you need do to solve the problem is to stop using the ointment, and the rash will gradually disappear in its own good time! Would you use the ointment again? Would it take willpower not to use it? Would you be miserable? Of course not, provided you knew for certain that this would solve the problem, you would be over the moon. However, if you had doubts you might be tempted to use the ointment again, and you would have to use willpower to resist the temptation. In such circumstances you would expect to be miserable and frightened. But even in those circumstances, once you realized for the first time that the rash was indeed getting smaller and less painful, you would know then that you had the answer: and even if it took a year for the rash to disappear completely, you would be happy from the start.

The same is true of any problem no matter how serious and varied the effects: the fear and misery are removed the moment you know that you have the remedy. You don't even have to wait to apply the remedy provided you know you have it.

Perhaps you feel that the analogy of the ointment and the rash is somewhat removed from your drinking problem. Is it? The rash is equivalent to the destructive effect that consuming alcohol has on your life. The ointment is alcohol itself.

Once you discovered that the ointment was the cause of the rash rather than the cure, you would be delighted that you had discovered both the cause and the cure, and you would never be tempted to use that ointment again.

There is no mystery or confusion here.

Before you even opened this book, you were fully aware that your problem was that you weren't in control of the volume of alcohol that you consumed. And you didn't need me to tell you that alcohol was the cause of that problem. So, like the ointment, you knew that alcohol was the cause of your problem. The only mystery is why you are still tempted to take it.

Perhaps you still suspect that the only conceivable explanation is that you do indeed have some innate physical or mental flaw which 'normal' drinkers don't have. It is essential that you realize that your failure to solve the problem isn't due to your physical make-up. It is due to your mental perception. But it is just as essential to realize that it is not an innate mental flaw like an addictive personality, and that with an open mind the flaw can be remedied. If you believe that there is no cure for a problem, then for you there is no cure. That is why it is essential to explode this red herring of an innate physical and/or mental flaw.

Let's assume for a moment that you do have some innate physical and/or mental flaw. Did you even notice it before you started to drink alcohol? Were you unable to enjoy life or handle stress before you got into the 'habit' of drinking alcohol? Before you drank alcohol, did you have any need or desire to drink alcohol? Did you find that you couldn't enjoy children's parties without alcohol, before you'd even touched the stuff? Doesn't it strike you as rather a coincidence that this 'inherent flaw' only made itself known after you began to consume alcohol, and that people who quit with Easyway find that it disappears just as magically when they stop consuming it?

Clear the confusion and it is so obvious! Alcohol is a foul-tasting, poisonous drug. That is a fact, whether you happen to be an alcoholic or just one of those 'lucky normal' drinkers. The only reason that anyone consumes that poison is that we have all been brainwashed from birth to see a drug called DEVASTATION as a friendly pleasure and a crutch.

Why is it that the majority of drinkers can control their intake? They are not in control! They've been brainwashed in exactly the same way as the rest of us. They also believe that DEVASTATION is a pleasure and a prop. It's just that they haven't yet reached the stage where the truth is blatantly obvious. But why is it that drinkers who *have* reached that stage don't see the situation like the ointment and the rash, and just quit? After all, we know that alcohol is the cause of our misery, and therefore we shouldn't drink it. But we don't drink for the reasons we shouldn't! We drink for the reasons that we do. And if you are convinced that you won't be able to enjoy social occasions or cope with stress without alcohol, then you won't be able to.

The solution then is to remove all of the brainwashing and return to the blissful state we enjoyed before we fell into the trap. Perhaps you believe it is not possible to go back to that state. After all, how can you eliminate knowledge once you have acquired it? That's just the point, as far as alcohol is concerned, we didn't acquire any knowledge, only fallacy and confusion. It is a fact that we could enjoy life and cope with stress before we fell into the trap. If we can be conned into believing that drinking a foul-tasting poison is some sort of pleasure and/or crutch, it shouldn't be too difficult to see the true situation. And it isn't. In fact it is very easy and enjoyable, provided you open your mind and follow all the instructions.

It is no good just reading the description of DEVASTATION at the beginning of Chapter 7 and telling yourself that everything is true. Would you have a desire to take strychnine? Of course you wouldn't! You wouldn't even be tempted to. And if there is no temptation, you don't have to feel deprived or use willpower to resist it. You need to see alcohol as it really is, stripped of all the hype. That way you will permanently remove any temptation to drink it. Do not make the common mistake of clinging on to some of the brainwashed image. Allow me to refer back to the frequent question:

"Could you have an occasional drink and not get hooked again?"

What the questioner is actually saying is:

"I can't face the thought of never having another drink."

Why not? Doesn't this mean that they have retained some of the brainwashing? Why is the thought so daunting? Only because we believe that we are giving up some genuine pleasure or crutch. Thinking about an occasional drink is trying to get the best of both worlds. But isn't that what we've been doing ever since we fell into the trap? Trying to get the so-called pleasure or crutch, while not doing too much damage to our ourselves in the meantime. The trouble is that the nature of any drug is to make you want to consume more and more, so there will always be more damage.

If you see one drink as a pleasure or crutch, you'll see a million drinks in the same light. It would be like walking a tight-rope across Niagara Falls: your whole life would consist of trying to avoid falling into the abyss. Sooner or later you would be bound to fall. Even if you succeeded, you'd be miserable: if you retain the desire to have an occasional drink, you'll spend the rest of your life trying to resist the temptation. And you won't be seeing alcohol like strychnine!

Perhaps you still find the thought of quitting forever a daunting prospect. I can understand that. It was to me. I won't deny that it can take courage to face up to that prospect. But I guarantee that if you can summon up that courage, you too will escape from a nightmare world of fear and depression and wonder why you spent so long in it. With alcohol, there aren't two worlds to get the best of. There is only one world: a world of misery. Get it absolutely clear in your mind once and for all: no one who feels compelled to drink one drop of DEVASTATION could describe themselves as being in control. The fact that drinkers are ignorant of the true facts about alcohol proves that they are not in control. The platitude I most abhor, usually used by people who should know better is "It's all right in moderation."

Imagine if the pilot of your plane said: "We are about to fly into fog. I'm sure nobody will object if I alter the calibration of my instruments ever so slightly." Would you regard such a man as being in control? Your 'lucky normal' drinker is in exactly the same position.

Where drugs are concerned "It's all right in moderation" is like saying "It's all right to get a tiny bit pregnant" or "By all means go over Niagara Falls, but don't go down more than 3 feet." The nature of all drug addiction is to fool you into believing that you are in control, to block your mind from the evil effects, and to drag you further and further down. The only difference between Niagara and alcohol is that with Niagara it takes just a few seconds for all victims to reach rock-bottom and disaster. The dangers are therefore very obvious and so very few people become victims. With alcohol we are actually persuaded that it is a good thing to be a victim.

Because 80 percent never reach rock-bottom and remain 'happy normal drinkers' throughout their lives, and because the degeneration of the 20 percent who do reach rock-bottom can be so gradual, the trap is not an obvious one. But remember that nobody ever chooses to become a drug addict; and every addict started with just one dose.

Observe other drinkers: start to see them as they really are. They are not enjoying a sociable drink: they have been conned into taking DEVASTATION. And be aware that just as you were never genuinely in control, neither are they. Remember 'The Critical Point' that we discussed in Chapter 10? Alcoholics believe that 'normal' drinkers are different to them because they can control their intake. The real difference is that the 'normal' drinkers are at the stage of the disease where they can cope with their intake. They believe that they enjoy a drink, it is no particular problem to them, so they have no need to exercise control. All alcoholics were once at that stage. You need to see them as they really are: just flies in the pitcher plant, slowly sliding down, oblivious of their fate. Rejoice that you are free of that trap forever.

"But since they are oblivious, isn't ignorance bliss? If they believe they are getting a genuine pleasure by drinking, surely they are?"

In fact they are not, but it is not always easy to see it that way. Let me use an example. A close friend and I regularly rent a holiday villa together in Spain. The high point of the holiday has always been the moment we arrive. For many years we have observed the following ritual, before we have even unpacked: we sit on the balcony which overlooks a picturesque beach, and down a bottle of champagne. When I told him that I'd quit drinking permanently, the first thing he said was: "We'll never be able to enjoy that ritual again." The remark surprised me because the conversation took place in mid-December when we were both embroiled in the preparations for Christmas, and neither of us had mentioned sunny Spain.

The ritual wasn't ruined when the next holiday duly arrived, but the pleasure was somewhat tainted. It wasn't because I didn't drink champagne, but because I insisted that my friend did. He was clearly uncomfortable about the situation, and every time I topped up his glass he would say: "Are you sure you don't mind me drinking champagne?"

If I had quit drinking by using the willpower method, I would have envied him.

But holidays are marvellous. And that moment was very special: we had arrived safely, put the worries of the world behind us, were relaxing with a refreshing drink, looking out over a beautiful scene and ruminating on the prospect of a pleasant week ahead. Was it less special for me because my drink didn't contain poison? Was the moment more special for my friend because his did? No. With or without the poison, what we had always enjoyed, and I hope will continue to enjoy for many years, was the rest of the scenario.

The point that I am making is that just because alcohol *seems* to give pleasure, that doesn't mean that alcohol makes an already pleasant occasion even better. Allow me to elaborate. Have a guess at how a non-drinker would feel in such a situation: relaxing at the beginning of a holiday, looking out over charming scenery on a beautiful summer's evening, the only responsibility for the next week being to have a good time. You got it in one: the non-drinker is feeling fantastic! I was over the moon! Now imagine how my friend, a drinker, would have felt if for some reason he couldn't drink alcohol. That's right: deprived. Now imagine how he would have felt if that reason was removed and he had a drink. That's right: fantastic! Over the moon! He'd be feeling exactly the same as me. Doesn't that indicate that alcohol can only make you miserable? It also illustrates how 'normal' drinkers are fooled into believing that it gives them genuine pleasure. These people drink alcohol not because it is pleasurable, but because in certain situations they feel miserable without it. In other words: they are already hooked!

Not only is the ignorance not bliss, it is not complete ignorance either. 'Normal' drinkers might not be fully aware of their situation, but there is no doubt that they suspect they have fallen into a trap. Their attitude tends to be: "It's not doing me any harm, and if ever I need to quit, I will." This is another subtle aspect of the trap that makes us put off the evil day. The friend I referred to was one of several acquaintances who had been dropping subtle hints about how much I had been drinking. Yet his first thought when I told him I had quit was not "Great News!" but "We'll never be able to enjoy that ritual again." And why was he so uncomfortable that he was drinking alcohol and I wasn't? Was it because he thought I might feel I was missing out and might be tempted? If so he must have felt somewhat guilty. Or was it that he didn't like to drink alone? He wasn't: I had a refreshing fruit juice. Perhaps he felt silly being the only one drinking poison.

You might feel put down if you offer someone a drink and they look at their watch and say something like, "I don't normally drink before 7pm!". You sense they are implying that you have a serious drink problem because you are in the habit of drinking before 7pm. The inclusion of the word 'normally' tells you that they are about to break their golden rule. They'll need a bit more persuasion, because they need to blame you. They might even go so far as to jokingly accuse you of getting them into bad habits. In truth, they are delighted that you have allowed them to break a rule without losing face. I used to envy people like that when I had a drink problem. I'd think, "Aren't you lucky to be able to discipline yourself like that?" I was so wrapped up in my own troubles that I never noticed that they broke the rule more times than they kept it. Neither did I realize that what they were actually telling me was that they also had a drink problem. What other reason could they have for such a rule? Another classic giveaway is:

"No thanks, I'm driving tonight."

Have you noticed that they can never say it without it sounding like they really mean "Aren't I a goody-goody?" Again you envy them and ask them if it bothers them not drinking.

"No problem, I can take it or leave it."

It's said in the same goody-goody tone. But if they could genuinely take it or leave it, why do they go to the trouble and expense of taking a taxi next time? All they are doing is trying to prove to themselves and to the rest of the world that they are not hooked. All they are actually proving is that they are. When they do take a taxi, they won't leave until 2am and can hardly walk to the vehicle. Note also that when they don't drink, they aren't actually enjoying themselves, and leave the party at 10 o'clock.

"Doesn't this prove that alcohol provides genuine pleasure?"

No! All it proves is that they are already hooked, that they cannot enjoy life without it. However, this raises a very relevant point which we need to address. Before I quit, a very good friend would occasionally go on the wagon. This man was one of the most interesting people that it has been my privilege to meet. But when he was on the wagon he was a miserable bore. I actually delayed quitting completely, for fear that it would have the same effect on me. I'm pleased to confirm that it didn't happen to me, or so my friends assure me, and it doesn't happen to other drinkers who quit by using Easyway.

The impression given is that it was the drink that helped him to get over his inhibitions and turned a miserable bore into a fascinating person. But if alcohol had the effect of turning bores into interesting people, all drinkers would be fascinating, and the more they drank the more enthralling they would be. Do you need me to tell you that there is nothing more boring than a drunk slurring his gibberish an inch from your nose? The truth is that in the case of my friend all the alcohol did was turn an otherwise interesting and happy man into a miserable bore when he was on the wagon, because he was just like many recovering alcoholics. He believed that he couldn't enjoy life without alcohol. And if you believe that, then you won't be able to. The fact that certain people can't enjoy certain situations without alcohol doesn't mean that alcohol provides genuine pleasure. They were perfectly capable of enjoying those situations before they fell into the trap.

I find that since I quit drinking, like the "No thanks, I'm driving tonight!" man, I tend to leave certain social functions earlier and not attend others at all. Initially this worried me. It seemed to indicate that I wasn't enjoying myself so much without drinking. I realized it was the exact opposite. The true reason was that they were boring functions. The only way I could suffer them previously was to inebriate myself. It just goes to emphasize the fact that alcohol does not make people happy but merely renders them temporarily oblivious to their sorrows. It doesn't cure those sorrows: it greatly magnifies them out of all proportion. Nowadays I just don't attend those boring functions. If I cannot avoid them,

I leave as soon as politeness allows, so I can spend more time doing things that make me genuinely happy; instead of watching other people enter oblivion.

Alcohol doesn't make boring people interesting, on the contrary, all it does is turn bores and interesting people into boors. Nor does drinking relieve boredom. Boredom is having nothing interesting to occupy your mind. Drinking is not a particularly mind-absorbing exercise, and therefore by definition it cannot relieve boredom. The fact that some people try to solve their boredom by rendering themselves oblivious is a sad fact, and even more so when they have to resort to it every day. What could be more boring than to have to drink all day, every day?

The clue that the majority of these 'lucky normal' drinkers already suspect that they are hooked lies in analysing not so much what they say, but why they even bother to say it. They always seem to be on the defensive, even when they are not under attack.

"Frankly, I can take it or leave it. Sometimes I go a month without a drink."

The statement is made in the usual goody-goody tone. You think, "You lucky so and so! If only I could control it like you." In fact regularly going on the wagon is a sure indication of a serious drink problem. If they genuinely enjoy a drink, why would they even want to go a month without one? Obviously because their drinking was causing them a problem. And if they can genuinely take it or leave it, why do they start drinking again and return to the problem? Equally obvious: they cannot enjoy life without alcohol. We think such drinkers have the best of both worlds. In fact they have the worst of all worlds. When they are drinking, they wish they didn't have to: that is why they go on the wagon. When they are on the wagon, they are miserable not drinking: that is why they start again. But isn't this the case the whole of our drinking lives? When we are allowed to drink, we either take it for granted, or wish we didn't; it is only when we won't allow ourselves to drink that it appears to be such a pleasant pastime.

Drinkers who go on the wagon are entitled to boast about it, because they have had to employ considerable willpower to survive a period without alcohol. The vast majority of attempts to go on the wagon are in fact attempts to quit completely. After all, if you've reached the stage where your drinking is causing you problems, what is the point of going through the considerable willpower needed to deprive yourself just for a month; only to go straight back into the pit? Why aren't we honest enough to admit it? For the same reason that all drug addicts have to lie to themselves and to other people. If we say "I'm going to quit permanently" and then fail, we've burnt our boats. Our friends know that we are drinking not because we choose to but because we are hooked. Far better to keep our options open. That way we can actually turn our failure into success. Hence the smug:

"Frankly, I can take it or leave it. Sometimes I go a month without a drink."

Ironically, such statements are intended to prove that the person is in control; in reality they prove the opposite. Why would anyone need to make such a statement in the first place? Imagine I said to you:

"Frankly, I can take them or leave them. Sometimes I go a month without carrots."

Would you think: "Lucky chap! If only I could do that?" Or would you think: "What a weird thing to say, Allen obviously has a bit of a hang-up about carrots"?

And have you noticed how, when we are learning to drink as youngsters and it tastes foul, we brag about the great volume we can consume; but once we have 'acquired' the taste and suspect we are hooked, we boast about how little we drink and the fact that we can take it or leave it? We don't do this about things that we genuinely enjoy. I wouldn't dream of saying "I enjoy playing a hole of golf", rather than "a round of golf". But people who regularly drink a whole bottle of wine with a meal invariably say, "I enjoy a glass of wine with my meal."

I'd like a pound for every time I've heard someone say, "Doctors say a glass of red wine is good for the heart." The statement is usually made by some grossly overweight chain-smoker who has already drunk a whole bottle; as if they are drinking not because they are hooked or even because they claim to enjoy it, but for purely medical reasons.

I recently had a conversation with a man whose father died from chronic alcoholism. His elder brother was a chronic alcoholic. He described the misery that the family had been through. I was amazed to learn that he himself was an "I enjoy a glass of wine with a meal" drinker. He insisted that he was in control and could take it or leave it. I said: "After the misery you experienced, and in view of the fact that two out of the three of your closest blood relatives are alcoholics, I find it difficult to believe that you even risk becoming one yourself, if you truly can take it or leave it." He and his mother had both quit completely for several months after his father's death. But even the fact that they had both started drinking again (which would indicate that they were both drinking not because they chose to but because they had failed to quit permanently) didn't shake his belief that he was in control.

We went through the process of exploding the myths about taste, quenching the thirst, and so on. He was finally reduced to "A glass of wine complements the meal." This is another classic that you have probably heard many times before. But just think about it: what does it actually mean? I like a sauce on meat because I find meat too dry and the taste somewhat bland. So provided I like its taste, the sauce does improve upon, or complement, the taste of the meat. It is true that some dishes are cooked in wine; but we don't pour the glass of wine over our food, so how can it complement the meal? It is just another excuse.

Statements like "Alcohol is OK in moderation" are no reason for consuming it! In fact, that particular statement is a frank admission that it is harmful. Why on earth would you need to moderate if it weren't harmful? "It isn't doing me any harm" is another classic excuse commonly given as a reason to justify drinking. We don't do things just because they don't do us any harm. I don't suppose it would do me much harm if I spent the remainder of my life blowing bubbles, but if I offered that as a reason for doing it you would regard me as a candidate for the funny farm. How much more ridiculous is it to claim that our reason for doing something is that it isn't doing us any harm, when it is blatantly obvious to ourselves and to the rest of the world that it is in fact doing us considerable harm?

I call such statements 'the Joey isn't in the cupboard' syndrome. When I was ten I was playing with my best friend Joey and his five-year-old brother Ronny. We spotted his other brother approaching the front door. Joey hid in a cupboard with me and told Ronny not to tell Tommy where we were. The moment Tommy entered, Ronny said "Joey isn't in the cupboard, Tommy." It was an example of saying something designed to deceive the listener, which actually conveys the exact opposite message. I have given several classic examples common to drinking, some almost as obvious. I could quote dozens of them. Start spotting them for yourself. Other drinkers, including these 'lucky' casual drinkers, can be the most powerful force of all to make you happy not to be one. In fact, if only all drinkers would open their minds and be honest, the whole miserable pastime would soon be history.

Another classic example is the subject of vintage wines. I find it just as fascinating as:

THE KING WHO WAS IN THE ALTOGETHER

24 *The King Who Was In The Altogether*

For those who are not familiar with the story, a rather devious tailor displayed a suit of clothes to the king and his courtiers. To a personage of refinement, taste and intelligence, the suit was quite obviously the finest ever made. But to a moron, the suit was completely invisible. I used to think Hans Christian Andersen was attempting to stretch our imaginations too far by expecting us to believe that the king could actually be fooled into parading stark naked. I offer my humble apologies to Hans. I realize now that his fantasy must have been based on fact: the liquor and wine trade.

Keep in mind that whether I'm mentioning beer, wine or spirits, in each case what I am actually talking about in the paragraphs that follow is a foul-tasting, highly addictive, poisonous drug, which is produced from decaying vegetable matter and provides no advantages whatsoever. Yet there are people who will pay hundreds of pounds for a bottle of wine! At least I hear stories of such people. I've never actually met one. Do you believe that the taste of any bottle of wine is worth hundreds of pounds? If you do you are either a fool, or in the wine business and making your living from fools!

I have seen people go through much pomp and ceremony when paying £25/$35 for a bottle of wine. Ironically, they were always people who were either scraping the barrel or had so much money that they didn't know what to do with it. I also admit that at times I have joined in the ritual. Not wishing to be impolite, I have congratulated them on the quality of their selection, while thinking to myself: "I can get better than this for a fiver in my local supermarket."

I used to be impressed with the whole ritual of 'enjoying' a bottle of wine with a meal: the elaborate discussion with the wine waiter, in order to select exactly the right wine for the meal. The fact that each person present has different tastes and is eating a different type of food makes it impossible anyway, but we all have to go through with the farce. Then there's the checking of the label and the sampling. Some 'experts' will sniff both the cork and the wine and swirl the wine around the glass before taking a swig. After a suitable pause they will nod approval. Is there a single recorded event in history when the wine was refused because it didn't swirl satisfactorily?

When I selected a wine I wasn't so much searching for one that actually tasted good, as trying to find one that was not too sweet or too 'dry', so that I could drink it without too much hassle. I found that a good result was usually more through luck than judgment, and that unless I stuck to the same wine, I seldom chanced on one that I liked. The whole ritual is a complete farce anyway, because after one or two glasses, the inebriating effect renders you oblivious to the taste!

In the RAF a corporal was in the habit of entering the billet at 5am shouting: "Shake a leg! Shake your Brasso!" I later discovered that if you didn't shake your metal polish regularly, the alcohol would drift to the top of the tin, and it was regarded as a delicacy by some connoisseurs. It's hard to relate such types, or the meths-drinking tramp, to the pomp and ceremony that I've described above, but it does explain why wine-tasting experts spit the foul stuff out. Nowadays when I watch people going through the wine selection ritual, I find it difficult to keep the smile off my face. I wonder what they would think of me if I went through the same performance to drink a bottle of fruit juice?

We are persuaded that wines improve with maturity. What a clever marketing ploy! If dealers over-buy, they don't have to dump it in a half-price sale at the end of the year; they let it collect dust and charge more. There are many vested interests that have tried to persuade me that wine improves with age, and I believed them. The ritual that caused me to question the claim is the hype about Beaujolais Nouveau. Apparently it's absolutely essential to drink it within 24 hours of being bottled, even if it means chartering a special plane; otherwise you might just as well pour it down the drain! Tell me a product improves with age and I might be stupid enough to believe you. But if you tell me the same product deteriorates with age, it is you that is being stupid. You insult my intelligence!

In truth I have nothing but admiration for professional wine connoisseurs. If you think about it, all you need to know about a drink is whether it tastes good. Since it's an acquired taste anyway and each individual has his own tastes, the expert can't even tell you whether you will enjoy it. Just think of the imagination and nerve it must take to build a whole profession on descriptions like precocious, audacious, unassuming, ambitious, robust and amusing. They are actually describing a bottle of addictive, dehydrating poison. The only amusing thing about it is that we actually fall for this codswallop.

At a clinic I offered a lady some refreshment. She said, "I would like a cup of tea; with no milk, sugar, or tea." It took a moment for the penny to drop, then I pointed out that it would just be a cup of hot water. She said: "That's right, I don't want to include the harmful ingredients, but I still like to think I'm enjoying a nice cup of tea." It struck me as being somewhat bizarre, but was it any more stupid than working hard to acquire a taste for a foul flavour like bitter just to get the alcoholic effect, then deciding we don't want that effect after all? So the manufacturers spend a fortune on research, perfecting a drink that has no alcohol but retains the foul taste. Just how gullible can we get? One brewer used the slogan "You won't like it!" as the basis of its advertising campaign. I bet the tough guys really went for that one. And have you heard about the latest gimmick? Organic lager. That's a really healthy way to take poison.

Do you have problems persuading your weight-conscious wife or girlfriend to try a little cream on her strawberries? Do you think you could persuade her to drink a small glass of cream? It's easy! You can make her drink several glasses and pay ten times as much as the cream would normally cost. Just buy her a bottle of one of these popular liqueurs that contain cream. If you enjoy the sweet taste of a wine or liqueur, what you are enjoying is the sugar additive, not the alcohol. The wine trade is a bit subtler than the beer trade: the opposite to sweet is bitter, but the opposite to a sweet wine is a dry wine. How can any wine be dry? I have heard wines described as cheeky, approachable, flippant and even mysterious! The only mystery is why we are stupid enough to fall for the hype.

On presentation nights at my golf club, the drinks would arrive quicker than I could down them. Occasionally I would knock back what I believed to be the dregs of a gin and tonic but which actually turned out to be neat gin. The effect is about as pleasant as sniffing ammonia. How often do you see whisky drinkers obliterate the taste with a mixer yet complain that the bar didn't stock their favourite brand of whisky? When blindfolded these so-called experts have difficulty in distinguishing between the taste of whisky and cold tea!

You will sense that you are getting near to the end of the book. I've spoken much about the confidence trick and explained why drinking alcohol does nothing for you whatsoever. I've explained why all the benefits that society has brainwashed us to believe alcohol provides are really just illusions. I've also explained how in each case it does the exact reverse. Perhaps you feel that what I haven't done is to explain:

HOW TO MAKE IT EASY TO QUIT

25 *How To Make It Easy To Quit*

You might find it hard to believe that any alcoholic can find it ridiculously easy to quit, particularly if you have been through the miseries of attempting to quit with the willpower method. If you are at rock-bottom, and have lost home, family, car and job, I cannot promise to replace those immediately. What I can promise is that I can help you to rid yourself immediately of the evil that has led you to rock-bottom. When I escaped from the evils of drug addiction, I expected the major benefits to be in physical health and wealth, and I wasn't disappointed in either respect. But there were several unexpected benefits which proved to be even greater than these.

One was the return of my self-respect. Another was my freedom: not to have my life dominated by something I despised. What sort of hobby is it, that when you are allowed to do it you feel ashamed and miserable, and when you are not doing it you feel deprived and miserable? To spend half your life waiting for 7pm and when it arrives: sentencing yourself to oblivion. Above self-respect and freedom I would rate regaining my courage and confidence, and feeling like the strong, healthy human being Mother Nature intended me to be. Finally it was great to feel like a mature adult yet at the same time like a young boy again. When you feel mentally and physically low, molehills became mountains. When you feel strong and in true control of all your faculties, mountains become the molehills they really are. But the greatest gain by far was the combined result: HAPPINESS! That's the only drug it's worth getting hooked on!

Why should it be difficult to quit? After all, no one forces us to drink. If we decide that we never want to be the slaves of alcohol again, why should there be any difficulty? What about the terrible withdrawal pains? Some people are under the illusion that delirium tremens – the shakes and seeing pink elephants – is caused by withdrawal from alcohol. In fact, it is caused by drinking alcohol. Non-drinkers don't suffer from delirium tremens! The actual physical withdrawal is so imperceptible that the vast majority of drinkers don't even realize they are addicted. The only pain that drinkers suffer when they try to quit is what AA so aptly describes as:

An overwhelming craving for the very thing that can only worsen the effects of physical suffering, irrational behaviour and increasing isolation.'

That's the only thing that makes it difficult to quit: the feeling of misery and deprivation caused by craving something that we won't allow ourselves to have, and it only becomes overwhelming if you have been conned by the illusion, or if you believe that because of some flaw in your physical make-up, you have no choice but to perpetually crave something that will destroy you.

It was the myth about the terrible physical withdrawal pains that helped me realize that Easyway would be equally effective for curing addiction to alcohol and other drugs. I was conducting a quit-smoking session. Midway through the session one of the group declared that he was a recovering alcoholic and heroin addict, and had been addicted to various other substances. He hadn't touched alcohol for several years and had managed to break free from the other addictions using his own willpower. His declaration prompted similar confessions from various other members of the group. Two others had managed to kick heroin under their own steam. This came as a revelation to me.

Society had led me to believe that heroin was by far the most difficult addiction to kick, mainly due to the terrible physical withdrawal symptoms. I expressed surprise that they had managed to kick heroin without assistance but hadn't been able to quit smoking. I asked them to describe the terrible physical symptoms caused by withdrawal from heroin. I emphasize that this was a group of highly intelligent people, who up to that point had experienced no difficulty in expressing their views in a clear and precise manner. But when attempting to describe those terrible symptoms, each one of them was reduced to waffle. I was hearing exactly the same feeble excuses I had heard thousands of times from smokers:

"It was terrible; I couldn't sleep at night or concentrate."

Me: "That's not physical and anyway, what's so terrible about not being able to sleep at night or concentrate? Everybody goes through periods like that."

"I kept breaking out in cold sweats."

Me: "I grant you sweating is physical, but there's no pain. Athletes sweat every time they perform. It's a perfectly natural function that's intended to cool your body."

Whether it was withdrawal from heroin, nicotine or alcohol, by far the most common statement was "It was like having flu." I could write a whole book on this aspect alone. It has been shown that imprisoned heroin addicts – who have no prospect of obtaining heroin whilst in prison – only suffer withdrawal pangs when they are released and return to their old haunts. The environment triggers associations of taking heroin, which in turn triggers the so-called physical withdrawal.

I've also heard it said that attempting to quit 'cold turkey' could actually kill a heroin addict. A certain doctor, widely considered to be the leading expert on nicotine addiction in the UK, has actually stated on national television that some heavy smokers, if they attempt to quit, may have to use nicotine substitutes for the rest of their lives. He fails to explain how thousands of smokers have stopped overnight without suffering any withdrawal symptoms whatsoever, physical or mental. I'm talking about the people who have quit with the help of Easyway, including myself and countless other chain-smokers.

I have no doubt that if you search hard enough, you will find what appears to be proof that chronic alcoholics suffer severe physical withdrawal symptoms. I am absolutely certain that addicts suffer no physical withdrawal pain whatsoever when they abstain, and that in fact the whole subject is a red herring. Let's assume for a moment that you did suffer something similar to flu. Practically all of us suffer from a bout of flu at some point in our lives. OK, perhaps we did feel like dying for a few days. But is that really such a tragedy? It's not pleasant, but most of us can handle it and take it on the chin. The physical pain we go through by remaining an alcoholic is a thousand times greater than a bout of flu. Imagine saying to someone who had admitted they were a drug addict: "You can have flu for seven days after which you will be completely free of your addiction." There's not a self-confessed drug addict on the planet who wouldn't jump at that opportunity.

So why do we believe that we suffer terrible physical pains when we try to quit? Partly because we've been brainwashed to believe it. Partly because we tend to blame anything that goes wrong in our lives on the fact that we have quit, even when it is pure coincidence. But mainly because the *mental* torture is so severe when using one of the variations of 'the willpower method'. But how can mental torture cause physical pain? In the short-term it doesn't. But let us not underplay the misery of mental torture. I used to get in a panic and suffer the shakes at just the thought of running out of cigarettes. And to take another example, if a tiger was chasing me, I might not be suffering actual physical pain before he caught me, but my mental terror would cause me to experience some pretty powerful physical symptoms.

Make no mistake, being unable to scratch an itch can drive you to distraction. Craving a drink hour after hour, day after day, when the only person who is preventing you from ending that misery is you, will also drive you to distraction. No one would question the fact that severe and prolonged mental stress causes the victim to become run down and more vulnerable to physical diseases. What further evidence do you need than shell-shock?

I would bang my head against the wall and scream at my wife and children, so that one of them would eventually say: "I can't bear to see you suffering like this. If life is so miserable without it, I'd rather you gave up trying to give up!" What a face-saver. I wasn't giving in. I was only starting again to make my family happy. I would even accuse them of being the only reason that I was still an addict. How many times have you heard smokers who have failed to quit say "I was so irritable. I felt I was being unfair to my family, friends or colleagues. So I started again."?

Addicts will often adopt such tactics, including feigning physical pain. Was I aware at the time that there was no physical pain, that I was merely trying to hoodwink myself and my family? I don't know. I know that in hindsight I can't remember any details about the location or extent of that physical pain. But if you knock your funny-bone or hit your thumb with a hammer, you never forget such details. I do know that I felt thoroughly ashamed of myself, which would imply that there was no physical pain: deep down I knew at the time that I was faking. But at the time I wasn't interested in analysing my motives. Having failed yet again, my level of self-esteem was already at rock-bottom and the last thing I needed was to make it lower. My only concern was to find some way of ending the misery I was going through without a further loss of face.

In hindsight, am I still ashamed of myself? For many years I found it impossible to forgive myself. I think of myself as a basically honest and compassionate person. What a terrible thing I did to my family. They knew the drug was killing me and ruining my life. It was also blatantly obvious to them that I was receiving no benefits whatsoever from it. They were so pleased during the periods I was able to abstain. I can only imagine what effect it had on them when I not only slid back into the pit again, but actually blamed them for it.

I now realize that I had no more reason to feel ashamed than a person suffering from shell-shock, or anyone else whose life is being ruined because their only crime was that they were unfortunate enough to fall into the alcohol trap. As I stated at the beginning of the book, the real culprit is ignorance. But my experience does serve to illustrate the level to which an otherwise honest and considerate person can be reduced when their life is dominated by a drug. It was a nightmare world of fear, panic and misery, and I am so grateful that I escaped.

Whilst on the subjects of nightmares and physical withdrawal pains, it is very common after successfully kicking any drug occasionally to dream that you are taking it again. Even after I discovered Easyway I would dream that I was smoking again. I knew before I stubbed out my final cigarette that I would never smoke again. Even so the dream did concern me. Did it mean that subconsciously I still wanted to smoke? When I wrote the book version of Easyway, I actually tried to get hooked again. Before you jump to the conclusion that I obviously did still want to smoke, allow me to explain why I did that.

At the group stop smoking clinics I would warn clients that they might feel somewhat disorientated for a few days but that there would be no severe physical withdrawal symptoms. Most clients would confirm that they found this to be true. Others would say that they experienced no withdrawal symptoms whatsoever. Occasionally one would complain that they were suffering unbearable physical pain. A few pertinent questions would bring forth nothing more than the "I can't sleep" type replies that I referred to above. But I began to doubt my own perception. Had I really not experienced any withdrawal symptoms whatsoever, or had I been so elated at being free that I just hadn't noticed them, rather like a rugby player is unaware of cuts and bruises in the excitement of the game?

Before completing the book, I wanted to get hooked again, so that I could quit again and be able to objectively assess the severity and existence, or non-existence, of any withdrawal symptoms. The experiment shattered my little world. No, it wasn't because I was stupid enough to deliberately get hooked again, and then found I couldn't quit. In fact, it was the exact opposite. I had been claiming that I knew more about quitting smoking than anyone else on the planet; and that just one puff will get you hooked again. But I couldn't get hooked! I could smoke; in fact after a month I managed to get up to twenty a day. But I was having to force myself. It was rather like smoking your first cigarette or drinking your first pint of beer. Even after a month I couldn't feel the need or desire to smoke. Then it dawned on me. I could never get hooked again even if I tried for the rest of my life; because what hooks you is not the drug itself, but the illusion that you get some crutch or pleasure from it. Like any other confidence trick, once you understand the trick, you can't possibly fall for it again.

The experiment did help to prove certain points. When I realized I could never get hooked again, I quit torturing myself; and I can confirm that I suffered no withdrawal effects, physical or mental. If addicts suffer any physical pain when they quit, it is a direct result of the mental anguish they are going through. Fortunately, with Easyway both the mental anguish and any physical withdrawal pains that might otherwise have resulted from it are removed before you take that final drink.

I continue to have occasional dreams in which I am still drinking or smoking. The second point my experiment proves is that such dreams do not indicate that I have a secret desire to drink or smoke. The fact that those dreams cause me consternation is further evidence. After I wake up there is often a short period before it dawns on me that it was just a dream. My reaction is never disappointment because I no longer drink or smoke. On the contrary, it is utter relief that it was just a dream and that I am free from the living nightmare of drug addiction.

The third point it proves is that the solution is entirely mental. It is only the misery of mentally craving for an illusory pleasure and/or crutch that keeps us hooked. But I must issue a warning here. Some people think Easyway is indeed a miracle: the experiment proves that even if I have the occasional drink, I can't get hooked. It proves the exact opposite. The reason I couldn't get hooked is because I had no desire to smoke. If you have no desire to drink, you'll have no desire to have an occasional drink. If you have a desire to have an occasional drink, you are already hooked.

What causes us to go on craving? Is it the incredibly powerful addictive effect of the drug? No, it is ignorance: the belief that we are making a genuine sacrifice, that social occasions will never be enjoyable without alcohol, or that we won't be able to cope with stress without it; and the belief that we can never be completely free.

Once a drinker always a drinker. Another completely groundless platitude that makes us believe we can never be free. At the last AA meeting I attended a man who had been dry for over 20 years repeatedly said: "I'm just one drink away from being a drunk." It was impossible not to admire his resolution. At the same time I felt so sorry for him to have felt so vulnerable for such a long period. With Easyway you'll feel more secure than someone who has never drunk alcohol. Once you understand exactly how a confidence trick works, you are not likely to fall for it again. But a person who doesn't understand it is always vulnerable.

Drinkers see alcohol as a tug-of-war. On one side fear: it's ruining my health and wealth. On the other side: it's my crutch and pleasure. In reality it is fear on both sides. There is no genuine crutch or pleasure. It is a case of: I can't enjoy life or even cope with it, *without* alcohol. The fears on both sides is caused by the alcohol: non-drinkers don't suffer from either set of fears. You didn't suffer from either set of fears before you had your first alcoholic drink.

Many people believe that quitting alcohol is about as difficult as climbing Everest. If you haven't prepared yourself properly, this will probably be the case. I can only imagine the elation that Sherpa Tenzing and Edmund Hillary felt when they reached the summit, but I cannot believe it was any greater than the intense feeling of relief and pleasure I felt when I knew I was free forever from the slavery of drug addiction. Perhaps you feel you have still got the hard preparation to do. I have very good news for you. You have not only completed the preparation but most of the climb. In fact you are only 100 feet from the summit.

Before I give you the final instructions ... Oh dear! I told you there were only seven instructions. I wasn't trying to deceive you; they were a set of instructions designed to help you understand Easyway and to get the maximum benefit while you were reading the book. The final instructions will show you how to make it easy to quit. Believe me, I hate giving instructions. I'm the sort of chap that finds it almost impossible not to defy signs like 'WET PAINT! DO NOT TOUCH!' or 'KEEP OFF THE GRASS' and I'm worried that you'll have the same reaction to my instructions.

It has been suggested that the instructions would be more acceptable if I referred to them as pieces of advice. That would be fatal. Let us extend the analogy of the maze. Imagine that there are sixteen junctions and that at each junction you have the choice of taking the left or the right fork. In order to leave the maze you need to choose the correct fork every time. Your chance of success on each attempt to leave the maze is less than one in 30,000. But if you had an official map of the maze that told you the correct turn at each fork, provided you exercised due care and diligence, success would be guaranteed.

Let me make it quite clear, I do not make it easy to cure alcoholism:

IT IS EASY TO CURE ALCOHOLISM

Now assume that the official map of the maze gave you the wrong fork at each junction. If you believed it and followed its advice, you would never leave the maze. And can you imagine the effect it would have on you if, when you came to the first junction, there was a notice saying:

THERE IS NO EXIT TO THIS MAZE BUT LIFE CAN BE SATISFACTORY IN IT!

It is the advice of the so-called experts that makes it so difficult, or even impossible, to escape from the alcohol trap. Some people have described Easyway as a set of useful tips that might help you to quit. It isn't. It is the correct map of the maze. If you follow it, it will guarantee your escape. Take just one wrong turn and you will remain stuck in the maze.

You might think that some of the instructions are so obvious as not to be worth mentioning. Let's use an example. One of the really important instructions is:

'Having made what you know to be the correct decision, NEVER EVER question that decision.'

That's pretty obvious. But how often have you heard people who are attempting to quit alcohol for good say something like: "I could murder for an ice-cold beer!"? What is the point of vowing on day one that alcohol will never touch your lips again, and then spending the rest of your life wishing for something that you hope and pray you will never have? Even if you believe you got some genuine pleasure from drinking, it's a stupid thing to do; but when alcohol has completely ruined your life, it is nothing less than sheer lunacy. So why do we do it? Because we have been brainwashed to react in certain ways when we attempt to quit. One of those ways is to believe that you have no choice but to crave for an ice-cold beer at certain times. You do have a choice. And if you continue to crave for an ice-cold beer, or any other alcoholic drink, you will be brainwashing yourself. So take nothing for granted. You ignore the instructions at your peril. Before reading them, I would like you to check the following points:

1. Are you clear that there are no advantages from taking alcohol? I don't mean that the disadvantages outweigh the advantages. I mean can you see that there are no benefits whatsoever?

2. Are you clear exactly why cutting down is not an option: why it has to be all or nothing?

3. Are you clear that there is no inherent flaw, either physical or mental, in the make-up of an alcoholic: that anyone who drinks alcohol is just another fly in the pitcher plant, and that an alcoholic is just a victim in the chronic stage of the disease?

If the answer to any of the above questions is 'No', you need to re-read the appropriate chapter. If you still have serious doubts, re-read the whole book. If your doubts are slight and you are anxious to quit as soon as possible, the next two chapters might well clear those doubts, but do not attempt to quit until you have read them.

There is just one object to everything that I have written, and that is for you to achieve:

THE CORRECT FRAME OF MIND!

The willpower method of quitting is to make a vow never to drink again and then to spend an indefinite period of desperation and misery trying to resist the craving, hoping that one day you will wake up feeling:

EUREKA! I'M FREE!

Easyway is the complete reverse. It is to remove the schizophrenia and brainwashing before you take your last drink, so that you know that there is nothing to give up; on the contrary, so you know that you are about to achieve something marvellous. Starting off with a feeling of doom and gloom would be like me leading you to the exit of the maze; but instead of walking out into the sunshine and freedom, you walk back into the maze. If you feel apprehensive because of fear of failure, or because you cannot believe that it is easy to quit, don't worry. When footballers come on to the pitch for the Cup Final, they have butterflies in their stomach. That doesn't prevent it from being the most exhilarating experience of their lives. You are about to achieve something equally exhilarating, and you have one great advantage over those footballers: follow the instructions and:

YOU CANNOT LOSE!

If you are not in the correct frame of mind because your answer to one or more of the above questions is 'No', clear up the doubts first: remember you can always consult an Easyway clinic. But do not fall for the most insidious aspect of the trap:

TIMING

The subtlest part of the trap is that it is usually years before you realize that you are in it. Most drinkers have lived and died never knowing they fell for the most ingenious confidence trick in history. But the most insidious part of the trap is this. However far you might have slid down the pitcher plant, it will try to make you block your mind to the true situation. It will try to fool you into believing that you are in control: that you can choose to drink whenever you want to. It will attempt to do this until it has destroyed you completely; just as it has fooled and destroyed millions of others.

I've described the tug-of-war of fear. The fear that it will destroy us is a fear of tomorrow. Perhaps it will never happen. But the fear of life without alcohol starts the moment you make an attempt to quit. So the natural tendency is to put off the evil day.

And there will always be an excuse to do so, if you want one. Isn't there always a wedding coming up, or Christmas, or some other social function? There will always be some stress in your life that you feel it might be better to be free of first. Please don't fall for that trap. Isn't that what you've been doing since you first realized you had a problem? Whilst you are hooked on alcohol you will never be free of stress. Get that clearly into your mind. You don't need to be frightened; you won't have to go through a transitional period of misery. You'll be able to enjoy social occasions and cope with stress immediately. Suppose you had a different disease, say lung cancer, and you heard of an instant cure: a cure that was inexpensive and painless! Would you hesitate? There is nothing bad happening. You've spent most of your life like the heroine in *Notorious*. You've got a wonderful opportunity today: to decide whether you are going to spend the rest of your life being dominated by that evil drug; or TO BE FREE !

Before we proceed with the final preparations, I need to clear my conscience. All drug addiction is a subtle confidence trick based on the following principles of deceit:

1. Massive brainwashing about the illusory benefits that the drug will provide. This brainwashing is inadvertently perpetuated by victims of the drug, who are merely trying to justify their own stupidity: and deliberately perpetuated by the colossal advertising from vested commercial interests.

2. A policy of supplying the first doses free of charge: until the victim becomes hooked.

Unfortunately the only way I can reverse this massive brainwashing is to convince you that it is all based on deceit. Obviously I cannot use deceitful tactics in order to help you to get free. So why do I need to clear my conscience? My book on smoking is called *The Easy Way to Stop Smoking*. So why isn't this one called *The Easy Way to Stop Drinking*? Because there are significant differences between drinking and smoking. All smokers are aware that it is completely unnatural to breathe lethal fumes into their lungs. Although heavy smokers envy casual smokers, even casual smokers would love to be completely free. All parents hate the thought of their children smoking: which means that all smokers wish they had never fallen into the trap.

But the act of drinking is not only natural, but essential for survival. Drinking alcohol is both unnatural and destructive. But we have been brainwashed to believe otherwise. Therefore casual drinkers do not have the same desire as casual smokers to be completely free. They believe they are in control, so why should they deny themselves what they consider to be a genuine pleasure? Chronic drinkers would love to be able to control their intake, but have learned by hard experience that it has to be all or nothing. In between there are the millions of drinkers who realize that they have a problem, but cannot face the prospect of life without alcohol; so they would also love to be able to control their intake.

If you are one of those drinkers, the title was deliberately designed to mislead you into believing that there is an easy way to be what AA describes as a 'normal' drinker. I make no apologies for doing that. My sole objective was to prevent you going through further misery only to reach the inevitable conclusion that it has to be all or nothing. Let me also make it clear that the title I have used is truthful. There is an easy way to control your drinking. It happens to be the only way to control your drinking:

TO BE COMPLETELY FREE

If you are still not clear why it has to be all or nothing, you have missed one or more important points. Would you get on the plane if you knew the pilot believed he could solve an emergency by making his instruments read incorrectly? If you still see 'just one drink' as some sort of crutch or pleasure, you are left with just two options: a lifetime of misery drinking alcohol, or a lifetime of misery not drinking it and feeling deprived. Not much of a choice is it? Fortunately, there's another option: to see drinking alcohol in its true light, and spend a lifetime rejoicing in the fact that you have escaped from that fearful prison. If you are still in doubt after you have read the final preparations, do not attempt to quit: instead re-read the book until the penny has dropped. Let us not delay your escape any longer. Provided that you have removed any doubts, we can now proceed with:

THE INSTRUCTIONS THAT MAKE
IT EASY TO QUIT

26 *The Instructions That Make It Easy To Quit*

WARNING!

To attempt to quit drinking by following these instructions without reading the rest of the book, would be equivalent to executing the perfect dive with no water in the pool.

If you feel the need for a second to last drink, take it now, but make sure that you are sober when reading the instructions. These are detailed instructions. An abbreviated version is included in Appendix B.

1. Do not think "I must never have another drink!" That would create a feeling of deprivation. Instead, start with a feeling of: "Isn't it great! My life is no longer dominated by DEVASTATION!"

2. Having made what you know to be the correct decision, NEVER EVER question that decision. This is one of the key differences between Easyway and the willpower method. The difficulty in quitting lies not in the physical withdrawal pains, but in continuing to mentally crave a drink, and in questioning your decision. With some decisions it's difficult to weigh up the pros and cons. But there are no pros whatsoever to drinking DEVASTATION! If you begin to question your decision, you will start to crave for a drink. You will feel miserable and deprived if you don't have one; and you will feel even more miserable if you do. If you begin to doubt your decision, you are on a loser either way.

3. Do not – I repeat, do not – try to avoid thinking about the fact that you no longer drink alcohol. Let me illustrate the futility of

such an exercise. I would like you not to think about a huge pink elephant. What have you started to think about? It is impossible to deliberately not think about something. It's like worrying about not being able to sleep at night: the more you worry about it, the more you guarantee that you won't be able to sleep. In any event, there is no need not to think about it. There is nothing bad happening. On the contrary, there is something marvellous happening. It is what you are thinking that is important. If you are thinking "I'd love a drink" or "When will I be free?" you will make yourself miserable. If you are thinking "EUREKA! I'M ALREADY FREE!", you will enjoy thinking about it, and the more you think about it the happier you will be.

4. Be aware that for a few days there will be a little monster inside your body, wanting to be fed. The feeling might register as just an empty, insecure feeling; or just the feeling of: "I want a drink!" Either way, don't worry about it. Remember, that is what you've been suffering ever since you fell into the trap and it is so slight we don't even know it is there most of the time. But you need to be aware that the little monster exists and that it will soon die.

Think of it that way. Imagine that little monster as an evil goblin perched on your shoulders, tightening its legs around your throat and demanding endless supplies of alcohol. It is him that is dependent on alcohol, not you. Once you realize that, he has lost his power over you; the situation is reversed. You now control him. You are going to starve him of alcohol and you are going to revel in his death throes.

5. Don't worry if you occasionally forget that you have quit. By that I do not mean that you can have the occasional snifter. That feeling of "I want a drink" might be due to the death throes of the goblin, or simply that you have forgotten that you have quit. Do not confuse it with doubting your decision. It's rather like when you buy a new car. The indicator switch is bound to be where the horn was on the old one: I'm convinced the manufacturers do it deliberately. For a few days whenever you try to indicate you blow

your horn. Every other motorist in sight is thinking: "What's he honking for? The idiot is doing a right turn and not even indicating!" I pride myself that I never indulge in road rage. On one rare occasion I hit the horn when another motorist cut me up. Not a sound came out; instead I was blinded by my own windscreen washer. The incident itself wasn't so bad, but now every time I'm cut up I have to put up with Joyce's: "Give him a squirt, Allen." The point I'm making is that it takes time to adjust, but it's nothing to worry about. I didn't want to squirt, I wanted to indicate. You might well get that feeling of a void or wanting a drink, particularly over the next few days. If and when it happens, reverse it immediately. Just remind yourself, "This is the death throes of that goblin on my back. It's what drinkers suffer throughout their drinking lives. Isn't it marvellous: I'M FREE!" That way the slight pangs immediately become moments of pleasure. Get into the habit of doing that over the next few days. Unless you reverse those pangs immediately, you will be doubting your decision. Remember, any slight aggravation that you might suffer over the next few days is not because you stopped drinking, but because you started. Non-drinkers don't have this problem. Any major alteration in your life takes time to adjust to: even an improvement, like a better home, job or car. You may feel a little strange or disorientated over the next few days, but don't worry about it; you'll soon adjust. If you start to worry about it, you'll create a phobia and never adjust.

6. Do not wait to become a non-drinker. One of the main problems of the willpower method is that you are never sure when you are free. In fact 'recovering' alcoholics believe they can never be permanently free. They are waiting to see if they will not drink again. They are actually waiting for something to not happen. It merely confirms that they are always in doubt. How can you be sure when you are free? Easy! Just follow these instructions; and one of the instructions is to realize that you will be free the moment you finish the last drink. 'Take one day at a time', and 'take each day as it comes' are meaningless platitudes. How can

you do anything else? They are part of the willpower method: 'Don't even attempt to face the rest of your life without alcohol, just take each day as it comes.' What a morbid prospect! Life is wonderful. Remember that you haven't given up living. You haven't given up anything. You've spent much of your life in prison. Don't waste another precious day!

7. Accept that just as drinkers, non-drinkers and ex-drinkers all have good days and bad days, so do people who have quit drinking. If alcohol genuinely made people happy, drinkers would never be unhappy. The tendency when people stop drinking is to blame everything that goes wrong on the fact that they've quit. All that does is to start you doubting your decision and moping for a situation that never existed. Be aware that time is on your side, nobody can prevent your escape; and as each day passes, you will feel more confident, happier, healthier and wealthier. But don't wish your life away. If it's a good day, enjoy it to the full. If it's a bad day, remind yourself that it would have been so much worse if you were still a drinker.

8. Realize that you are in control of the craving and not the other way around. The most common questions that I am asked are: "How long will it take for the little monster to die?" and "When will the craving go?" It is not possible to tell when the little monster dies, because that very slight empty feeling is inseparable from a hunger for food or normal stress. This is one of the reasons why drinkers using the willpower method are never quite sure when they are free. Long after the little monster has died, their brains misinterpret normal hunger or stress as: "I need a drink." The point is: the feeling is so slight anyway that you don't need to worry about it. For convenience I have referred to the little monster as craving alcohol. In reality the little monster never craves alcohol any more than your body craves food. Your body merely signals the empty feeling to your brain. It is only your brain that is capable of craving anything. At some point in the near or distant future your brain may well say: "I need a drink." YOU ARE

STILL IN CONTROL. Whether the thought was triggered by the little monster, or the fact that you had temporarily forgotten that you no longer drink, or for any other reason, you are still in control. You have the choice of either reminding yourself that you are now free from the nightmare, or starting to mope for a drink.

9. Do not mourn. If a close friend or relative dies, you have to go through a grieving process. No matter how great the pain, time does begin to heal the wound. Life goes on, but that wound will never completely heal. Drinkers go through a similar trauma when they attempt to quit by using the willpower method. They know that they will be better off as non-drinkers, but they still retain the brainwashing. They believe that they are losing a genuine friend or crutch. Some do manage to escape, but they never feel completely free, they remain vulnerable. The problem is that they are still surrounded by the demon drink and the brainwashing is as bad as ever. It only needs a tragedy or just one little slip, and in no time at all they find themselves not just back in the pit, but at rock-bottom. But if an enemy dies, there is no need to mourn. On the contrary, you can rejoice from the moment of his death and you can continue to rejoice for the rest of your life. It is your choice. You can spend the next few days moping because you can no longer drink; or for the rest of your life, whenever the subject of alcohol crosses your mind, you can think:

EUREKA! I'M FREE!

10. Do not alter your life in any other way purely because you've quit drinking. Some 'experts' advise you to avoid pubs, restaurants, the company of drinking friends, and other situations in which you might be tempted. No wonder drinkers find it so difficult to quit using such tactics. The best policy is to go to a pub or a party immediately: to prove to yourself that you don't have to wait in order to enjoy yourself without drinking. It doesn't matter if you are the only non-drinker at the party. There is a covert mental battle between drinkers and non-drinkers. Drinkers that love you

will be delighted that you have quit but part of their brain will hate you for quitting. They will sense that you are truly free and this will make them feel insecure. In that battle the non-drinker has a hand of four aces. The drinker doesn't have a pair of twos. It is at such times that you might forget that you've quit. You've just been explaining how great you feel since you quit drinking. Someone asks you what you are drinking and without even thinking you say: "I'll have my usual." You feel absolutely ridiculous and the guffaws of your friends don't help. It's at times like these that you can start doubting whether you really are free. Don't worry: the fact that you have forgotten that you didn't drink – surrounded by drinkers and in a situation where you would previously have been drinking – is actually proof that it doesn't bother you. But don't just stand there looking glum. Say to those drinkers: "Do you know, I feel so relaxed about it that I'd forgotten I quit. You should try it." I guarantee they'll start assuring you how much they enjoy it and how they can take it or leave it. They will expect you to be miserable and when they see you relaxed and happy they will think you are Superhuman. More important: you will be feeling Superhuman!

11. Resist the temptation to convert your friends. When you are truly free it is only natural to want to help your friends to escape. You might also be tempted to explain the true facts about alcohol as a defensive manoeuvre in the covert battle between yourself and your drinking friends. Try to resist the temptation. It will just provoke a heated argument, cause you frustration and actually make it harder for your friend to quit. Trying to persuade a drinker who doesn't understand the alcohol trap to quit is like trying to force someone who suffers from claustrophobia into a small lift. However, you will find that when they see that you are a truly free spirit, they will start to ask questions. This means that they too would like to be free. You are now dealing not with panic but an open mind. Even then go softly-softly. You can get almost as much pleasure helping someone else to escape as you do from escaping yourself.

12. If possible alter the parts of your lifestyle which you do not like. This might appear to be a contradiction of instruction No.10. Let me use an example. Avoid drinking friends, but not friends who happen to drink. Perhaps I still need to elaborate. Don't change or even avoid a true friend because he drinks. If you do, you will be making a genuine sacrifice. But if, for example, you were in the habit of calling into the same pub after work, just to have a drink, you might well have become friendly with similar lost souls. If your only common interest was to drink alcohol, to continue the habit would only frustrate and bore you. But if you enjoyed a game of darts or snooker at the venue and you wish to carry on, by all means continue to do so. Once you have removed the goblin from your back you'll probably find that you have been in the habit of wasting a lot of your time. At first you may find you don't know how to fill this time. Don't worry about it. Four things you can't have too much of are time, energy, love and money. Alcohol ravages all these things. You will have so much more of each of these valuable commodities. Spend them wisely on activities that give you genuine pleasure. Enjoy the challenge of restructuring your life. I like to exercise daily, not because I've quit drinking, but for the purely selfish reason that all aspects of life are so much more enjoyable when you feel fit and healthy. Do not confuse occupying yourself usefully with substitutes.

13. Do not use substitutes; whether that substitute is an activity, a non-alcoholic drink, an item of food, or anything else. Let me make this quite clear. I'm not saying, don't eat! I'm not saying, don't drink! I'm saying, don't use excess food or beverages as substitutes for alcohol. If you enjoy a certain activity, go for it! But do it because you enjoy it, not as a substitute for drinking alcohol. By even thinking of using a substitute, you are subconsciously telling yourself that you are making a sacrifice. Get it clear in your mind that you don't need a substitute. Drinking alcohol didn't fill a void in your life; on the contrary, it created one. When you get over a bout of flu, do you search for another disease to take its

place? Your object is to be rid of two monsters. The little monster is so slight that it is not a problem. The real problem is the Big Monster in the brain. You know you didn't need to drink alcohol before you became hooked: the whole key is to prove to yourself as quickly as possible that you can enjoy life and cope with it without alcohol.

14. Enjoy breaking false associations. At one time I couldn't imagine a wedding, a party, a holiday, Christmas, a game of golf or even a meal without alcohol. The truth is that I couldn't imagine life without alcohol. I truly believed that if ever I did manage to quit, I might just as well spend the rest of my life in a monastery. But all of those things that I mentioned are pleasant occasions in their own right. However, if you tell yourself that you can't enjoy them without poisoning and inebriating yourself, then you won't be able to. Not only is it enjoyable to purge the poison from your body, but it can be even more enjoyable to break these associations and free yourself from the slavery in the mind. It is essential to break these false associations now.

15. Never envy drinkers. They all suffer from a disease called alcoholism. The fact that they are oblivious to it, and might remain so throughout their lives, is their loss. Would you envy someone who was HIV positive but wasn't aware of it? Get it clear that whenever you see anyone drink alcohol, on any occasion, they are not doing so because they choose to, but because they have fallen for an ingenious, subtle confidence trick. Also remember that you are not being deprived. It is the drinkers who are being deprived: of their health, their money, their energy, their courage, their concentration, their self-respect, their peace of mind and their freedom. Drinking alcoholic drinks is nothing more or less than addiction to alcohol. You wouldn't envy a heroin addict. Heroin kills an infinitesimal number of people in the UK, compared to the 40,000 that die annually from alcoholism. Like all drug addiction, alcoholism doesn't get better. It gets worse and worse. I

have excellent news for you. You are about to drink the only alcoholic drink that can bring true enjoyment:

YOUR FINAL DRINK

27 *Your Final Drink*

At the clinics some clients question the need for the final drink. Perhaps it does sound somewhat contradictory for me to say that alcohol does absolutely nothing for you whatsoever, and then actually recommend that you have a final drink. I do so for good reasons, not least of which is that the main difficulty in quitting is the doubt: when do you become a free spirit? It is important that you realize that you will have achieved your goal the moment you finish your final drink.

This is a very special day. It might well be the most momentous day of your life. We like to ritualize and celebrate special days like birthdays and weddings, and this is certainly a day that you will want to remember, so why not make a ritual of that last drink? You can even use the last drink to toast the fact that it is the last drink. But does this mean that you can never toast or celebrate again? Of course not: you merely toast with a drink that doesn't contain alcohol. But isn't that substituting? Not really; drinking is a normal and natural function. However, this does raise a problem which we need to address.

Many drinkers who quit find it a problem deciding what to drink at social events. For health reasons, most prefer to drink fruit juices rather than cola, but find that they tend to taste sickly after they've had a couple. That's no problem; once you've quenched your thirst you have no need to go on drinking. The only reason that most people permanently have a glass in their hands at parties is that they are drinking alcohol, which dehydrates them. Because most people drink alcohol, an illusion has been created that you can't be enjoying yourself unless you have a drink in your hand. We are also in the habit of eating at parties, but we don't feel the need to eat throughout the party. If you attempt to drink the same volume of soft drinks as you did alcohol, you will be substituting and you will give your body unnecessary problems. Drinking alcohol is a common cause of obesity and another considerable benefit of quitting can be to reduce weight. This benefit will be lost if you attempt to substitute.

Ironically, this problem of what to drink doesn't only affect drinkers who have quit. Many casual drinkers, who would prefer to drink soft drinks, also switch to alcoholic drinks because they have been brainwashed to believe that you must keep drinking something, and fruit juices tend to get sickly. I wonder how many people have been accelerated down the road to alcoholism because of this.

You might already have experienced what I refer to as 'The Moment of Revelation'. It is truly a wonderful experience. It is the moment when you know that you are free. With some people it happens even before they take the last drink. Sometimes during group sessions at one of the clinics, long before the therapy is over, a client will say something like: "You needn't say another word. I can see it all so clearly. I know I'll never drink again." Perhaps you have already experienced that moment. If not, don't worry; some people have to wait for the proof of the pudding. But it is important not to try to make that moment happen, that would be like trying not to think about drinking and would just create a phobia. 'The Moment of Revelation' usually happens after one of those occasions that you once couldn't imagine without alcohol. It might be a social occasion or a trauma: you suddenly realize that not only did you enjoy the occasion or cope with the trauma, but the thought that you no longer drink never even crossed your mind.

Before you take that final drink I need to issue a warning. It's one thing escaping from the alcohol trap, but you also need to ensure that you don't fall into it again. There are two main dangers and you need to prepare for them both. One is that some tragedy should occur in your life, usually the death of a loved one. There will always be some helpful soul, with the best of intentions, that will try to force a brandy down your throat. That brandy will neither bring back your loved one nor will it ease your loss. What it will do is to create another tragedy. Just remember that.

But the bigger danger is that because Easyway makes it easy to quit, you can fall into the trap of thinking:

"What possible harm can there be in having just one drink? Even if I did get hooked again, I'll find it easy to quit again."

The moment you even start to ponder the thought of having just one drink, you are no longer using Easyway and it will have lost its protection. Make a habit of regularly reminding yourself how miserable you were as a slave to alcohol and of reliving the euphoria of 'The Moment of Revelation'. Then serious alarm bells will ring in your mind if you ever find yourself starting to think along the lines of having just one drink.

And remind yourself that there is no such thing as just one drink. Even if there were, when would you drink it? Next year? Twenty years from now? Do you really want to spend the rest of your life waiting for the next dose of poison?

So let's get it out of the way now so that you can be free for the rest of your life. Don't make it your favourite tipple. Another object of the last drink is to ingrain into your mind what a foul-tasting poison alcohol is. Don't worry, I'm not going to ask you to drink pure alcohol, or meths, or metal polish. Choose a spirit, preferably the one that you find tastes the most foul. Pour yourself a generous measure of neat spirit. Before you drink it, take time out to close your eyes and make a solemn vow that it will be your last ever alcoholic drink. Concentrate on the foul taste, and ponder on how you were once conned into paying a fortune just to pour that filthy poison down your throat. Then:

GET ON WITH ENJOYING YOUR LIFE!

APPENDIX A

THE INSTRUCTIONS

1 FOLLOW ALL THE INSTRUCTIONS

2 DON'T JUMP THE GUN

3 START OFF IN A HAPPY FRAME OF MIND

4 THINK POSITIVELY

5 DON'T QUIT OR CUT DOWN UNTIL THE END OF THE BOOK

6 ONLY READ THE BOOK WHEN YOU ARE SOBER

7 KEEP AN OPEN MIND!

APPENDIX B

THE INSTRUCTIONS THAT MAKE IT EASY TO QUIT

1 Cultivate the attitude: "Isn't it great? My life is no longer dominated by DEVASTATION!"

2 Never, ever doubt your decision: there is absolutely nothing to give up!

3 Do not try not to think about drinking.

4 Be aware that the little monster exists, but don't worry about him.

5 Don't worry if occasionally you forget that you no longer drink.

6 Don't wait to become a non-drinker.

7 Accept that you will have good days and bad days.

8 Be aware that you control the craving and not the other way around.

9 Do not mourn the death of an enemy.

10 Don't change your lifestyle just because you have quit drinking.

11 Don't try to convert your friends unless they first seek your help.

12 Change those parts of your lifestyle which you do not like, but for purely selfish reasons.

13 Do not use substitutes.

14 Enjoy breaking the associations.

15 Never envy people who drink alcohol.

16 Last but not least:

ENJOY LIFE!

THE EASYWAY CLINIC LIST

The following pages list contact details for all Allen Carr Stop Smoking Clinics worldwide where the success rate, based on the money back guarantee, is over 90%. Selected clinics also offer sessions that deal with alcohol and weight issues. Please check with your nearest clinic, which is listed, for details.

Allen Carr guarantees you will find it easy to stop smoking at his clinics or your money back.

AUSTRALIA
VICTORIA, TASMANIA:
Tel: 03 9894 8866 or 1 300 790 565 (Freecall)
Email: info@allencarr.com.au
Website: www.allencarr.com
Therapist: Gail Morris

SYDNEY, NEW SOUTH WALES:
P.O. Box 309, Balmain, NSW 2041
Tel and Fax: 1300 785180
Email: nsw@allencarr.com.au
Website: www.allencarr.com
Therapist: Natalie Clays

SOUTH QUEENSLAND:
– OPENING 2006
P.O. Box 174, Annerley, QLD 4103
Tel: 1300 855 806 (Freecall)
Fax: 07 3892 4223
Mobile: 0402 854 946
Email: sqld@allencarr.com.au
Website: www.allencarr.com
Therapist: Jonathan Wills

AUSTRIA
Sessions held throughout Austria
Central Information and Booking line:
0800 RAUCHEN (0800 7282436)

Triesterstraße 42, Spielberg
Tel: 03512 44755
Fax: 03512 447755-14
Email: info@allen-carr.at
Website: www.allencarr.com
Therapists: Erich Kellermann and Team

BELGIUM
ANTWERP:
Koningin Astridplein 27 B-9150 Bazel
Tel: 03 281 6255 *Fax:* 03 744 0608
Email: Easyway@dirknielandt.be
Website: www.allencarr.com
Therapist: Dirk Nielandt

CANADA
Seminars held in Toronto and Vancouver. Corporate programs available throughout Canada
Central Information and Booking Line:
1 866 666 4299 (Toll free)
Email: info@theeasyway tostopsmoking.com
Website: www.allencarr.com
Office: 75 Brookfield Road, Oakville, ON, L6K 2YB
Tel: 905 8497736 *Fax:* 905 849 9237
Email: nicole@theeasyway tostopsmoking.com
Therapist: Damian O'Hara

CARIBBEAN

GUADELOUPE, ANTILLES:
Tel: 05 90 84 95 21
Email: allencaraibes@wanadoo.fr
Therapist: Fabiana de Oliveira

COLOMBIA,
SOUTH AMERICA

BOGOTA:
Tel: (571) 2365794 or 571 5301802
Email:
info@esfacildejardefumar.com
Website: www.allencarr.com
Therapist: Jose Manuel Duran

DENMARK

COPENHAGEN:
Asger Rygsgade 16, 1th, 1727
Copenhagen V, Denmark
Tel: 519 03536
Email: mette@easyway.dk
Website: www.allencarr.com
Therapist: Mette Fonss

ECUADOR,
SOUTH AMERICA

QUITO:
Gaspar de Villarroel E9-53y Av.
Shyris 3er piso, Quito.
Tel & Fax: 02 2820 920
Email: toisan@pi.pro.ec
*Website:*www.allencarr.com
Therapist: Ingrid Wittich

FRANCE

Sessions held throughout France
Central Booking Line:
0800 FUMEUR (Freephone)
11b rue St Ferreol, 13001 Marseille
Tel: 33 (4) 91 33 54 55
Email: info@allencarr.fr

Website: www.allencarr.com
Therapists: Erick Serre and Team

GERMANY

Sessions held throughout Germany
Free line telephone for Information and Booking: 08000 RAUCHEN
(0800 07282436)

Kirchenweg 41, D-83026
Rosenheim
Tel: 08031 463067
Fax: 08031 901 9090
Email: info@allen-carr.de
Website: www.allencarr.com
Therapists: Erich Kellermann and Team

ICELAND

REYKJAVIK:
Skeidarvogur 147, 104 Reykjavik
Tel: 553 9590 *Fax:* 588 7060
Email: easyway@easyway.is
*Website:*www.allencarr.com
Therapist: Petur Einarsson

ITALY

MILAN:
Via Renato Fucini, 3, 20133 Milano
Tel/Fax: 02 7060 2438
Email: info@easywayitalia.com
Website: www.allencarr.com
Therapist: Francesca Cesati

JAPAN

TOKYO:
Roop Toranomon 5F 2-9-2
Nishi-Shinbashi Minato-ku Tokyo
105-0003
Tel: +81 3 3507 4020
Fax: +81 3 3507 4022

Therapist: Miho Shimada
Email: info@allen-carr.jp
Website: www.allencarr.com

MAURITIUS
Tel: 00230 727 5103
Email:
allencarrmauritius@yahoo.com
Website: www.allencarr.com
Therapist: Heidi Houreau

MEXICO
Tel: (5255) 5330 7351
Email: info@allencarr-mexico.com
Website: www.allencarr.com
Therapist: Jorge Davo

NETHERLANDS
Website: www.allencarr.com

AMSTERDAM:
Pythagorasstraat 22, 1098 GC
Amsterdam
Tel: 020 465 4665 *Fax:* 020 465 6682
Email: amsterdam@allencarr.nl
Therapist: Eveline de Mooij

UTRECHT:
De Beaufortlaan 22B, 3768 MJ
Soestduinen (gem. Soest)
Tel: 035 602 94 58
Email: soest@allencarr.nl
Therapist: Paula Rooduijn

ROTTERDAM:
Mathenesserlaan 290, 3021 HV
Rotterdam
Tel: 010 244 07 09 *Fax:* 010 244 07 10
Email: rotterdam@allencarr.nl
Therapist: Kitty van't Hof

NIJMEGEN:
Van Heutszstraat 38, 6521 CX
Nijmegen
Tel: 024 336 03305
Email: nijmegen@allencarr.nl
Therapist: Jacqueline van den Bosch

NEW ZEALAND
AUCKLAND:
472 Blockhouse Bay Road,
Auckland 1007
Tel: 09 626 5390
Mobile: 027 4177077
Email: vickie@easywaynz.co.nz
Website: www.allencarr.com
Therapist: Vickie Macrae

CHRISTCHURCH:
P.O. Box 29363, Christchurch
Tel: 021 737810
Email: easyway@allencarr.co.nz
Website: www.allencarr.com
Therapist: Maria Roe

NORWAY
OSLO:
Bygdøy Allé 23, 0262 Oslo
Tel: 23 27 29 38
Fax: 23 27 28 15
Email: post@easyway-norge.no
Website: www.allencarr.com
Therapist: Laila Thorsen

POLAND
WARSAW:
Ul. Wilcza 12 B m 13, 02-532
Warszawa
Tel: 22 621 36 11
Email: annakabat@hotmail.com
Website: www.allencarr.com
Therapist: Anna Kabat

PORTUGAL

OPORTO:
Edificio Zarco, Rua Goncalves
Zarco 1129B, sala 109, Leca de
Palmeira, 4450-685 Matosinhos
Tel: 22 9958698
Email:
info@comodeixardefumar.com
Website: www.allencarr.com
Therapist: Ria Slof

REPUBLIC OF IRELAND

DUBLIN & CORK:
Lo-Call (From ROI):
1 890 ESYWAY (37 99 29)
Tel: 01 494 9010 (4 lines)
Fax: 01 495 2757
Email: info@allencarr.ie
Website: www.allencarr.com
Therapist: Brenda Sweeney and
Team

SLOVAKIA/CZECH REPUBLIC:
B. Smetany 10, CZ-301 35 Plzen
Tel: 00421 905 325248/
00421 905 FAJCIT
Email: info@easyway-sk-cz.com
Website: www.allencarr.com
Therapist: Leo Baier

SOUTH AFRICA

Central Booking Line: 0861 100 200
HEAD OFFICE & CAPE TOWN
CLINIC: 15 Draper Square, Draper
St, Claremont 7708
Tel: 021 851 5883
Mobile: 083 600 5555
Email: easyway@allencarr.co.za
Website: www.allencarr.com
Therapist: Dr. Charles Nel

PRETORIA:
Tel: 084 (EASYWAY) 327 9929
Email: info@allencarr.co.za
Website: www.allencarr.com
Therapist: Dudley Garner

SPAIN

MADRID and BARCELONA:
(other areas also available)
Central Office: Felisa Campuzano,
21, 39400 Los Corrales de Buelna,
Cantabria
Tel: 902 10 28 10
Fax: 942 83 25 84
Email: easyway@comodejarde
fumar.com
Website:
www.comodejardefumar.com
Therapists: Geoffrey Molloy & Rhea
Sivi and Team

SWEDEN

Website: www.allencarr.com

SWITZERLAND

Free line telephone for Information and
Booking:
0800 RAUCHEN (0800 7282426)
Schöntalstr. 30, Ch - 8486
Rikon-Zurich.
Tel: 052 383 3773 *Fax:* 052 3833774
Therapists: Cyrill Argast and Team
SESSIONS: Suisse Romand and
Svizzera Italia
Tel: 0800 728 2436
Email: info@allen-carr.ch
Website: www.allencarr.com

TURKEY

Tel: 0090 212 3585307
Email: info@allencarrturkiye.com

Website: www.allencarr.com
Therapist: Emre Ustunucar

UK
Stop Smoking Helpline: 0906 604
0220 (Premium rate – 60p per min.)
Information Line: 0800 389 2115
(Freephone)
Website: www.allencarrseasyway.com

LONDON:
lc Amity Grove, Raynes Park,
London SW20 OLQ
Tel: 020 8944 7761
Fax: 020 8944 8619
Email:
postmaster@allencarr.demon.co.uk
Website: www.allencarr.com
Therapists: John Dicey, Sue Bolshaw,
Sam Carroll, Colleen Dwyer,
Crispin Hay, Jenny Rutherford

BIRMINGHAM:
415 Hagley Road West, Quinton,
Birmingham B32 2AD
Tel & Fax: 0121 423 1227
Email: easywayadmin@tiscali.co.uk
Website: www.allencarr.com
Therapists: John Dicey, Colleen
Dwyer, Crispin Hay

BOURNEMOUTH &
SOUTHAMPTON:
Tel & Fax: 01425 272757
Website: www.allencarr.com
Therapists: John Dicey, Colleen
Dwyer, Sam Carroll

BRIGHTON:
Tel: 0800 028 7257 (Freephone)
Website: www.allencarr.com

Therapists: John Dicey, Colleen
Dwyer, Sam Carroll

BRISTOL & SWINDON:
Tel: 0117 950 1441
Email: stopsmoking@easyway
bristol.co.uk
Website: www.allencarr.com
Therapist: Charles Holdsworth
Hunt

BUCKINGHAMSHIRE: MILTON
KEYNES, HIGH WYCOMBE,
OXFORD & AYLESBURY
Tel: 0800 0197 017 (Freephone)
Email: kim@easywaybucks.co.uk
Website: www.allencarr.com
Therapist: Kim Bennett

EXETER:
Tel: 0117 950 1441
Email: stopsmoking@easyway
exeter.co.uk
Website: www.allencarr.com
Therapist: Charles Holdsworth
Hunt

KENT:
Tel: 01622 832 554
Email: easywaykent@yahoo.co.uk
Website: www.allencarr.com
Therapist: Angela Jouanneau

LANCASHIRE AND SOUTHPORT:
Tel: 01722 739 849
Email:
mark@easywaylancashire.co.uk
Website: www.allencarr.com
Therapist: Mark Keen

MANCHESTER:
0800 804 6796 (Freephone)
Email: stopsmoking@easyway
manchester.co.uk
Website: www.allencarr.com
Therapist: Rob Groves

NORTH EAST:
Tel/Fax: 0191 581 0449
Email: info@stopsmoking-uk.net
Website: www.allencarr.com
Therapist: Tony Attrill

NORTHERN IRELAND:
P.O. Box 243, Derry, N. Ireland,
BT48 0WX
Tel: 0800 587 5212
Email: ciara@easywayni.com
Website: www.allencarr.com
Therapist: Ciara Orr

READING:
Tel: 0800 028 7257 (Freephone)
Website: www.allencarr.com
Therapists: John Dicey, Colleen
Dwyer, Sam Carroll

SCOTLAND
Sessions held throughout Scotland
Tel: 0131 449 7858
Email: info@easywayscotland.co.uk
Website: www.allencarr.com
Therapist: Joe Bergin

SOUTH WALES:
CARDIFF/SWANSEA
Tel: 0117 950 1441
Email: stopsmoking@easyway
cardiff.co.uk
Website: www.allencarr.com
Therapist: Charles Holdsworth
Hunt

STAINES/HEATHROW:
Tel: 0800 028 7257
Website: www.allencarr.com
Therapists: John Dicey, Colleen
Dwyer, Sam Carroll

YORKSHIRE:
Tel: 0800 804 6796 (Freephone)
Email: stopsmoking@easyway
yorkshire.co.uk
Website: www.allencarr.com
Therapist: Rob Groves

USA
Seminars held regularly in New
York and Los Angeles
Corporate programs available
throughout the USA
Central information and bookings:
1 866 666 4299 (Toll Free)
Email: info@theeasyway
tostopsmoking.com
Website: www.allencarr.com

NEW YORK:
1133 Broadway, Suite 706, New
York. NY 10010
Tel: (212) 696 6768
Therapist: Damian O'Hara

DISCOUNT VOUCHER
for
ALLEN CARR'S
EASYWAY CLINICS

Recover the price of this book when you attend an **Allen Carr's Easyway to Stop Smoking** Clinic anywhere in the world!

Allen Carr has a global network of clinics where he guarantees you will find it easy to stop smoking or your money back.

The success rate based on this money back guarantee is over 90%.

When you book your session mention this voucher and you will receive a discount to the value of this book. Contact your nearest clinic for more information on how the sessions work and to book your appointment.

Details of Allen Carr's Easyway Clinics can be found at

www.allencarr.com
or call 0800 389 2115

Easyway To Stop Drinking Alcohol sessions are available at limited locations. **Call +44 (0)20 8944 7761 for latest listings.**

This offer is not valid in conjunction with any other offer/promotion.